From Creation
To Unification

*The Complete Histories Behind
The Ch'ang Hon (ITF) Patterns*

*CheckPoint
Press*

From Creation To Unification

The Complete Histories Behind The Ch'ang Hon (ITF) Patterns

By Stuart Anslow

From Creation To Unification
The Complete Histories Behind The Ch'ang Hon (ITF) Patterns

By Stuart Anslow

Cover Design by Liam Cullen
Layout by Stuart Anslow
Edited by John Dowding

Copyright © 2013 Stuart Paul Anslow

All rights reserved

No parts of this publication may be reproduced, stored in a retrieval system, or transmitted in any form or by any means, electronic, mechanical, photocopying, recording or otherwise without the prior permission of the copyright owner.

British Library Cataloguing In Publication Data
A Record of this Publication is available from the British Library

ISBN 978-1-906628-55-0

First Published 2013 by
CheckPoint Press, Republic of Ireland,
Tel: 00353 949032758   www.checkpointpress.com

Disclaimer: Many pictures within this book have their copyright expired due to age or are in the public domain, for others, every effort has been made to obtain any necessary permissions with reference to copyrighted material, both illustrative and quoted; should there be any omissions in this respect we apologise and shall be pleased to make the appropriate acknowledgments or remove the material in any future editions.

*This book is dedicated to
my Grand Parents;*

Margery and Glanville Anslow

Eliza Jones and Victor Raeburn

History never forgotten

"Most of us spend too much time on the last twenty-four hours and too little on the last six thousand years."

- Will Durant

Acknowledgements

As with all my books, I like to acknowledge and thank all those that have helped in some way to shape it, whether directly or indirectly.

First and foremost I would like to thank those who have written the books on Korea and its history, that I have used in the course of my research. Without these important works, this book could never have been compiled as fully as it has been and I would never have learnt all I have during the course of my research. I would also like to thank those that allowed the use of their pictures and photographs to illustrate the chapters within this book.

I would like to thank and acknowledge the hard work of my proof reader John Dowding who, as with my previous books; reads, re-reads and re-reads again, each and every chapter, not only correcting typing errors, but also providing me with valuable feedback on how the book comes across to the reader and whether certain aspects could do with extra clarifications.

My thanks and appreciation to Liam Cullen for designing the books fabulous cover, it really portrays just what I wanted it too.

A big thank you to Dr. George Vitale for the wonderful photo's he allowed me to use for this book, all from his personal collection. As well as reviewing the chapters and sharing his insights, thoughts and knowledge with me; writing one of the great forewords to the book; and lastly for arranging the translation of the Jeju Island monument by Grandmaster Phap Lu, Minh Luong and Jerry Potts - many thanks to you all as well.

My thanks and appreciation to Master Ray Gayle for reviewing this book and agreeing to write one of its fantastic forewords, which upon reading it, made me feel very chuffed and solidified that my hard work researching this project had been valuable and worthwhile.

Thank you to Master Doug Nowling for his useful insights in regards to some information within this book, some Hangul translations and

From Creation To Unification
The Complete Histories Behind The Ch'ang Hon (ITF) Patterns

allowing me the use of some of his great pictures, which is all very much appreciated.

A big thank you to Bert Edens for sharing with me the report he wrote for his first degree which enriched this book further, just when I thought it was all finished!

My thanks also goes to Sanko Lewis for his refreshing insights into certain aspects of Taekwon-Do history, which I have quoted in this book.

Thanks and appreciation to Patrick Steel, Yi Yun Wook and Brian Jongseong Park for helping me to gain a better understanding on the nuances of the Korean language, with Yi Yun Wook once again providing me with the Hangul for the pattern names.

Lastly, but by no means least, many thanks to my instructors Master David Bryan and Mr John Pepper for helping me during my formative years of Taekwon-Do and of course to General Choi Hong Hi, Grandmaster Park Jung Tae and all those that helped them create the patterns we now practice today within Ch'ang Hon Taekwon-Do.

Foreword By
Master Ray Gayle, VIII

This is a book that every Taekwon-Do enthusiast will surely want to read and own. If you have been training in the art for some years, you will no doubt be aware that Taekwon-Do is not just about punching and kicking; the art goes far deeper than that and like most things in life the more you look the more you find, and the more you find the more your understanding of the subject can be enhanced. I'm happy to be writing this foreword because the content of this book is of great interest to me and I believe that many students have been looking for such a book for many years.

Stuart Anslow writes books that Taekwon-Do students and instructors want to read. I believe that this book is no exception. There are many books in the marketplace that have been written about the technical aspects of Taekwon-Do, but there are very few books that have been written (and perhaps none until now) that have the depth of research about this particular aspect of Ch'ang-Hon Taekwon-Do. This book is certainly well over-due. In fact this book has been over-due since 1955 when the inauguration of Taekwon-Do was announced.

So what makes Stuart Anslow qualified to write such a book? The first qualification needed and arguably the most important qualification for any book is a real passion for the subject and Stuart Anslow has passion in abundance - not just for patterns, sparring and destruction that form the basis of Taekwon-Do training - but for all the wider and

From Creation To Unification
The Complete Histories Behind The Ch'ang Hon (ITF) Patterns

intriguing aspects of the art such as real applications, Korean history and the link between Karate and Taekwon-Do.

I first came to know Stuart through his excellent monthly magazine, 'Totally Taekwon-Do', which features articles on all aspects of the art that I love and have been teaching for many years. Since then I have had the pleasure of seeing his passion for the Art while watching a number of his competition appearances. Finally, reading and enjoying his books that deal with the real applications of the Ch'ang-Hon pattern set have further fuelled my admiration for Stuart.

This book will certainly prove a valuable tool to any serious Taekwon-Do student who would like to know more about the history of the names behind their Taekwon-Do patterns. The Ch'ang-Hon patterns were named by General Choi using names of famous people and events from Korean history. In my early years of training it wasn't the done thing to question why we did this and why we did that, so as far as most of us were concerned we learnt the meanings of patterns to enable us to progress to the next level. When I had progressed to a certain level within the art, I was then told that the people within the meanings were there for us to take inspiration from and in some cases they had given their lives in the pursuit of the right principles and that this should give us strength to follow our own beliefs and to uphold that which we know is good and right and that by knowing about these individuals it would also help us to follow the tenets of Taekwon-Do. Of course it was always difficult to take any inspiration from the meanings, as the story of these individuals were told using one or two sentences; Won-Hyo was a noted monk who introduced Buddhism into the Silla Dynasty in 686 AD; but what inspiration could I draw from that? Was that all he did?

Stuart Anslow has certainly done his research, and he answers many of the questions for you. There are now some great stories to draw that inspiration from; it certainly brings a new life to each pattern within the Ch'ang-Hon set. I am a self confessed Taekwon-Do geek so it's the perfect read for me and I'm sure many others will find some of the missing links of their own knowledge that they have been searching for.

Foreword By
Master Ray Gayle, VIII

My particular favourite chapter is the meaning and life of Choong-Moo. What a warrior he was! You can now see why even today, the Korean people hold him in such high esteem. Stuart covers the meaning with page after page of interesting facts, dates and historical information about the life and battles of this fearless warrior. After you finish reading about Choong-Moo you have a wider understanding of what type of person he must have been and how loyal he was to his king and country. It finally puts those last pieces of missing jigsaw in to place and completes the whole picture for the reader. Stuart's style of thoroughly researching his subject to ensure accuracy is in full evidence. While reading you'll experience all the emotions that I'm sure General Choi intended his students to feel when he first put names and meanings to the patterns.

Master Gayle is an VIII degree black belt and currently chairman of the Professional Unification of Martial Arts. He has been training in Taekwon-Do for 35 years and has been a full-time instructor for 27 years. Even with his busy schedule, he still manages to continue to teach all levels of student at least 4 - 5 nights each week. He has a real passion for the technical elements of Taekwon-Do and martial arts philosophy. He has also had a very successful career as a competition fighter.

Master Gayle with General Choi Hong Hi and Grandmaster Hee Il Cho

Master Gayle was graded from 10th kup to 2nd degree by FGM Rhee Ki Ha. Graded to 3rd then 4th degree by GM Hee Il Cho. Graded to 5th degree under the T.A.G.B. Graded to 6th degree by General Choi Hong Hi. Awarded his 7th

From Creation To Unification
The Complete Histories Behind The Ch'ang Hon (ITF) Patterns

degree by Master Choi Jung Hwa. Awarded his 8th degree in 2012 by senior members who attended the 2nd P.U.M.A. Open World Championships.

Foreword By
Master George Vitale, VIII

It is indeed my great pleasure to write the foreword for this book. It is also a humbling experience and feeling as well. Master Stuart Anslow is an accomplished martial artist, who is very dedicated to his work and his students. Yes I do use the title Master in reference to this wonderful Taekwondoin and teacher, even though he is a V Dan (5th Degree) Black Belt. Of course in my ITF (International Taekwon-Do Federation) or the Original Taekwon-Do, we consider VII Dan (7th Degree) to be the threshold level for the Master title. But then again many independent groups refer to IV Dans (4th Degrees) as Masters. Some in the WTF (World Taekwondo Federation) or Kukkiwon also consider that as the level for Master, while some accounts use V Dan as the threshold. So in my personal view, someone who has worked as hard as Stuart has, for as long as he has and has produced both quality students and ground breaking written works, truly deserves the title of Master.

This present publication is yet another much needed resource for all students of Korean Martial Arts. Yes all Korean Martial Arts! While many Korean stylists do not do the ITF Patterns, often referred to as the Chang Hon (Gen. Choi's penname) or Chon-Ji (the 1st Pattern) set, they are involved to some extent in learning about Korea, Koreans, their culture and history. This latest masterpiece by a true master of Taekwon-Do will help all those who are interested in learning more about these very topics. Exposure to the knowledge

From Creation To Unification
The Complete Histories Behind The Ch'ang Hon (ITF) Patterns

imparted to those that read this book, will most definitely help the readers get a greater sense of the Korean roots of their respective Arts. This knowledge certainly has the potential to enhance the rewards of an individual student's training once they become more informed of the history and culture of the place and people who shared their Art with the world.

Patterns, as devised by 2 Star Major-General and Ambassador Choi Hong Hi are a sequence of attack and defense fundamental techniques set to a fixed and logical sequence. These sequences of fundamental movements were given labels that were named after great Korean patriots, significant historical events or Korean themes. In many instances the number of movements contained in each pattern had significance as well. Also the pattern or diagram made when moving on the floor performing these fundamental movements often had meaning that added to the student's knowledge about the subject the Tul was named after.

General Choi did this for a specific set of reasons. Of course he wanted to make his Martial Art of Self Defense more Korean and by naming his new Patterns, the first Korean ones ever, after important connections to Korea it helped to do just that! Doing so in the aftermath of the long and brutal occupation of Korea by Imperial Japan also helped to reinvigorate Korean pride, as he was a proud Korean patriot. It also served the purpose of drawing other Koreans to practice his Patterns (Tuls in Korean), as compared to the Karate based Kata's learned in Japan from the hated Japanese.

The first President of the Republic of (south) Korea (ROK) had a policy in place that made it illegal to embrace anything Japanese. In the Democratic People's Republic of (north) Korea (DPRK) harsh purges of anything Japanese and anyone who embraced or collaborated with the Japanese Imperial authorities were commonplace. General Choi lived under the Japanese occupation and suffered because of it. He was made to take a Japanese name and forcefully conscripted into their military. He stated publicly that connecting his Patterns to Korea and giving them definitions for students to learn as part of their training, also insured that Korean history could never again be eradicated by any invading occupying

Foreword By
Master George Vitale, VIII

force, as they were spread around the entire globe via his Original Taekwon-Do's Tuls.

My use of the term "Original" Taekwon-Do is meant not as a derogatory term or to relay a sense of superiority, but rather to simply distinguish the style of Taekwon-Do that first applied the label of Taekwon-Do to the system of self defense devised in the ROK Army by General Choi. He was of course assisted by the many talented soldiers under his command that he had access to as the result of his important position, that yielded great power and influence. At first, all of the Korean striking arts that were being practiced resembled the Karate roots from which they came. There was of course some Chinese Martial Art influence as well. The way General Choi started to move away from those Japanese roots were primarily at first, the new Patterns that he was developing in the ROK Army and while he was dispatched to Malaysia as Korea's first Ambassador to that Country and finalized when he returned to Seoul after his diplomatic assignment ended.

Others developed away from the common Karate roots in their own way. The Tae Soo Do practitioners on the civilian side moved away from those same roots with their new sport competition rules they developed. The many independents made their journey away from those roots in their own ways and to different levels or varying extents. Some of these independents practice the Chang Hon Patterns and will find this book invaluable. But as stated above, all Korean Martial Artists, including the WTF or Kukki Taekwondo students, will find value in this book. There is no doubt it will help expand the information they have on the birthplace of their Art as well.

General Choi looked at his Patterns as the signature of his Korean martial art of self defense. In essence it was what helped make his Taekwon-Do a martial art in it's own right. These patterns, the unique way that he insisted they be performed, with the chambers and previous positions he incorporated, along with many other changes, additions and updates to his system, made his Taekwon-Do a distinctive art.

This book however is not about movements or techniques. But rather

From Creation To Unification
The Complete Histories Behind The Ch'ang Hon (ITF) Patterns

it is a comprehensive expansion on all 25 of the Pattern definitions of the Tuls that General Choi devised. While his 15 volume Encyclopedia of Taekwon-Do (unprecedented by any other martial art) contains several pages of step-by-step instruction and numerous photos, the definitions he wrote are a paragraph at most! So the latest gem written by Stuart is the result of an in-depth research into what these patterns represent. And yes I said 25 Tuls, as this new book contains both Ko-Dang and Juche. In fact the section on Ko-Dang and Juche go into great depth on the reasons why Juche replaced Ko-Dang! My contribution to Taekwon-Do is through the teaching and sharing I do. Since I was never was blessed with much physical talent, I gravitated to diligent study so I could hold my own with the much more physically talented in a very physical martial activity. I have also pursued higher education and have earned 2 Associate Degrees, 2 Bachelor Degrees (with one in History), a Master Degree and was the first and only American to ever earn an academic Doctorate (PhD) Degree from the DPR Korea (*see first photo*).

I can say without any reservation that during my review of this book I have learned so very much from Master Anslow's work. Please remember that this assertion is from someone who reads, studies and conducts research an awful lot! I was also honored to be able to offer input along the way, sharing what I have learned as well. While a few organizations or groups have added more knowledge to the definitions, none to my knowledge have done it on all 25 and most limit it to the first 9 Gup Tuls. While some are good, like the one compiled by the Irish Taekwon-Do Association (ITA) from research conducted by my cousin Mr. Michael Clune, they are often not widely available or even known about. Additionally, an earlier book put out by Master Richard Mitchell of the United States Taekwon-Do Federation (USTF) is no longer in print and only goes up to the 9th Pattern (Chung-Mu). In fact a recent search on Amazon yielded only 10 used copies starting at $97.39!

So I hope you enjoy this book as much as I have. Please take note of the order of the patterns when they were finalized and who assisted General Choi in devising them. Pay particular attention to the mistakes made in General Choi's writings as far too many others repeat them in their own versions and Stuart's research corrects these.

Foreword By
Master George Vitale, VIII

Delve into the greatly expanded and rich information contained on the pages that follow. Stump your students by asking questions that cannot be answered with the limited knowledge that is contained in other sources. Better yet, keep your instructors and seniors on their toes by asking them questions or impressing them with the new knowledge you have gained as a result of reading this wonderful addition by Master Stuart Anslow. I am proud to have him as a fellow martial artist, a friend, a peer and of course an instructor.

Clockwise from top left: Master Vitale with General Choi (in the late 1980's); with Grandmaster Kim Bok Man who was instrumental in the formation of many of the patterns and with Colonel Nam Tae Hi, General Choi's right hand man.

"History is a guide to navigation in perilous times. History is who we are and why we are the way we are."

- *David C. McCullough*

About The Author

Stuart Anslow received his black belt in the art of Taekwon-Do in 1994 and is now 5th degree.

He is Chief Instructor of the renowned Rayners Lane Taekwon-do Academy, which was established in 1999 and is based in Middlesex, UK.

During his martial arts career, Stuart has won many accolades in the sporting arena, including national and world titles. His Academy is very successful in competition as well, winning many gold medals at every martial arts championship his students enter, a testament to his abilities as an instructor.

In 2000, Stuart won a gold and silver medal at Grandmaster Hee, Il Cho's 1st AIMAA Open World Championships in Dublin, Ireland and in 2004 he returned with 14 of his students to the 2nd AIMAA Open World Championships where they brought home 26 medals between them, 7 of them becoming World Champions in their own right, 2 became double world gold medallists, all from a single school of Taekwon-do. In 2012 he took 13 students to the PUMA World Opens and collectively his students won 28 medals, 6 of which were gold's, with one student again becoming a double world gold medallist.

In 2002, Stuart founded the International Alliance of Martial Arts Schools (IAOMAS) which drew martial artists from around the world together, growing from a few schools to over 400 in under a year. This non-profit organization is an online student and instructor support group that gives travelling students the ability to train at hundreds of affiliated schools worldwide and is truly unique in the way it operates.

Stuart has been a regular writer for the UK martial arts press, having written many articles[1] for *'Taekwon-do and Korean Martial Arts', 'Combat', 'Martial Arts Illustrated'* and *'Fighters'* magazines, as well as taking part in interviews for some of them. He now mainly writes for *'Totally Tae*

From Creation To Unification
The Complete Histories Behind The Ch'ang Hon (ITF) Patterns

Kwon Do' magazine. His numerous articles (which can be found on the Academy web site) cover the many related subjects of martial arts from training to motivation, but his main love is Taekwon-do. As well as his Academy, Stuart is the Chief martial arts instructor for a private school, which was the first school in the country to teach martial arts as part of its national curriculum.

In 2002, Stuart received an award from the Hikaru Ryu Dojo, a martial arts academy in Australia, presented by their Chief Instructor and fellow IAOMAS member Colin Wee when he visited Stuart's Academy in the UK. In recognizing Stuart's contribution, Colin stated (referring to IAOMAS) that *"nothing to date has been so foresighted and effective as Stuart's work in establishing this worldwide online martial arts community."*

In October 2003, Stuart was inducted into the world renowned Combat Magazine *'Hall Of Fame 2003'* for his work within the field of martial arts on a worldwide level. Combat magazine is the UK and Europe's biggest martial arts publication.

In 2004 he was selected as the Assistant Coach for the Harrow Borough Karate Squad, to compete at the prestigious London Youth Games held at Crystal Palace each year. This position he held for 5 years before having to give it up due to time constraints with his work in Taekwon-do. During the same year Stuart also received various Honorary awards for his work in the International field of martial arts. From the USA he received a *'Yap Suk Dai Ji Discipleship'* award for his innovative work within IAOMAS and *'T'ang Shou`* society award for promoting martial arts on a worldwide scale.

Stuart receiving his 'Hall of Fame 2003' award by Combat magazine editor, Paul Clifton

In 2006 he was presented with a *'Certificate Of Appreciation'* from the members of IAOMAS Canada which read *'In recognition of your un-dying contribution to the evolution of martial arts and your inspirational and innovative*

About The Author

formation of the International Alliance Of Martial Art Schools'. Though just a humble instructor or student as he refers to himself, he continues to inspire others, as other martial artists have inspired him through his career so far.

Also in 2006 he released his first book relating to Taekwon-do; *'Ch'ang Hon Taekwon-do Hae Sul: Real Applications To The ITF Patterns Vol: 1'* which explored the applications of patterns techniques contained within the Ch'ang Hon patterns, away from what was considered the *'norm'* for applications in favour of more realistic (and ultimately more beneficial) techniques. The book was extremely well received and became an instant success, seen as a 'must have' by both instructors and students worldwide.

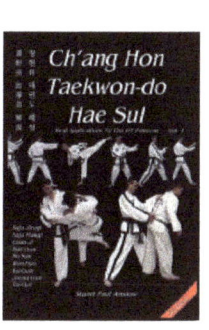

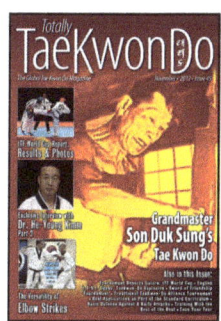

In 2009, his love for Taekwon-do and disappointment with the coverage in the various Taekwon-do magazines led him to publish his own online magazine *'Totally Tae Kwon Do'*; which ran free for 40 issues and was for all students of the art. Supported by his friends, Tae Kwon Do instructors and students around the world it too became a worldwide success and continues to delight and educate those interested in Tae kwon Do with each new issue that comes out.

In 2010 he released 3 more books titled *'The Encyclopedia Of Taekwon-Do Patterns:: The Complete Pattern Resource For Ch'ang Hon, ITF & GTF Students Of Taekwon-Do'* which featured all 25 of General Choi's patterns, as well as those of Grandmaster Park Jung Tae and the knife pattern by Grandmaster Kim Bok Man, plus the 3 Saju exercises - a feat that had

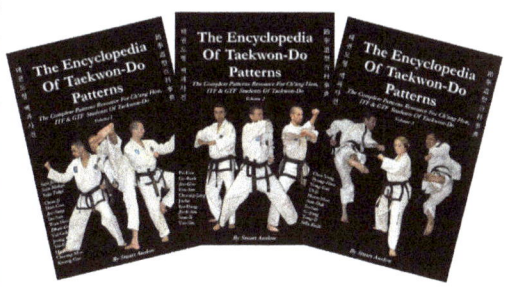

xxi

From Creation To Unification
The Complete Histories Behind The Ch'ang Hon (ITF) Patterns

never been published before. All were extensively detailed in a way that had never been done before either, setting the template for how future books on patterns and kata should be done. These books received worldwide acclaim as well.

In 2012 he released the much anticipated 2nd volume of *'Ch'ang Hon Taekwon-do Hae Sul: Real Applications To The ITF Patterns'* which followed on where Vol. 1 had left off, exploring realistic applications for the patterns from 2nd Kup to 2nd Degree.

Stuart is well known in the UK and internationally and apart from being a full time instructor of Taekwon-do, running local Self Protection courses, writing and publishing books on the art of Taekwon-do and publishing the monthly *Totally Tae Kwon Do* magazine, he is the father of four beautiful children, whom he supports and cherishes,

His work in Taekwon-Do, both through his teaching of the art as well as his articles and books, is not only held in high regards by those who practice the Ch'ang Hon system (ITF), but also respected by many in the WTF (World Taekwondo Federation) as well, including its former President, Dr. Choue.

Citation of Appreciation, signed by Dr. Choue, President of the WTF, which reads: *'In recognition of your dedicated service and outstanding contribution to the development of Taekwondo'*

Table of Contents

Acknowledgements vii
Foreword By Master Ray Gayle, VIII ix
Foreword By Master George Vitale, VIII xiii
About The Author..xix
Introduction.. 1

Chapter 1: **Kings, Kingdoms, Emperors and Dynasties** 9
Chapter 2: **Romanization of Korean** 13
Chapter 3: **A Brief History of Korea**...................... 17

Chapter 4: **Chon-Ji** 39
Chapter 5: **Dan-Gun** 43
Chapter 6: **Do-San**... 49
Chapter 7: **Won-Hyo** 59
Chapter 8: **Yul-Gok** 69
Chapter 9: **Joong-Gun** 75
Chapter 10: **Toi-Gye** 89
Chapter 11: **Hwa-Rang**.. 95
Chapter 12: **Choong-Moo** 109

Chapter 13: **Kwang-Gae**... 129
Chapter 14: **Po-Eun** 137
Chapter 15: **Ge-Baek** 143

From Creation To Unification
The Complete Histories Behind The Ch'ang Hon (ITF) Patterns

Chapter 16: **Eui-Am** 149
Chapter 17: **Choong-Jang** 155
Chapter 18: **Ko-Dang** 161
Chapter 19: **Juche** 167

Chapter 20: **Sam-Il** 175
Chapter 21: **Yoo-Sin** 185
Chapter 22: **Choi-Yong** 195

Chapter 23: **Yong-Gae** 203
Chapter 24: **Ul-Ji** 209
Chapter 25: **Moon-Moo** 219

Chapter 26: **So-San** 225
Chapter 27: **Se-Jong** 233

Chapter 28: **Tong-Il** 243

Appendix i: **Patterns of the GTF** 249
Appendix ii: **Revising the Definitions** 261

Bibliography 265
Other Books By The Author 268

Introduction

As a young student of Taekwon-Do, I was first exposed to the definition of patterns by way of a piece of paper, handed out to students, in order to give them the information they needed to revise for their next grading. Along with the physical aspects required, this paper would also list the Korean terminology we had to learn as well as, from 9th Kup, the definition of the pattern we were required to perfect and later demonstrate as part of the grading, that would allow us to move up to the next Kup grade should we pass, and from there, we would receive a new sheet to coincide with the new grade, showing the new requirements, new terminology and of course, the new definition for the new pattern we were about to learn.

And so it continued; I trained, revised and graded, each time learning what I needed to know without giving it much thought. To be honest, at that time, I never really even considered that there was more to the definition than what was on the paper; I simply trained hard and learnt what the organisation I was under required of me.

What I didn't know at the time, was that the pattern definitions I was learning at each grade level were exact copies of what was written in General Choi's 15 volume *Encyclopedia of Taekwon-Do*, copied word for word much the same as it is done today.

My first 'awaking' to the fact that there is more to the pattern definitions than we are required to learn came not from any copied

The author as a 2nd kup, performing Hwa-Rang tul at a tournament in 1993

From Creation To Unification
The Complete Histories Behind The Ch'ang Hon (ITF) Patterns

resource of General Choi, but actually from Grandmaster Hee Il Cho, when, at sometime during my formative years, I brought one of his books to help me revise my patterns outside of classes. This book, *The Complete Tae Kwon-Do Hyung, Vol 1,* covered what I wanted by way of step by step photographs of the patterns and of course, had an introduction to each pattern to accompany them. However, unlike the definitions I had previously studied, the pattern definitions were not just a single sentence or two, but had a whole page dedicated to them, with more information that I had ever previously read.

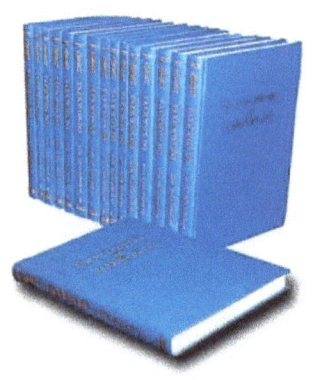

Yet, whilst I found all this interesting and was happy to know a bit more about the people the patterns were named after, I still never gave it too much thought! Roll on to after I graded to 1st degree black belt and I obtained a copy of General Choi's 15 volume *Encyclopedia of Taekwon-Do,* where of course the pattern definitions I had learnt in the previous years were listed, exactly the same as on those sheets of paper. In the first volume General Choi listed 12 principles behind his patterns and yet, whilst most of the principles are easy to understand and put into practice, the twelfth one always confused me! It stated *"Each movement in the pattern must express the personality and spiritual character of the person it is named after"* and my confusion lay in the fact of, how could anyone perform a pattern in a way that expresses the personality or character of the person they are named after, with so little information on that person!

Furthermore, if we look at each pattern as a whole, though they contain different techniques, in different orders, with a few variations in rhythm (slow motion, connecting motion etc.), they are basically performed in a manner that is identical to one another and give no inclination of anything relating to the 'character' of the person they are named after! In fact, to this day, the only thing I have ever come

Introduction

across relating to the performance of one of the Ch'ang Hon patterns in a manner befitting whom it was named after was in a draft version of a manuscript by Sabumnim Colin Wee[1] titled *"Fighting Heaven and Earth; Unlocking the secrets of martial arts through form interpretation"* which Colin shared with me when I was at the end of writing my first book (Ch'ang Hon Taekwon-do Hae Sul, Vol.1). In this manuscript he examined the movements of the patterns alongside the historical figure they were named after, finding 'realistic applications' to the techniques, based upon the personality of the character they were named after. Whether or not this was General Choi's intention when he wrote the twelfth principle is anyone's guess!

The author with Sabumnim Colin Wee, when he visited the Rayners Lane Taekwon-do Academy dojang in 2003

Whatever the exact meaning of the twelfth principle, the fact remains that General Choi named his patterns after famous Korean people or events for a reason and in the first instance, that was to restore Korean national pride amongst the Korean people, who were rising from the ashes of over 36 years of brutal occupation by the Japanese, an occupation that amongst other things, tried to destroy Korean culture and history entirely.

Being Korean, General Choi was obviously proud of his heritage and it was through Taekwon-Do that he was able to spread his pride throughout the world. When asked[2] how the patterns of Taekwon-Do came about, General Choi answered *"When the Japanese invaded Korea they tried to remove the Korean nationality. You could not go to school and be educated if you were not Japanese. I was left a man with no country and therefore*

---

[1] Sabumnim Colin Wee is a 6th degree Taekwon-Do Instructor based in Australia, with 30 years experience, whom I have known for over a decade.

[2] "Interview with General Choi Hong Hi, Founder of Taekwon-do". By Maria Heron. The Times, 1999

From Creation To Unification
The Complete Histories Behind The Ch'ang Hon (ITF) Patterns

no national pride. The Patterns of Taekwon-Do represent the history of Korea from time in legend to this century. The propagation of Taekwon-Do throughout the world has also enabled, through the patterns, a small part of Korean history to be learned by its practitioners. A part of Korea therefore now exists across the whole world and Korea's nationality and history can never be removed by oppressors again".

General Choi Hong Hi [3]

Through the patterns of his Taekwon-Do, thousands of students learn more about Korea and its history than through any other resource. When Master George Vitale, VIII, stayed at my house during a visit to the UK in 2012, he told me that Koreans were constantly surprised and amazed at his knowledge of Korean history and this is not just the odd Korean he may meet in his home country of the USA, but during his extensive travels to both North and South Korea, as well as some Korean Societies he attends, something he attributes almost solely to Taekwon-Do.

Master George Vitale, VIII and the author, 2012

In 2006, as I drew near completion of my first book, *Ch'ang Hon Taekwon-do Hae Sul*, I too wanted an introduction to the patterns that were represented within its pages. Though it wasn't a history book per se, I did some light research and wrote some interesting introduction pages to each pattern, covering more about their background than most books had done before. Whilst doing this research, I came across an error in one of the patterns and that was that Do-San's birth date wasn't 1876, as we learnt in the *'standard'* pattern definition; that is copied directly from General Choi's Encyclopedia of Taekwon-Do, but rather it was 1878. Now, whilst this is just a simple error, what surprises me to this day, bearing in mind that the book was released in 2006, plus I have

---
[3] Photo courtesy of Master George Vitale, VIII

Introduction

also had numerous discussions on the internet about it, is that hardly anyone seems willing to change the date to the correct version.[4] Even in newer books released, some by very high ranking Taekwon-Do Masters, the same incorrect dates appear and I find this a shame, not only because Do-San is a celebrated figure in Korean history and so should have his details recorded as correctly as possible, but also because he is someone that General Choi wanted highlighted by way of his patterns, such was his importance and significance to the General. Whilst I can understand an error by General Choi, as he was not a historian himself and when he chose his pattern names he was busy with both formulating Taekwon-Do and as a General within the newly formed Republic of Korea Army, it defies me that so many are unwilling to make such a simple correction, even though the history elements, through the patterns were, and are, an important part of them for General Choi and Taekwon-Do itself, some even attempt to make excuses or reason away the error, rather than just acknowledging it and correcting it!

Performing Ge-Baek tul in the dojang, 2005

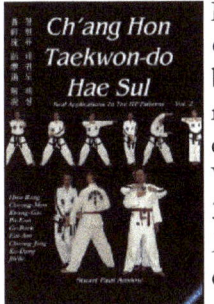

Moving forwards to when I started to put together *Ch'ang Hon Taekwon-do Hae Sul, Vol.2*, I decided, because the introductions were such a big hit with readers of *Hae Sul 1*, that I would again include in-depth introductions to the start of each chapter in Volume 2. In between volumes 1 and 2, I released a 3 book series *'The Encyclopedia Of Taekwon-Do Patterns'*, which were books on the more technical elements of solo pattern performance. This series would have been a great place to put these in-depth introductions, but due to the amount of detail presented on each pattern, space did not permit it, so I decided to keep with what I had

---

[4] Interesting enough, during the course of my research for the 2nd volume of *Ch'ang Hon Taekwon-do Hae Sul*, I re-read Grandmaster Hee Il Cho's pattern introductions in his *The Complete Tae Kwon-Do Hyung* books and noticed that he had Do-Sans birth date correct..

From Creation To Unification
The Complete Histories Behind The Ch'ang Hon (ITF) Patterns

done previously and put them in the 'Hae Sul' book. This time however, my research far exceeded what I did for Volume 1 and presented me with a new problem! A lot of the research I had done amounted to far more than was required for a short, albeit in-depth, introduction chapter to a book, which again was not really a history book per se (despite containing much historical information anyway). I wanted a page or two of details on the history behind the patterns, but some were nearly 20 pages long and had to be edited down for the book, which is part of the reason this book now exists.

During the course of this exhaustive research, I came across more errors in the history, from incorrect dates, to slightly misleading information if taken word for word by the 'standard' pattern definitions, as well as new and interesting information that I had never heard before! Some will see these corrections as a 'bad thing', as it's almost sacrilege to go against the words of the General, even if that information is blatantly incorrect in this day and age. But, as I said before, General Choi wasn't a historian and can be easily forgiven and understood for any errors, as apart from his various roles formulating Ch'ang Hon Taekwon-Do, within the ROK Army, and later his duties as South Korean Ambassador to Malaysia etc. he never had the resources we have today, in fact, the occupation of Korea probably destroyed much of any research material or books about Korean history anyway!

Performing Yoo-Sin tul at a tournament, 2005

As I finalised this book, I was on a phone call with Master Doug Nowling, VII (a wealth of Taekwon-Do and ITF historical information himself), clarifying some information he had given me in the past that I was using for this book as well, and during the course of our conversion, I brought up the fact that I had found quite a few errors pertaining to General Choi's pattern definitions with regards to my current research and gave my thoughts on the matter; why I thought that was so and how it may be perceived by some and he told me of an interview with General Choi, that he was present at some

Introduction

years ago. The interview was by none other than renowned Korean historian Dr. He-Young Kimm and during the interview, Dr. Kimm questioned General Choi about the historical definitions of the patterns and (I presume) the 'in-exactness' of them! General Choi said to Dr. Kimm something along the lines of *"These are the histories as I learnt them as a young man and others will correct them in the future"* - so in a way, this book is following the thoughts and wishes of General Choi himself and I hope that by knowing this small piece of information, students, instructors, chief instructors, grading examiners and association heads will no longer be unwilling, afraid or wary of updating the information they present to students or require as part of their syllabus and gradings.

Ready to begin Ul-Ji tul at a tournament, 2007

Whilst Ch'ang Hon (ITF) Taekwon-Do is well documented in many areas, there are a few areas that fall short; one is realistic applications to the patterns which I address in the *Ch'ang Hon Taekwon-do Hae Sul* books and another is a more in-depth history behind the patterns, which I cover in this book.

From Creation to Unification: *the Complete Histories Behind The Ch'ang Hon (ITF) Patterns* reveals the full historical background to each pattern; from Chon-Ji to Tong-Il. As you read this book, you will gain a deeper understanding of the people and events that were the inspiration for General Choi; the people and events he personally selected to name his patterns after. I guarantee you will learn more than you ever knew about them before, with more in-depth, up to date and exact information. Small errors are corrected, new information has come to

Performing Se-Jong tul at the PUMA Black Belt World Championships, 2011

From Creation To Unification
The Complete Histories Behind The Ch'ang Hon (ITF) Patterns

light, which I hope you will enjoy and find interesting, but above all, I hope you will be inspired by the deeds and events of Korea's illustrious figures from its past, just as General Choi was, just as I was and just as General Choi intended when he named the Ch'ang Hon patterns of Taekwon-Do!

Kings, Kingdoms, Emperors and Dynasties

Over the course of this book you will read about the many historical figures (or events) that the patterns are named after. These historical figures lived during certain periods of Korean history and we often read text that states (for example) *"...originated in the Silla dynasty"* or *"...19th King of the Koguryo Dynasty"*. As well as that, many students learn that originally Korea was divided into Three Kingdoms; Silla, Paekche and Koguryo, and its important (or at least useful) to understand the difference between them.

The first is the difference between a kingdom and a dynasty. Basically a kingdom is the amount of territory and people ruled over by a king (or queen), which grew and diminished throughout history and could be conquered by other rulers or dynasties, such as the Tang Dynasty of China and thus the land and people were absorbed by the new rulers and became part of their kingdoms. Within the main Three Kingdoms of Korea, smaller states also existed, such as The Gaya Confederacy and Buyeo (amongst others) and sometimes these are also referred to as 'kingdoms'.

A map showing the 3 ancient Kingdoms of Korea as they were in 576 AD [5]

On the other hand, a dynasty is a sequence of rulers that are considered to be from the same family, ruling in succession, though it is not always as clear cut as a 'father to son' ascension, though any heir to the throne would usually be connected by blood. If a dynasty is conquered, it is usually the end of the family line and thus the end of

---

[5] Picture by Historiographer. Cc-by-sa-3.0-up

From Creation To Unification
The Complete Histories Behind The Ch'ang Hon (ITF) Patterns

the dynasty and a new ruler and ruling dynasty takes over.

In one example (below) we have the Kingdom of Koguryo, which was one of the Three Kingdoms of Korea. The Koguryo Dynasty was founded in 37BC and lasted until 668AD when it was defeated by a Silla-Tang alliance. During its rule of over 7 centuries, it had 28 monarchs, including Kwang-Gae the Great who was the *"19th King"* out of 28. During its time, each King was somehow related to the last by blood, yet its territory (the kingdom) was constantly in flux, as battles for territory were fought, won and lost, expanding and decreasing its size as time went by. At that time, when a dynasty ended due to defeat, the land was taken by the kingdom that conquered it, however, once Korea was finally unified as an (almost) whole country, a dynasty would end when the bloodline ended and a new dynasty would take its place, for example in 1392, the Goryeo Dynasty ended and the Joseon Dynasty began.

1. **King Dong-Myeong** (37BC to 19BC) – Founder of Goguryeo
2. **King Yuri** (19 BC to 18 AD) – Son of King Dong-Myeong
3. **King Dae-Musin** (18 AD to 44 AD) – 3rd son of King Yuri
4. **King Min-Jung** (44 AD to 48 AD) – 5th son of king Yuri
5. **King Mobon** (48 AD to 53 AD) – 1st son of King Dae-Musin
6. **King Taejo** (53 AD to 146 AD) – Grandson of King Yuri
7. **King Chadae** (146 AD to 165 AD) – Younger brother of King Taejo
8. **King Sindae** (165 AD to 179 AD) – Half-Brother of King Taejo and King Chadae
9. **King Goguk-Cheon** (179 AD to 197 AD) – 2nd son of King Sindae
10. **King San-Sang** (197 AD to 227 AD) – 3rd son of King Sindae
11. **King Dong-Cheon** (227 AD to 248 AD) – 1st son of King San-Sang
12. **King Jung-Cheon** (248 AD to 270 AD) - 1st son of King Dong-Cheon
13. **King Seo-Cheon** (270 AD to 292 AD) – 2nd son of King Jung-Cheon
14. **King Bong-Sang** (292 AD to 300 AD) – 1st son of King Seo-Cheon
15. **King Micheon** (300 AD to 331 AD) – Grandson of King Seo-Cheon and Nephew of King Bong-Sang
16. **King Gogug-Won** (331 AD to 371 AD) - 1st son of King Micheon
17. **King Sosurim** (371 AD to 384 AD) - 1st son of King Gogug-Won
18. **King Gogug-Yang** (384 AD to 391 AD) – 2nd son of King Gogug-Won
19. **King Kwang-Gae** (391 AD to 413 AD) – 1st son of King Gogug-Yang

The Koguryo Dynasty from its Founding to the reign of King Kwang-Gae the Great., showing the bloodline connection between each monarch

Kings, Kingdoms, Emperors and Dynasties

Finally, some monarchs are referred to as kings or queens, whilst others as emperors or empresses, but what's the difference? Technically it seems quite clear cut – a king or queen was the ruler of a single territory aka their kingdom, be it a whole country or part of a country (such as Paekche), while an emperor or empress would rule over multiple territories or countries aka their empire.

However, the distinction between the two isn't actually as clear cut as a standard dictionary definition would lead us to believe, as it often became a matter of personal choice. In the West, king or queen was the preferred title in most cases, for example, during the height of the British Empire, which ruled over multiple territories around the world, the queen was still known as Queen Victoria as opposed to Empress Victoria. In the East however, the dynasties of China and Japan preferred the terms emperor or empress as to them, the title alluded to more grandeur and even if they didn't have multiple territories under their rule, many Asian kings and queens, including those in Korea often used the terms, irrespectively.

King Se-Jong the Great

"It is not the literal past, the 'facts' of history, that shape us, but images of the past embodied in language."

- *Brian Friel*

Romanization of Korean

Prior to King Se-Jong creating the Korean alphabet (Hangul), Korean people wrote in Hanja (the Korean word for Kanji), a Chinese script language. The problem was, that whilst the Korean people spoke Korean, when it came to writing, all texts were written in a different language; that of Classical Chinese, so a person would have to learn a whole new language to be able to write using it!

Only scholars, kings and the aristocracy learned how to read (and thus write) Classical Chinese, from their study of the Chinese Classics (such as the I-Ching) but it remained far away from the general populations grasp, leaving most of the Korean people illiterate until Hangul was introduced. Hangul, which was also a script language, was simpler to read and write but most importantly it was unique to the Korean people as it was based on the Korean language itself.

Below is a poem titled *'The Song of Cheoyong'* attributed to the 9th Century Korean poet Cheoyong. The poem was recorded in the *'Memorabilia of the Three Kingdoms'* by the Buddhist monk Iryeon, during the Goryeo Dynasty.

處容歌	처용가
東京明期月良	동경볽은둘애
夜入伊遊行如可	밤들어노녀다가
入良沙寢矣見昆	들어사자리에보곤
脚烏伊四是良羅	가롤이네히러라
二兮隱吾下於叱古	둘은나이엇고
二兮隱誰支下焉古	둘은누이언고
本矣吾下是如馬於隱	믿이내이다마론
奪叱良乙何如爲理古	빼앗어늘엇디ᄒ리잇고

The Song of Cheoyong

The left column is the poem in its original written form (Hanja) and the right column is the same poem reconstructed in Hangul by the Japanese Scholar, Shimpei Ogura (1882-1944), which was published in

From Creation To Unification
The Complete Histories Behind The Ch'ang Hon (ITF) Patterns

1929. Side by side it clearly illustrates that the Hangul version is much simpler and thus easier to read and understand.

When translating Hangul so Westerners are able to read it, there are two methods often used:

1. McCune–Reischauer Romanization of Korean
2. Revised Romanization of Korean

In brief, *McCune–Reischauer* Romanization of Korean doesn't translate Hangul in a literal sense, but rather uses phonetic pronunciation. When writing using the McCune–Reischauer method, letters are used with breves (˘) over characters, apostrophe's (') between them and occasionally hyphens (-) between words, to distinguish words that look similar, but are pronounced differently. This system was created by George McCune and Edwin Reischauer, two Americans, in 1937. A variant of this system was adopted by the South Korean Government from 1984 to 2000, before they changed to the Revised Romanization version. A variant of the McCune–Reischauer method is still used by North Korea.

Revised Romanization of Korean (meaning using Roman letters aka the English alphabet) is now the official Romanization language of South Korea. It was developed by the National Academy of the Korean Language and introduced in 2000. In short, this version limits itself to only the official English alphabet, with only the occasional use of a hyphen (-) when needed to make syllables clearer (though it is a common practice to use hyphens in Korean names). Therefore it doesn't rely on breves (˘) and apostrophe's (') to distinguish sounds within similar words, which was one of the main reasons the South Korean Government changed to it, as many wouldn't bother going to the extra hassle of adding breves when typing and thus, certain words would come out differently (and mean different things) when read out loud!

However, though there are preferred (modern) ways to translate Korean text into English, there is no actual 'correct' way, which is why you will see so many variations of the same word e.g. Dan and Dhan or Kup and Gup. The only truly correct way to write the Korean

Romanization of Korean

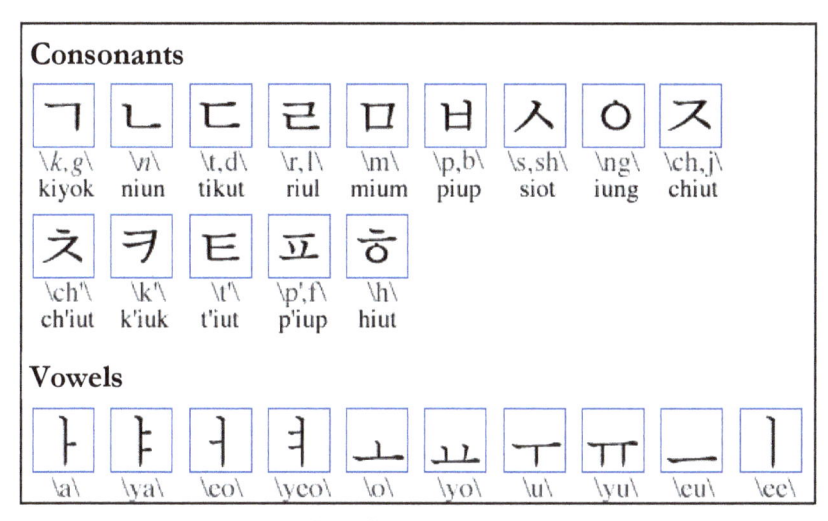

Consonants

ㄱ	ㄴ	ㄷ	ㄹ	ㅁ	ㅂ	ㅅ	ㅇ	ㅈ
\k,g\	\n\	\t,d\	\r,l\	\m\	\p,b\	\s,sh\	\ng\	\ch,j\
kiyok	niun	tikut	riul	mium	piup	siot	iung	chiut

ㅊ	ㅋ	ㅌ	ㅍ	ㅎ
\ch'\	\k'\	\t'\	\p',f\	\h\
ch'iut	k'iuk	t'iut	p'iup	hiut

Vowels

ㅏ	ㅑ	ㅓ	ㅕ	ㅗ	ㅛ	ㅜ	ㅠ	ㅡ	ㅣ
\a\	\ya\	\eo\	\yeo\	\o\	\yo\	\u\	\yu\	\eu\	\ee\

Hangul - as it is used today

language, is by writing it in its official 'Hangul', which obviously isn't too useful for those that do not read it!

When General Choi (actually pronounced Chae) wrote his books, he chose to write his words in a way of his choosing, using phonetics and based on whatever form of Romanization was popular at the time. For example, in his first book, he mostly used the *McCune–Reischauer* method, writing the names of his patterns as Ch'ŏn-Ji, Tan-Gun, Chung-Gŭn etc. but when he released his later books, his method changed to be more like the *Revised Romanization* method i.e. Chon-Ji, Dan-Gun, Joong-Gun etc. doing away with the breves and apostrophe's, though he still reverted to the *McCune–Reischauer* method on occasion; for example, in Toi-Gye '*Yi-Hwang*' should be written as '*I-Hwang*' when the *Revised Romanization* method is used.

In the following chapters you will read the pattern description exactly as General Choi wrote them in his encyclopaedia's (the bolded text), irrespective of which *Romanization* he used. This is then followed by more in-depth information about whom or what the pattern is named after, as well as any notes regarding corrections.

Why is all this important?
It is important when reading the various descriptions of the historical

From Creation To Unification
The Complete Histories Behind The Ch'ang Hon (ITF) Patterns

characters, both within this book and elsewhere, to understand that the time period (dynasties), areas (kingdoms) and even their names, may have different spellings, when in fact they are the same thing. Below are some examples that are listed in the following order:

a. *McCune–Reischauer* Romanization of Korean
b. *Revised Romanization* of Korean
c. General Choi's Version

Kokuryŏ – Goguryeo – Koguryo
(one of the three kingdoms of ancient Korea)

Paekche – Baekje – Baek Je
(one of the three kingdoms of ancient Korea)

Silla – Silla – Silla
(one of the three kingdoms of ancient Korea)

Koryŏ – Goryeo – Koryo
(One of Korea's ruling dynasties)

Chosŏn – Joseon – Yi
(One of Korea's ruling dynasties – sometimes referred to as the Yi Dynasty)

Kyebaek – Gyebaek – Ge-Baek
(Famous Korean General and Ch'ang Hon pattern name)

Suffice to say, for the context of this book, with the exception of General Choi's original definitions, I have either used General Choi's method of spelling in the descriptions, so as not to confuse the reader and for the rest I have used the *Revised Romanization* method, as it simply looks more elegant whilst keeping in line with how I believe General Choi would have written it himself.

Finally, as a extra note, if you refer back to the hangul chart, you will notice that General Choi named some of the techniques in Taekwon-Do based on the shape of the Hangul characters, for example:

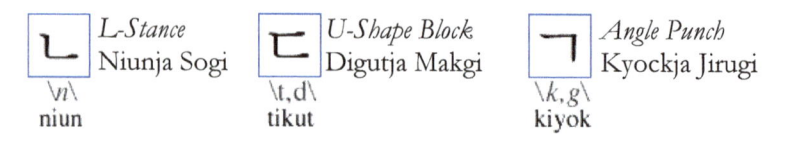

ㄴ *L-Stance* Niunja Sogi	ㄷ *U-Shape Block* Digutja Makgi	ㄱ *Angle Punch* Kyockja Jirugi
\n\ niun	\t,d\ tikut	\k,g\ kiyok

A Brief History of Korea
(And how the patterns relate)

Upright man (Homo Erectus) is thought to have existed in Korea some 400,000 to 700,000 years ago, during the Stone Age or Palaeolithic period; however the predominant view today is that the Korean people are not direct descendants of the Stone Age man that inhabited Korea originally. Instead, the origins of the Korean people are thought to possibly be from Mongol tribes who populated the area and eventually formed into three distinct groups or kingdoms.

A postcard depicting Dan-Gun [6]

According to the **Dan-Gun** legend, Korea was founded in the year 2333 BC in the north of the Korean peninsula, with lake **Chon-Ji** being his first home. Dan-Gun was said to have founded Korea and thus the first dynasty known as the *Gojoseon period.* [7]

---

[6] Picture courtesy of David A. Mason. *www.san-shin.org*. Reproduced with thanks.

[7] Originally called the Joseon Dynasty, the addition of the word 'Go' which means Ancient, was used to distinguish it from the later Joseon Dynasty which was founded over 4,000 years later.

From Creation To Unification
The Complete Histories Behind The Ch'ang Hon (ITF) Patterns

In 1122 BC *Dan-Gun* returned to Heaven leaving an uncle of the Chinese Shang King, who had fled to Korea, to rule until 193 BC (according to legend), this is known as the *Gi-Ja Joseon period*. Gi-Ja Joseon eventually became *Wiman Joseon period* after its ruler was overthrown by one of its Generals; Wiman, which existed until 108 BC.

Putting It In Context
1292 BC to 1290 BC was the reign of Rameses II of Egypt, better known as Rameses the Great.

Around the 3rd or 2nd century BC, in the south of the Korean peninsula the *Jin state* was founded; *Wiman Joseon* and the *Jin State* bordered each other. Both the *Wiman Joseon* and the *Jin state* had disintegrated by the 1st century BC becoming a collective of smaller kingdoms. Known as the *Proto-Three Kingdoms period*, these small kingdoms would eventually form the three best known kingdoms of Korea: Silla, Goguryo and Baekje – these kingdoms would war with each other for the next 700 years.

A map showing Gojoseon in decline in 108 BC[8]

The Kingdom of Silla was founded by King Park Hyeokgeose[9] around 57 BC. Originally it was called *Saro* until it was changed to Silla in 505 AD. The Goguryo Kingdom was founded in 37 BC by Go Jumong, a Prince from Buyeo (a state in the Proto-Three Kingdoms era) after he fled Buyeo during a

Putting It In Context
From 69 BC to 30 BC Cleopatra ruled Egypt and in 27 BC, the Roman Empire was founded.

---

[8] Picture by Historiographer. Cc-by-sa-3.0

[9] This is the origins of the Korean surname 'Park'

A Brief History of Korea
(And how the patterns relate)

power struggle. Upon founding Goguryo he changed his name to King Dong-Myeong meaning *'Holy King of the East'*, and finally the Kingdom of Baekje was founded by Onjo, the 3rd son of King Dong-Myeong in 18 BC.

Though Silla, Goruryo and Baekje are the three main kingdoms which this period is named after (***The Three Kingdoms period***) there was in fact a 4th kingdom called the Gaya, which was founded in 42 AD. Gaya was a collection of smaller kingdoms, overseen by a centralized government and is often referred to as *'The Gaya Confederacy'*. It existed sandwiched between Silla and Baekje until it fell apart due to pressure from Goruryo and became absorbed as part of Silla in 562 AD.

Korea in 476 AD (Wa is Japan) [10]

It was during the *Three Kingdoms period* that **Kwang-Gae** became the 19th King of Goguryo, expanding its territory so much, it became the largest kingdom ever seen in Korea.

Each of the three kingdoms had their own elite warriors; Goguryo had the Sonbae[11], Baekje the Ssaurabi[12a,b] and Silla had the **Hwa-Rang** warriors, which over time included kings and generals within their ranks, such as **Yoo-Sin** and even **Won-Hyo** at one point, before he spent his life introducing Buddhism to the Silla Dynasty.

---

[10] Author unknown. Cc-by-sa-3.0-Up

[11] Meaning 'Elder' and often translated as 'a man of virtue who never retreats from a fight'

[12a] A disputed term - see footnote [12b] on the next page for full details as to why!.

From Creation To Unification
The Complete Histories Behind The Ch'ang Hon (ITF) Patterns

Goguryo bordered China and had constant threats of invasion from the Chinese Dynasties over its borders, and it was in 612 AD that General **Ul-Ji** would defend the Goguryo Kingdom against a Sui invasion force of over one million Chinese soldiers! This crushing defeat led to the fall of the Chinese Sui Dynasty and they were succeeded by the Tang Dynasty and with them, a new threat to Goguryo came. Goguryo's **Yong-Gae** countered this threat by building a *'one thousand unit'* wall along Goguryo's border and whilst doing so, also fought Silla's forces, led by **Yoo-Sin** in the South. In the same year that *Ul-Ji* defeated the Sui Dynasty, a boy was born in the neighbouring Kingdom of Baekje – he would grow up to be their most famous General; **Ge-Beak**, who would fight for the kingdom until its final days, when he was himself defeated by *Yoo-Sin* at the famous battle at Hwangsan Field in 660 AD.

Yoo-Sin - One of Korea's most esteemed Generals

Putting It In Context
In 43 AD the Romans invaded Great Britain, but by 476 AD the Roman Empire had fallen in the West (The Fall of the Roman Empire).

Korea had seen its first Queen in 632 AD; Queen **Sun-Duk**, who took control of the *Hwa-Rang* warriors, then, when Baekje invaded, she allied Silla with Goguryo, but when Goguryo turned on Silla as well and she cleverly strengthened the dynasty by allying it with the Tang Empire.

After Baekje's defeat in 660 AD, the 29th King of Silla died and its 30th king was crowned – this was King **Moon-Moo**, who continued the relationship with the Tang Empire, first fostered by Queen *Sun-Duk*, and with their help, along with the help of *Yoo-Sin* once more, went onto to defeat the Goguryo Dynasty just 7 years later, uniting Korea

---

[12b] In reference to the term 'Ssaurabi', Baekje's warrior caste - This is a widely disputed, as despite the fact some Korean martial arts organisations claim they were the warrior caste of Baekje, the word 'Ssaurabi' is a modern term, not found in the language of the Three Kingdoms era, though undoubtedly, as with the other two Kingdoms, Baekje would have had its own elite warriors by a different name.

A Brief History of Korea
(And how the patterns relate)

for the very first time under one ruler.

This period is often called by its modern name of *Unified Silla*, but some historians prefer the term *North and South States Period,* as despite the modern term now used, just 30 years after Silla defeated Goguryo, a new kingdom emerged in the north of Korea (and included parts of Southern China and Russia). It was known as Balhae and this kingdom would last for over 200 years, falling to the Khitan's[13] in 926 AD, before being absorbed between the Liao Dynasty of China and the emerging Goryeo Dynasty of Korea.

Balhae in 830 AD

Unified Silla remained the dominant kingdom in Korea for a further two centuries, but began to weaken during the reign of Queen Jin-Seong (Silla's 3rd Queen) and, with its weakening state, new kingdoms were founded by some who claimed links to the earlier kingdoms of Baekje and Goruryo. These kingdoms were originally named Hubaekje and Hugoguryeo, but later reverted to the historical names of Baekje and Goruryo and this was called the **Later Three Kingdoms Period**.

Hugoguryeo (Goruryo) became the dominant kingdom, but when its ruler, King Gung-Ye turned into a despot he was overthrown by his own General (Wang-Geon) and Wang-Geon renamed the kingdom as Goryeo. A weakened Silla surrendered to Wang-Geon in 935 AD and just a year later, Goryeo conquered Hubaekje (Baekje), once again unifying the country.

General Wang-Geon became known as King Taejo and the **Goryeo**

---

[13] The Khitan tribe were nomads located in Manchuria and similar in nature to the Mongols. They became the Liao Dynasty of China.

From Creation To Unification
The Complete Histories Behind The Ch'ang Hon (ITF) Patterns

Dynasty he founded in 918 AD lasted for just under 500 years. It was during the *Goryeo Dynasty* that **Choi-Yong** would protect the kingdom against internal rebellions, Japanese pirates and Mongol invasions, driving them back to the famous Je-Ju island, the island where many years later, **General Choi Hong Hi** would famously locate his 29th Infantry division and start his work formulating Taekwon-Do.

King Taejo, founder of the Goryeo Dynasty

Putting It In Context
1095 AD to 1099 AD was the time of the First Crusade and in 1162 AD, Ghengis Khan was born.[14]

It was during the Goryeo Dynasty that **Po-Eun** was born. *Po-Eun* would go on to become a faithful servant to Goryeo's King U. However in 1388, one of King U's own generals; Yi Seong-Gye, revolted and turned on the king. The king was defended by General *Choi-Yong* and his army, but was defeated. The *Goryeo Dynasty* continued for just a few more years with puppet kings controlled by Yi Seong-Gye, before he took the throne himself and became the 1st ruler of the *Joseon Dynasty* (sometimes referred to as the Yi Dynasty). Despite Yi Seong-Gye taking the throne, *Po-Eun* was still held in high regards by the new king and an attempt to 'convert' him to the new *Joseon Dynasty* was made by one of Yi Seong-Gye's sons, but when Po-Eun refused, by way of his famous poem *"I will not serve a second master"*, Yi Seong-Gye's son had him murdered!

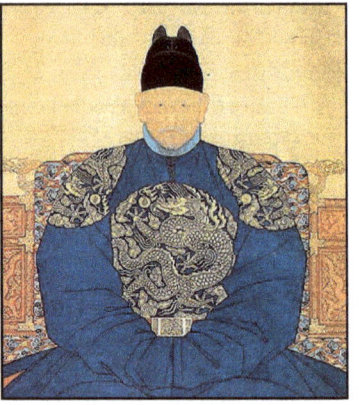

Yi Seong-Gyee who also became King Taejo[15], founder of the Joseon Dynasty

Putting It In Context
In 1266 Marco Polo travelled to China.

---

[14] Some historians put his date of birth at 1155 AD

[15] 'Taejo' was a name traditionally given to the 1st King of a new dynasty.

A Brief History of Korea
(And how the patterns relate)

Korea would derive its modern name from Goryeo, as when Marco Polo returned from his travels in Asia, he used the term *Goryeo* (*Koryŏ*) to describe the country. In Italian it was pronounced as *Cauli* and *Cauli* eventually became the English word *Corea*, which we now know as *Korea*.

The *Joseon Dynasty*[16] was founded in 1392 and lasted for over 500 hundred years. It was to be the last dynasty of Korea and produce some of its greatest people, such as **Se-Jong** the Great, who invented the Korean Alphabet, **Toi-Gye** and **Yul-Gok**, both of which became known as authorities on Neo-Confucian (with slightly differing view points) which became popular above Buddhism with the Government at that time.

> **Putting It In Context**
> It was during the Joseon Dynasty that Christopher Columbus travelled to the new world (South America) in 1492, that Henry VIII reigned in England (1509 to 1547) and Sir Francis Drake helped to defeat the Spanish Armada in 1588.

Yul-Gok's suggestion on training a 100,000 man reserve army to support the regular army was ignored and in under a decade, Japan invaded Korea and the Imjin War[17] started! With the land forces of the current *Joseon* King making little impact, possibly due to the premature execution of Kim Duk-Ryang, in favour of less competent generals, it was left to a soldier called Yi Soon-Sin, to form a Navy and defend the coast of Korea. This soldier would go on to become perhaps the greatest Admiral in the history of sea warfare, but it wasn't until hundreds of years after their deaths, that they were awarded the posthumous titles of **Choong-Jang** and **Choong-Moo** as we know them today!

However, it wasn't just Generals and Admirals of the *Joseon Dynasty* who fought against the Japanese during the Imjin war, civilians

---

[16] Korea is sometimes referred to as *'The Land of the Morning Calm'* which is loosely based on the Hanja for Chosŏn (Joseon).

[17] The Imjin War refers to two invasions of Korea by Japan. The first was between 1592 and 1596 as a newly unified Japan invaded Korea with the goal of not only conquering Korea's Joseon Dynasty, but also Manchuria, the Ming Dynasty of China and even the Spanish Empire! The second invasion occurred in 1597 (until 1598) with the smaller goal of conquering only the Joseon Dynasty. Collectively, they are known as the 'Seven Year War' or the Imjin War.

From Creation To Unification
The Complete Histories Behind The Ch'ang Hon (ITF) Patterns

formed guerrilla armies to fight the invasions and even a monk, known as **So-San**, formed a 5000 strong guerrilla 'monks' army of his own, despite being 72 years of age at the time!

The Imjin war ended in 1598, as *Choong-Moo* defended the sea and a combined Joseon and Ming army rid the land of the Japanese forces. The following years saw attacks by both the Jurchen (later to become known as Manchu's) and the Qing Empire of China, forcing Joseon to make treaties with both of them for the sake of the kingdom. These invasions made the Joseon Dynasty become an isolationist kingdom which allowed it to have relative peace for nearly 200 years.

During the 18th Century Christianity found its way to Korea and in the 19th Century Catholicism also entered Korea. Both of these were ignored until King Gojong came to the throne in 1863. King Gojong re-enforced the kingdoms isolationist policies and led a crackdown on outside influences, especially western influences, in Korea. At that time there were 12 Catholic priests from France practicing in Korea and so far, they had converted around 23,000 Koreans to Catholicism.

> **Putting It In Context**
> During this peaceful period in Korea, the Industrial Revolution took place, starting in 1760, Captain James Cook discovered Australia (1770) and America declared its Independence from Great Britain (1776).

King Gojong and his son, the Crown Pince Sunjong in Joseon Dynasty dress

King Gojong ordered the head priest, Bishop Berneux, to his court, arrested him, tortured him, then executed him. He then tried to round up the rest and execute them also, as well as thousands of the Korean converts. All but 3 of the priests were caught and executed. One of the priests managed to escape to China where he was fortunate to run into a visiting French Admiral. Upon hearing the news, the Admiral, supported by the French

Bishop Berneux

A Brief History of Korea
(And how the patterns relate)

Consul in Peking, was put in charge of punishing Korea for its actions against them.

Rear Admiral Roze was put in charge and he said at the time *"Since Joseon killed nine French priests, we shall avenge by killing 9,000 Corean's."*, however, he knew next to nothing about Korea and very few maps or charts of the surrounding seas existed, so he sent a small survey fleet to the Korean coast first. From his survey, he decided that taking a large fleet to the capital (Seoul) wouldn't work, due to the shallow waters of the Han River, so instead, decided to seize control of Gwanghwa Island, which was at the entrance to the Han River and thus, stop Korean ships sailing through.

Rear Admiral Roze

Admiral Roze along with 800 soldiers took control of the island fort fairly easily, but when his soldiers crossed from the island to mainland Korea, the resistance was much fiercer and the French troops retreated back to Gwanghwa Island and had to be content with bombarding the coast from their ships.

From his fortified position on the island, Admiral Roze sent letters to the King of Joseon, demanding the release of the final two French priests, but he received no reply. Korean resistance on Gwanghwa Island was growing quickly, winter was coming and then, when news that the two priests had in fact escaped to China was received, Admiral Roze and his troops left the island, razing the Government buildings and taking as many supplies and artefacts as they could.

The French fleet returned to their base in Japan before being deployed elsewhere to fight for France's interests. After the small invasion, Admiral Roze said *"The expedition I just accomplished, however modest as it is, may have prepared the ground for a more serious one if deemed necessary. The expedition deeply shocked the Korean Nation, by showing her claimed invulnerability was but an illusion. Lastly, the destruction of one of the avenues of Seoul, and the considerable losses suffered by the Korean government should render it more cautious in the future. The objective I had fixed to myself is thus fully accomplished, and the murder of our missionaries has been avenged."*

From Creation To Unification
The Complete Histories Behind The Ch'ang Hon (ITF) Patterns

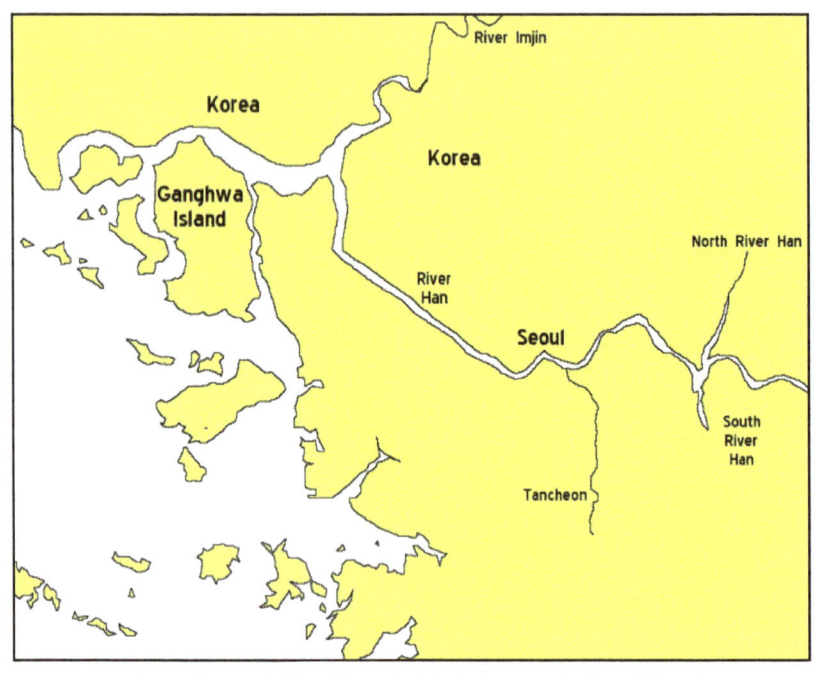

A map showing the Han River, which leads directly to the Capital (Seoul) and Gwanghwa island, at its entrance

Korea's isolationist policies continued[18] and they defended their waters with renewed vigour. In 1866 a US Navy ship, the General Sherman, had come to Korea to establish relations and trade. However, the Korean Court was suspicious of its intentions, feeling it was more likely a treasure hunting ship sent to plunder Korea's treasures. The General Sherman was a metal clad gunship and fully armed and in Korea, the only ships to be clad in metal were warships! In any case, local Korean officials met the Captain of the General Sherman (Captain Page) and following talks, refused to trade but said they would supply food and provisions for its journey home. They told the ship to wait where it had anchored whilst they informed the Joseon court and brought the supplies. However, once the officials were gone, the ship moved closer to Korea but became stranded. When this happened, word was sent to the ship to leave Korean

---

[18] Giving rise to the nickname *'The Hermit Kingdom'* by author William Elliot Griffis, in his 1882 book *'Corea: The Hermit Nation'*

A Brief History of Korea
(And how the patterns relate)

waters immediately or all the crew would be killed and though accounts of what happened next vary, the ship ignored the orders and apparently opened fire instead, which wasn't received well and the eventual outcome was that the General Sherman was sunk and all the crew killed.[19]

Five years later US ships returned to Korea again, to establish diplomatic relations, open trade and find out what had happened to the General Sherman and its crew. Upon initial contact with Korea, no information was forthcoming about the General Sherman and the US informed them that they intended to peacefully explore the coast. However, the policy of the Joseon Dynasty was that no foreign ships were allowed in its waters and the US ships were fired upon. What should have been peaceful diplomatic talks turned into an armed conflict, with Gwanghwa Island once again becoming the base of operations for foreign forces.

With its superior weapons, the US took control of the island fairly easily, despite some casualties. Hoping to use the Korean's they captured as a bargaining tool to open up talks, the US Ambassador was told to keep the prisoners they had captured, as the Korean court considered them cowards for being defeated. The Kings isolationist policy became even more resolute and unable to achieve its objectives, the US left the island and returned home.

The closed door policy to trade and relations with outsiders continued until in 1876, five years after the US left Gwanghwa Island, the Japanese made their attempt to open Korea's doors to trade. Japan used a strategy formerly used on them a few decades earlier by US Admiral Perry, which had forced Japan to open itself to foreign trade. The Japanese sent a ship near Gwanghwa Island, knowing that it would be defended due to the early attacks by the French and USA. Whilst the main Japanese ship stayed out of range of the island's guns, it launched a small boat towards it on the pretence of finding drinking

---

[19] Two months before the General Sherman arrived in Korea a similar incident had happened with a German ship. Also armed, it had travelled to Korea and requested trade. As would happen with the Americans, trade was denied but the Captain reported that he was well treated by the Koreans, when he returned to China. Also, a month before that, an American ship was shipwrecked off the coast of Korea and its crew were rescued and sent to China as well.

From Creation To Unification
The Complete Histories Behind The Ch'ang Hon (ITF) Patterns

water. As planned, the island opened fire on the ship, allowing the Japanese to retaliate and use its superior firepower on the island's defences. The Japanese ship attacked another fort on the island and then returned to Japan, blaming Korea and the Joseon Dynasty for the incident. A year later, a large Japanese fleet would sail to Korea and demand an apology for the incident at Gwanghwa Island, accepting in recompense a treaty between Korea and Japan.

> **Putting It In Context**
> During this time the world had witnessed the French Revolution (1789 to 1799); the Battle of Waterloo (1815); Victorian Britain had begun (in 1837); Abraham Lincoln had become President of the United States of America (1861); the Suez Canal had been built (opening in 1869); and the Satsuma Rebellion[20] had taken place in Japan.

The treaty is known as the *'Japan-Korea Treaty of Amity'* and it allowed Japanese citizens in Korea extraterritorial rights as well as forced Korea to open three of its ports to Japanese ships for trade. King Gojong decided to sign the treaty as he felt threatened by the superior technology[21] of the Japanese, and in part he hoped Korea would benefit by having access to the Japanese technology.

The *'Treaty of Amity'* did not sit well with the people of Korea, who already felt oppressed by their own king and it sowed the seeds for the Donghak rebellion in 1894. **Eui-Am** would become the rebellions 3rd leader some years later. Farmers rose up against the tyranny of the

---

[20] The Satsuma Rebellion was basically a civil war in Japan between the Satsuma Samurai Clan and the Meiji Government and is what the Tom Cruise film *The Last Samurai* is loosely based upon. Takamori Saigo, head of the Satsuma Clan originally supported the Meiji Government and in 1873 offered to go to Korea to insult its people, so as to provoke an assassination attempt on him and thus provide a justified reason for Japan to invade Korea. Just 3 years later Japan would achieve its aim anyway by way of the Gwanghwa Island incident.

[21] As an interesting aside, if it wasn't for a Scotsman, Thomas Glover, Japan may never have invaded Korea in 1910, as he was almost directly responsible for arming the Japanese with modern weapons as part of the Meiji Restoration. After a visit by US Admiral Perry, which forced the Japanese to open up trade with the West, Japan realised it was technologically behind in both weapons and machinery and could not compete as a world power. Thomas Glover offered to provide modern ship building and coal mining methods to Japan and later would provide guns to the Satsuma clan, but eventually gave them to both sides. This allowed the country to realise it ambitions of becoming an Empire, which led to the Sino-Japanese war and thus, the invasion of Korea. Thomas Glover even sent Hiro-Bumi Ito (along with 12 others) to secretly study in Great Britain, so they could learn how 'western ways' could develop their country.

A Brief History of Korea
(And how the patterns relate)

ruling classes, attacking Government offices and killing outsiders. They petitioned King Gojong for reforms, but he ignored them and the revolution grew. Unable to crush the rebellion himself, King Gojong called on China for assistance and they sent 3,000 troops to Korea. This led to conflict with Japan who sent in their own troops who fought with the Chinese, and it all took place on Korean soil.

In 1895, the Chinese signed a treaty with Japan and removed its troops from Korea, relinquishing all rights it once claimed over Korea. Feeling more threatened than ever before, King Gojang instituted reforms and in 1897 declared that Korea was now **'The Korean Empire'** and the Joseon Dynasty ended.

In 1904 the Japanese presence in Korea intensified, as Russia had placed troops in Manchuria and war erupted between them, once more fought on Korean soil. When the war ended in 1905 with the signing of a treaty, Japans influence over Korea was almost absolute and King Gojang signed the *'Elusa Treaty'*, commonly known as the *'Protectorate Treaty'*, which made Korea a protectorate of Japan and basically relieved it of its sovereignty.

Emperor Gojong and his son, the Crown Prince Sunjong in Korean Empire dress

The rebellions of the Korean people grew and it was during this era that **Do-San** would return to Korea from the United States to promote Korean Independence and **Joong-Gun** would assassinate Hiro-Bumi Ito. Japan strengthened its grip further by way of the *'Annexation Treaty'* in 1910, bringing *The Korean Empire* to an end and the start of **Colonial Korea**, which would last for another 35 years.

> **Putting It In Context**
> In 1912 the Titanic sank and in 1914 World War I begun and lasted for 4 years. Korea was occupied before World War I and remained so throughout World War II.

When Emperor Gojong died, a demonstration was planned to lobby for Korean independence, to co-inside with his funeral. This would be

From Creation To Unification
The Complete Histories Behind The Ch'ang Hon (ITF) Patterns

known as the **Sam-Il** Movement and whilst Korea didn't gain its independence from Japan, it did effect some major changes in the country. In the same year, *Choi Hong Hi* was born (on 9th November, 1919) in Hwa Dae, which is now in present day North Korea – although at this time, Korea was still one country under Japanese colonial rule.

A Sam-Il protest march

Choi Hong Hi in a karate gi

Choi Hong Hi travelled to Japan to further his education and it was here he would learn Karate, where he reportedly attained or claimed to attain the rank of 2nd degree. Upon returning home, he was forced to undergo a physical examination by the Japanese and was conscripted, against his will, into the Japanese Army, where he would serve under the Japanese name 'Nishiyama'. He was sent to Pyong-yang to serve and later tried to escape after helping plan a rebellion of Korean student soldiers (the Hahk-Byung Uprising). During the escape, *Choi Hong Hi* and his comrades were captured, imprisoned and eventually sentenced to be executed.

Korea's liberation from Japanese rule came when Japan surrendered to the Allied Forces in 1945, marking the end of World War II. This was just 3 days before *Choi Hong Hi's* execution was to be carried out, but now he was free.

As Japan relinquished its control of Korea, the country was divided up into two halves, to be administered by the USA and the Soviet Union until it could stand on its own two feet again. The Soviet Union

A Brief History of Korea
(And how the patterns relate)

(USSR)[22] took control of the North and the USA took control of the South, with the dividing line being the famous 38th Parallel. 1945 was also the year that 50 Governments formed the United Nations (which the GTF pattern **Pyong-Hwa** pays homage to) to ensure a world war never happens again.

In the North, **Ko-Dang**, an activist during the Korean Independence Movement, was asked to take control of the provinces to avoid problems as the Japanese left, however, against the wishes of the United Nations, who wanted democratic elections to decide Korea's new leadership, the Soviet Union instituted a communist state, choosing to place their choice of former guerrilla army leader[23] Kim Il-Sung in power, which led to the **Juche** idea. At that time in Korea, as within much of Asia, communism had a strong attraction for the population, which were mainly poor peasants and attracted to the ideology of communism with its claims to *'distribute wealth evenly'* they had nothing to lose and everything to gain by supporting it, even in the South! If it had not been for the roles of the USA and the UK when Korea was liberated, it is thought that Korea would have ended up a totally communist country altogether as, even with

Ko-Dang, circa 1947

Following liberation from Japanese rule Soviet Commander Andrei Romanyenko introduces Kim Il-Sung to the crowds, 1945

---

[22] *'Union of Soviet Socialist Republics'* known as the USSR or Soviet Union – a collective of 15 republics with a centralized communist Government based in Moscow, Russia, which existed between 1922 and 1991.

[23] At age 24, Kim Il-Sung was in command of his own guerrilla unit, the *'Kim Il Sung division'*, as part of the Communist Party of China's anti-Japanese groups that operated in North Korea, coming across the border from China to attack Japanese soldiers, before retreating back. His unit did take the Japanese controlled town of Poch'onbo, but while it is confirmed he was a resistance fighter, further accounts of his exploits are disputed due to the *'over-inflated'* history of Kim Il-Sung's *'prowess'*, put out as North Korean propaganda to its people, aimed to make them think that he almost single handily saved North Korea from its invaders.

elections looming, it was hard to find someone who didn't lean towards communism, which is why the US influenced election supported Syngman Rhee, who hadn't been in Korea for some time.

Opposed to communism, *Choi Hong Hi* enrolled in the 1st Military Training School in Korea, which would become the 'West Point' of South Korea, producing officers for the future South Korean Army. General Choi was one of the 110 officers who made up the first class[24] from the Academy who were the founding members of the ROK[25] army.

General Choi rose through the ranks quickly and by 1948 the US and the Soviet Union forces began to withdraw from Korea, however in 1950, after two years of bloody cross border fighting between North Korea and South Korea (incidentally, with more skirmishes started by the South), resulting in thousands of casualties, with the North suffering the heaviest losses, North Korea realised there was a lack of heavy weaponry deployed in South Korea at the time, and the North Korean President Kim Il-Sung saw this as a weakness and attacked South Korea[27] with a massive invasion on 25th June, 1950, which was the official start of the Korean War.

Lieutenant Choi Hong Hi, 1946 [26]

The Korean War lasted for 3 years, ending in July 1953, following the signing of an armistice, which basically restored the dividing line of the country; the 38th parallel. It was after the war that *Choi Hong Hi* took charge of his own military division and within this, using his knowledge of Karate, he developed Taekwon-Do along with the soldiers under his command and those that would later follow him.

---

[24] His serial number was #44

[25] Republic of Korea

[26] Photo courtesy of Master Doug Nowling VII, *Kido Kwan Martial Arts International.*

[27] Possibly after obtaining the go ahead from Stalin and Chairman Mao first.

A Brief History of Korea
(And how the patterns relate)

Korea remains divided[28] to this day and whilst the patterns of Taekwon-Do are named after illustrious figures or major events in Korean history, the final pattern represents General Choi's wish to see his country as one again and this pattern is of course **Tong-Il**.

Whilst North Korea has passed control of the country from father to son[29], South Korea had supposedly been democratic since Syngman Rhee became its 1st President in 1948, as the elections in the South were overseen by the United Nations.[30] However, whilst most see the two Korea's how they are today; one as a closed communist country and the other as an open democratic country, this has not always been the case in South Korea.

Kim Il-Sung with his son Kim Jong-Il

Originally, the US championed Syngman Rhee and he became its first president in 1948, but his two terms as president of South Korea were plagued with political turmoil and dissent, as he became more and more oppressive and dictator-like, brutally crushing any opposition, which resulted in protest marches against his

US General MacArthur and Syngman Rhee, 1948

---

[28] Interestingly, in South Korea a 'pre-divided' Korea is called *Hanguk*, whilst in North Korea they refer to it a *Chosŏn* (Joseon), after the last great dynasty of a 'whole' Korea, as well as Korea's first dynasty, Gojoseon. South Korea also retains the original Korean flag from pre-division days, whilst North Korea created a new one for itself!

[29] From Kim Il-Sung to Kim Jong-Il to Kim Jong-Un, its current leader.

[30] Despite being overseen by the United Nations, the choice of candidate was heavily influenced by the USA due to its official policy drafted to contain communism. i.e. They wanted someone who would definitely support their stand against communism.

From Creation To Unification
The Complete Histories Behind The Ch'ang Hon (ITF) Patterns

presidency and in 1960 he resigned and fled to Hawaii, where he lived in exile until he passed away in 1965. For the next year the country was run as a republic, with a parliamentary cabinet that only allowed any president minimal control.

However, in 1961 a military coup took place and Major General Park Chung Hee took control. Facing pressure from the USA, Park Chung Hee eventually held elections, though many questioned the elections legitimacy due to Parks control of the government. He suspended the constitution, then revised it over and over and in 1972 (at the height of his brutality as he pushed for absolute control - the same year General Choi and others fled Korea) he amended the constitution to allow him to remain president for life, leaving Park Chung Hee to rule over Korea for the next 18 years.

President Park Chung Hee

At first President Park's rule stimulated the South Korean economy substantially, later he would support the USA in the Vietnam War as well as conduct negotiations with North Korea. However, like his predecessor, his rule became more and more dictatorial and brutal; he created the KCIA (South Korea's secret police) to detect and eliminate any opposition, placing Lt. Colonel Kim Jong Pil (a man related to Park by marriage and the mastermind of the coup) as its director, restricting his people more and more. He removed those in opposition to him and minimized anyone who he didn't trust. The people of Korea protested against his presidency and he declared martial law on the country, using his secret police to crack down on those that opposed him.

General Choi Hong Hi originally supported the coup as it was being carried out in the name of Lt. General Chang, the South Korean Army Chief of Staff. However, Park Chung Hee never relinquished control of the government and started removing those in positions of power that were not part of his 'inner circle'. General Choi began to vocally oppose Park Chung Hee's reign as well and he was removed from his

A Brief History of Korea
(And how the patterns relate)

powerful army assignment and dispatched to Malaysia as Korea's first Ambassador there, a move designed to minimize General Choi's vocal opposition, but as General Choi became more and more critical, both his family and himself became threatened, forcing General Choi to leave the country secretly in 1972, where he self-exiled himself to Canada. Following this, the WTF[31] (World Taekwondo Federation) was established in South Korea in 1973.

> **Putting It In Context**
> In 1972, Richard Nixon was President of the USA and Sir Edward Heath was Prime Minister of the UK.

After 18 years of virtually unchecked power, on 26th October, 1979[32], Park Chung Hee was assassinated by the director of the KCIA which he had created and the Prime Minister Choi Kyu Hah took control of the government, but his reign was short-lived as once again a military coup took place by a Major General Chun Doo Hwan, who seized power. Chun Doo Hwan presidency was much the same as Park Chung Hee's, with military crackdowns, KCIA arrests and even martial law once again declared due to protests against him. The protests against him resulted in the Gwangju massacre, in which over 2000 protestors were killed by the army, lead by General Roh Tae Woo, under Chun's direction and control.

Prime Minister Choi Kyu Hah

President Chun Doo Hwan

In 1987 a Democracy Movement occurred, which forced the Government to amend the constitution so that no South Korean

---

[31] Interestingly, the term 'Kukki' (which means National) and is now synonymous with the Kukkiwon (World Taekwondo Headquarters - built in 1972) and WTF (World Taekwondo Federation - founded in 1973), was used much earlier, in relation to Taekwon-Do, by General Choi Hong Hi in 1965, where he named his travelling demonstrations the 'Kukki Taekwondo Goodwill Tour'.

[32] Ironically, 26th October, when President Park was assassinated was the same date that Joong-Gun shot Hiro Bumi-Ito in 1910

From Creation To Unification
The Complete Histories Behind The Ch'ang Hon (ITF) Patterns

President could serve more than one, 7 year term and in 1987, when his term was up, President Chun Doo Hwan stepped aside and his hand picked successor, General Roh Tae Woo became the country's next President. Shortly after, the 1988 Seoul Olympics were held, which saw Taekwondo (under the WTF) become a demonstration sport paving the way to it becoming a full Olympic Sport in 2000, much to the annoyance of General Choi who continually lobbied the IOC to include 'original' Taekwon-Do instead. Ironically, as with the Donghak rebellion years earlier, that used the Emperors State Funeral to let the world see the wrongs that were happening in Korea, once again the eyes of the world were focused on Korea in its build up to the 1988 Olympic Games which were the perfect opportunity let the world know of the atrocities happening in the country.

President Roh Tae Woo

The next term was by Kim Young Sam in 1992 and he became the first civilian democratically elected president the country had seen for over 30 years. Under his term, both former presidents General Roh Tae Woo and General Chun Doo Hwan were arrested and imprisoned for bribery and soliciting illegal funds and in Chun's case, the Gwangju massacre. Roh was sentenced to 22 years and Chun was sentenced to death but the sentences were commuted to 17 years and life imprisonment respectively.

President Kim Young Sam

The next president was Kim Dae Jung, who, just prior to his presidency convinced Kim Young Sam to release Roh and Chun as he didn't want his administration to start with the issues of the past and wanted a new future for South Korea. This was despite the fact that 20 years earlier, (then) President Chun Doo Hwan had sentenced Kim to death under his regime, but

President Kim Dae Jung

A Brief History of Korea
(And how the patterns relate)

following intervention by Pope John Paul II[33] his sentenced was commuted to life imprisonment. Kim Dae Jung went on to institute the *Sunshine Policy*[34] towards North Korea, meaning increased talks in the hope of finding a way to reconciliation and *Tong Il*, for which he received the Nobel peace Prize in 2000.

Roh Moo Hyun would become the next president in 2002, followed by Lee Myung Bak in 2008, who took a hard-line approach towards North Korea meaning, at least for his term, General Choi's dream of *Tong-Il* remained far from becoming a reality.

President Roh Moo Hyun

President Lee Myung Bak

In 2013 South Korea saw its first ever female leader, President Park Geun Hye, who is the daughter of former president General Park Chung Hee, who came to power via the military coup on May 16, 1961, which is commonly referred to as the '*May 16 Revolution*' by Koreans. Her father lived through two assassination attempts by North Korea, including one that killed her mother, South Korea's 1st Lady. It will be interesting for the Taekwon-Do community on how she deals with *Tong-Il* and the co-operation of the Taekwon-Do groups in the two Koreas.

President Park Geun Hye

General Choi Hong Hi passed away on 15th June, 2002, aged 83. Following an Official State funeral, honouring his role in creating and spreading the art of Taekwon-Do globally, the General was buried in the 'Patriotic Martyrs Cemetery' in Pyong-yang, North Korea, along

---

[33] Reported by CAN (Catholic News Agency) in 2009

[34] Part of the Sunshine Policy included outreach and interaction with North Korea, in the hope of fostering improved relations and understanding between both Korea's, which included an exchange of Taekwon-Do/Taekwondo Demo teams from both Country's.

From Creation To Unification
The Complete Histories Behind The Ch'ang Hon (ITF) Patterns

side other Korean patriots who resisted the Japanese occupation of Korea.

During one of his last interviews[35] he was asked if he ever regretted dedicating his life to Taekwon-Do, to which he replied: *"I taught Taekwon-Do without regard to race, religion, nationality, or ideology. In this respect, I am the happiest man in the world, and I am proud to have left my footprint in this world."*

From the Father of Taekwon Do

The life of a human being, perhaps 100 years, can be considered as a day when compared with eternity. Therefore, we mortals are no more than simple travellers who pass by the eternal years of an aeon in a day.

Here I leave Taekwon-Do for mankind as a trace of man of the late 20th century. The 24 patterns represent 24 hours, one day, or all my life.

---

[35] Interview by Dr. He-Young- Kimm. Taekwondo Times, 2000.

천지
Chon-Ji

Chon-Ji means literally 'the Heaven the Earth'. It is, in the Orient, interpreted as the creation of the world or the beginning of human history, therefore, it is the initial pattern played by the beginner. This pattern consists of two similar parts; one to represent the Heaven and the other the Earth.

General Choi, Hong Hi standing next to Lake Chon-Ji [36]

Chon-Ji is the first pattern of Ch'ang Hon Taekwon-Do, usually taught at 9th Kup, White belt. It has 19 moves and was developed in Malaysia between 1962 and 1964 with the help of Master Kim, Bok Man and Master Woo, Jae Lim.

Chon-Ji is named after a lake situated on the Baektu (White-Headed) Mountain in the Ryanggang Province of what is now North Korea and is actually an extinct volcano crater. The Hanja for Chon-Ji (천지), when separate have a different meaning to when they are joined.

---

[36] Photo courtesy of Dr. George Vitale, VIII

From Creation To Unification
The Complete Histories Behind The Ch'ang Hon (ITF) Patterns

'Chon' (천) means 'Heaven' and 'Ji' (천) means 'Earth' However, when combined together Chon-Ji actually means *'Heavenly Lake'*

Legend has it that Lake Chon-Ji was where Dan-Gun, Korea's legendary founder, first lived and is the highest peak in Korea and often referred to as the *'Roof of Korea'*.

Chon-Ji lake on Baektu Mountain [37]

It is said that General Choi, named the pattern after the lake because the water is so clear and calm that you can literally see the heaven meeting the earth, so the two parts of Chon-Ji tul represent this.

In Korean philosophy, *'Heaven and Earth'* are represented on the South Korean flag (the Taegeukgi), with the actual symbol called *Taegeuk* [38] (meaning Ultimate Reality), the symbol is similar to the well known Chinese symbol for *'Yin and Yang'* (Um and Yang in Korean), except that the Korean Taegeuk is Red for Heaven and Blue for Earth and represents Korean Taoism.

The South Korean flag (Taegeukgi), with the Taegeuk in the centre

The Taegeuk symbol goes back over a thousand years in Korea, with the oldest ever artefact found decorated with the symbol, dating back over 1,400 years, which was found in South Jeolla Province, Korea. Other evidence of this age old Korean symbol have been found in the

---

[37] Photo by Bdpmax. Cc-by-sa-3.0

[38] Taegeuk refers to the ultimate reality from which all things and values originate and is the Korean pronunciation of the Chinese characters (i.e. Hanja) for T'ai Chi. It is also the symbol that makes up the centre of the South Korean Flag (The Taegeukgi).. Source: en.wikipedia.org/wiki/Taegeuk

천지
Chon-Ji

Gameunsa Temple, which was built during the reign of King Jin-Pyeong of the Silla Dynasty, in 628 AD as well as other places.

In an article by Sanko Lewis[39], he notes that Chon-Ji, whilst having *'two similar parts'* representing *Heaven* and *Earth,* also has a third part representing *Humanity*, which is consistent with another, similar, Korean symbol called the *'Sam Taeguek'* meaning *'Triple Grand Ultimate'*. In this, again, Red represents Heaven, Blue represents Earth and Yellow represents Humanity.

The Sam Taegeuk, surrounded by the 8 trigrams or Palgwe.

Each of the *'two similar parts'* in Chon-Ji are made up of eight moves, which equal the number of Trigrams in the *Palgwe*[40] which surround the *Sam Taegeuk*. The final 3 moves are equal to the numbers of bars within each Trigram making the total of 19 moves found in Chon-Ji.

Furthermore, Sanko writes *"These last three movements consist of one forward punch and two retreating punches. If one considers the first forward punch as offensive and the two retreating punches as defensive, then one is presented with a trigram that starts with one solid bar, followed by two broken bars. This trigram symbolizes "Mountain" in the Palgwe."* – and a mountain is where lake Chon-Ji is situated but more so, where Dan-Gun, the legendary founder of Korea is reputed to have first lived.

With Chon-Ji being seen as the birthplace of the Korean nation, it is no wonder General Choi choose it to be the first of the patterns, despite not actually being the first pattern designed.

Finally, students often confuse which part represents 'Heaven' and which part represents 'Earth', mistakenly thinking that the first part represents the 'Earth' due to the Low Outer Forearm Block pointing

---

[39] *'An Introduction To The Philosophy Of Chon-Ji'* by Sanko Lewis - Issue 18 of Totally Tae Kwon Do magazine.

[40] *Palgwe* or *bagua* in Chinese, meaning literally "eight symbols". These are eight diagrams used in Taoism and represent the fundamental principles of reality using eight interrelated concepts. Each consists of three lines, each line either "broken" or "unbroken," representing yin or yang, respectively. Due to their tripartite structure, they are often referred to as "trigrams" in English..

From Creation To Unification
The Complete Histories Behind The Ch'ang Hon (ITF) Patterns

Sunrise over the Paektu plateau sets the eastern sky ablaze in the colours of molten iron, tinting it in a gold and silvery glow, as the dazzling rays from the sun spread out across the sky

downwards and the second part representing 'Heaven' due to the Middle Inner Forearm Block pointing upwards, when in fact it is the other way around, as this is also based on a trigram.

A trigram is made up of 3 lines – in this case it has heaven at the top, Earth at the bottom and, as Mr. Lewis pointed out, there is a third part to this pattern, which represents 'Humanity' and this is represented in the middle line of the trigram which is where the 'blocks' point to. The first part of the pattern has the Low Outer Forearm Block pointing down towards humanity, from heaven and thus represents 'Heaven'. The second part of the pattern has the Middle Inner Forearm Block pointing upwards from earth towards 'Humanity' and thus represents 'Earth'.

Finally, some feel that the 19 moves in Chon-Ji tul represent the 10 Kup ranks and 9 Dan ranks in Taekwon-Do, however, this cannot be the case as in his 1965 book 'Taekwon-Do' General Choi only listed 8 kup grades, starting from 8th Kup and covered by the following Kup belts: White belt (8th to 7th Kup), Blue belt (6th to 5th Kup) and Brown belt (4th to 1st Kup).

단군
Dan-Gun

Dan-Gun is named after the holy Dan-Gun, the legendary founder of Korea in the year of 2,333 B.C.

Dan-Gun is the second pattern of Ch'ang Hon Taekwon-Do, usually taught at 8th Kup, Yellow belt. It has 21 moves and was developed in Malaysia between 1962 and 1964 with the help of Master Kim, Bok Man and Master Woo, Jae Lim.

The legend of Dan-Gun dates back to the 12 Century, and has been used since that time to revive or bolster national unity and pride amongst the Korean people.

The legend goes that there was a time when heaven and earth were one and animals could speak like humans. The God Hwanin sent his son Hwang-Ung to the East to build a new country. Hwang-Ung settled on the Baektu Mountain (see Chon-Ji), the highest peak on the peninsula which is between the borders of what is now North Korea and China. This was in 2,333 BC during the 25th reign of the Yao Emperor in China.

Dan-Gun [41]

One day a tiger and a bear appeared in front of Hwang-Ung and asked if they could be transformed into human form. After much thought Hwang-Ung informed the animals that their wish could be granted,

---

[41] Courtesy of David A. Mason. *www.san-shin.org*. Reproduced with permission and thanks.

From Creation To Unification
The Complete Histories Behind The Ch'ang Hon (ITF) Patterns

The picture above is a depiction of the Dan-Gun legend and shows Hwang-Ung (son of the God Hwanin) under the Sandalwood tree (mentioned in Kim Pu-Sik's version of the legend) with the tiger and the bear that wanted to become human.[42]

but it would be difficult and would take much patience. The animals agreed that they would do whatever it took to become human and make their wish a reality.

Hwang-Ung gave the tiger and the bear twenty cloves of garlic and some mugworts and they were told to eat them whilst they stayed in a cave and prayed earnestly for 100 days.

After twenty days the tiger became hungry and could no longer continue, so he left the cave the next day in search of food and so stayed a tiger. When the 100 days were almost at an end, the bear began to lose its fur and its rear feet began to change, until at the end of the 100th day the bear had fully transformed into a beautiful woman. She became known as Ung-Yo which means *'the girl incarnated from a bear'*. Hwang-Ung, so taken by her beauty, married Ung-Yo and she gave birth to a son, who they named Dan-Gun. This child gave rise to the first Korean Dynasty in 2,333 BC, which was originally called the Joseon Dynasty but is now called the Gojoseon Dynasty to

---

[42] Picture courtesy of David A. Mason. *www.san-shin.org*. Reproduced with permission and thanks.

단군
Dan-Gun

distinguish it from the later 'Joseon Dynasty' which was founded in 1392 AD and given the same name as the earlier dynasty.

Another version of the legend (possibly the very first), by the 12th century scholar General Kim Pu-Sik, who wrote the *'Sam-Guk-Sagi'* or *'Annals of the Three Kingdoms'*; the earliest surviving source of history on the three kingdoms of Korea, tells a similar story except that Hwang-Ung told the tiger and bear to retire from the sunlight for 21 days with the food, in order to become men. The tiger, being fierce couldn't endure staying in the cave and left, but the bear had more faith and patience and stayed in the cave for the full 21 days and so was transformed into a beautiful woman.

According to the legend, Dan-Gun was found sitting under a tree on Mt. Baektu by the *'Nine Wild Tribes'* and they made him their king. He introduced many new things to them, such as religious worship (it is said he built the first alter in 2265 BC), the rite of marriage, tree felling, agriculture, house building, cooking, as well as the subject-king relationship. Dan-Gun eventually led them down the mountain to establish the first capital city called 'Asadal'[43] near or at Pyongyang where he lived his life with his wife, Pi So-Ap and had children. His sons are also said to have built a fortress at Chung-Dung island, known as Sam-Nang fortress.

Dan-Gun's alter at Muni-San (the highest peak) on Kang-Hwa island.

Pyongyang is now also the name of the DPRK's[44] (North Korea) capital city, so it was originally thought that Asadal was built there. However, this is now disputed by researchers who say there was more than one city named Pyongyang back then, as it was common for a

---

[43] Asadal meaning *'Morning Mountain'*

[44] *Democratic People's Republic of Korea* - herein referred to as North Korea

From Creation To Unification
The Complete Histories Behind The Ch'ang Hon (ITF) Patterns

ruler to have two capital cities and with North Korea's capital of *Pyongyang* being the most Southern of them, it is more likely the other *'Pyongyang'* was located in Manchuria (now China) as it was closer to Mt. Baektu. The original second *Pyongyang* would have been renamed in Chinese.

In 1122 BC the Shang Dynasty of China was overthrown and this had a dramatic consequence for Dan-Gun, as the uncle of the former Shang King (Gi-Ja) escaped and fled to Korea with 5,000 followers and Dan-Gun, who had reigned for 1,211 years fled from Gi-Ja's army to the town of Mun-Wha before finally resuming his spirit form and disappearing from the earth altogether. This left Gi-Ja to rule Korea, which he and his dynasty did from 1122 BC to 193 BC and in that time it is said he taught the people of Korea about Chinese culture, art, medicines as well as reading and writing.

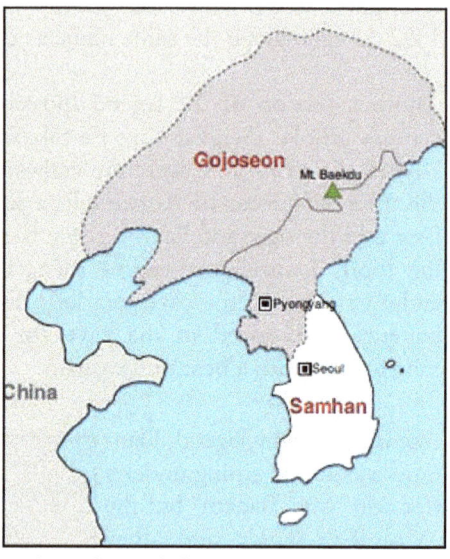

A map showing the location of Dan-Guns first home on Mt. Paektu, the area covered by the first Dynasty of Korea (Gojoseon) which is mostly in modern day China and the location of Modern day Pyongyang.in North Korea.[45]

There is a shrine in Mun-Wha (which is in North Korea) which is said to contain his 410-foot (in circumference) *'grave'* and contains two skeletons - that of Dan-Gun and his wife, Pi So-Ap - though no archaeologists outside of North Korea have ever been allowed to inspect it to verify its authenticity.

It is thought that this legend of Dan-Gun came about from the very founding of Korea itself, where various tribes from Mongolia, China and Manchuria came together as the first sons of Korea. These

---

[45] Picture courtesy of David A. Mason. Reproduced with permission and thanks.

단군
Dan-Gun

The Tomb of Dan-Gun and the reputed original stone monument, telling the history of the 'Tomb of King Dan-Gun', found at the site with the buried ruins of the original tomb. Two large skeletons are now enshrined inside the reconstruction; they are said to be King Dan-Gun and his wife.[46]

various tribes either worshipped the sun, or under a system of beliefs known as totemism[47], the tiger or the bear. Historians feel the myth may have started with the tribes of the *'sun'* and *'bear'* joining together and that union bore the child 'Dan-Gun' - who later united the races and founded one nation. Whilst the *'tiger'* worshipping tribes were either excluded or defeated by the *'Bear'* and *'Sun'* unified tribe – hence the bear, tiger and sun references in the legend itself. To elevate his position and thus help strengthen the unified tribes, Dan-Gun was elevated to the almost deity status of *'Grandson of the Lord of Heaven'* and thus the legend was born.

Although the legend of Dan-Gun has been used throughout the years to bolster national pride, it became extremely prominent in 1909 when Na Cheol[48] founded a religion based on Dan-Gun, known as *Daejonggyo* (The Religion of the Divine Progenitor or Great Ancestral Religion). It is also known as *Dangungyo* (Religion of Dan-Gun) and its main tenet is that, as Koreans already have a 'God' they have no need to worship other foreign Gods!

The 21 movements in this pattern are thought to refer to part of the legend of Dan-Gun (depending on which version you go with), where

---

[46] Photo's courtesy of David A. Mason. Reproduced with permission and thanks.

[47] Totemism is a belief system which humans feel they are connected and have kinship with the spirit-beings of animals or plants.

[48] Na Cheol (1863–1916), was also known as a leader of the Korean independence movement - See Sam-Il chapter.

the mythical tiger couldn't endure the 21 days he was meant to, for transformation into human form.

The pattern Dan-Gun only uses high section punches which is unique for a pattern of the Ch'ang Hon system, they are said to represent Dan-Gun climbing a mountain, perhaps descending from Lake Chon-Ji to establish his capital city (Asadal) or ascending to Muni-San to build the first altar. Some feel that the 3 punches in a row also may represent the 3 weeks (21 days) that the bear endured in the cave in Kim Pu-Sik's version of the legend.

Dan-Gun remains a spiritual figure that has helped maintain a strong Korean culture and it is this strong belief in identity that has helped Korea protect itself from invasion throughout its history. October 3rd is celebrated as a national holiday, commemorating the founding father, Dan Gun.

Statue of Dan-Gun [49]

---

[49] Photo courtesy of David A. Mason. *www.san-shin.org*. Reproduced with permission and thanks.

도산
Do-San

Do-San is the pseudonym of the patriot **Ahn Chang-Ho (1876-1938)**.[50] The 24 movements represent his entire life which he devoted to furthering the education of Korea and its independence movement.

Do-San is the third pattern of Ch'ang Hon Taekwon-Do, usually taught at 7th Kup, Yellow belt. It has 24 moves and was developed in Malaysia between 1962 and 1964 with the help of Master Kim, Bok Man and Master Woo, Jae Lim.

Ahn Chang-Ho was born a farmers son, on Torong Island, on the Taedong River which is near Pyongyang, on 9th November, 1878.[51] In 1894, still a teenager, Ahn Chang-Ho was influenced by a reverend he met and converted to Christianity, becoming a Presbyterian.

In 1897, at the age of 19, Ahn Chang-Ho became a member of *Tongnip Hyophoe* (Independence Association), but as the aims of the association started to falter around 1899/1900, Ahn Chang-Ho focused his efforts on improving education and established the first co-educational elementary school in Korea, called *Cheomjin* (meaning Gradual).

In 1902, Ahn Chang-Ho got married and emigrated to San Francisco

---

[50] The Encyclopaedia of Taekwon-do and countless other references are wrong, as Ahn Chang-Ho was actually born in the year 1878 and not 1876. Consequently, Master Hee Il Cho's *The Complete Tae Kwon-Do Hyung, Vol 1* has it correct!

[51] Dedicated Do-San sites in Korea also list his date of birth as 9th November, 1878.

From Creation To Unification
The Complete Histories Behind The Ch'ang Hon (ITF) Patterns

Ahn Chang-Ho, Pyongyang, 1898

in the United States with his new wife, Lee Hae-Ryon with the aim of receiving a western education, that in turn would allow him to further his education of Koreans, back in Korea, he was just 24 years old. Ahn Chang-Ho was one of the first Koreans to emigrate to the United States of America and it is said that during his journey there by steamship, as he approached Hawaii, he saw its volcanic peaks rising from the Pacific Ocean and decided to call himself 'Do-San' (Island Mountain), resolving to *'stand tall above the sea of turmoil existing in Korea at that time'*. However, upon his arrival he was disappointed and shocked at the lives of Korean Americans, who often fought amongst themselves and lacked any unity. So instead he focused his efforts on creating enlightenment and unity between Koreans living in the United States.

Ahn Chang-Ho's wish to improve the lives of his fellow Koreans living in the USA was not just rousing words and he took a 'hands on' approach, travelling around house to house, helping with any household chores that were needed to improve their appearance, such as washing windows, planting flowers, sweeping and even cleaning toilets. Though at first, many questioned the sanity of what he was doing, little by little the Korean houses became more respectable and thus those that lived there did too, taking more pride in their

도산
Do-San

appearances and that of their houses and thus raised the perceptions of Koreans by non-Koreans in America.

In Riverside, California, the orange orchards surrounding the area offered work to many, however, in a mirror of his homeland, the Japanese labour contractors controlled the jobs and excluded most Koreans. In an effort to balance the injustice for Korean workers Ahn Chang-Ho set out to resolve the problems and somehow convinced one orchard owner, Cornelius Earle Rumsey to loan him $1,500 to set up a Korean employment agency. Mr Rumsey was impressed with Ahn Chang-Ho's character and moral strength and so loaned him the money. Within a month

Cornelius Earle Rumsey with his wife.

Ahn Chang-Ho had repaid the loan which impressed Mr Rumsey even more, so much so that from that point on he only employed Korean workers. Along with Ahn Chang-Ho, Cornelius Rumsey helped to provide affordable housing to his Korean workers which led to the first Korean village in California.

By the age of 24, Ahn Chang-Ho was known as a leader of his countrymen within the United States as he organized the *Kungminhoe* (Korean National Association) which inspired his fellow countrymen (in the United States) to hope for the national independence of Korea.

In January, 1907, Ahn Chang-Ho returned home to Korea and formed an independence group known as the *Shinmin-Hoe* (New Peoples Association) after learning of the Japanese Protectorate Treaty; a treaty which enforced the right of the Japanese to legally occupy his

From Creation To Unification
The Complete Histories Behind The Ch'ang Hon (ITF) Patterns

country. The *Shinmin-Hoe* promoted Korean independence via the cultivation of nationalism in education, culture and business.

By 1910, the *Shinmin-Hoe* had grown in size considerably and soon became the focus of the Japanese occupier's attempts to close down such organizations as they threatened the occupation. In December of the same year the Japanese fabricated a fake plot to assassinate the Japanese Governor-General of the time, Masatake Terauchi, who was due to attend a dedication ceremony of a bridge on the Amnok river. The Japanese used this fabricated plot as an excuse to arrest every one of the *Shinmin-Hoe* leaders as well as six hundred innocent Christians. One hundred and five Koreans were tried after horrific torture during which many of those arrested died. This incident

Masatake Terauchi [52]

and the fact that the charges and plot were obviously fabricated concerned the worldwide community so greatly that they applied international pressure on the Japanese, which eventually allowed most of the accused to go free.

After the assassination of Hiro-Bumi Ito (see Joong-Gun chapter) Japan tightened its grip on Korea's leaders and, with the country on the verge of collapse, Ahn Chang-Ho was forced into exile in Manchuria before finally returning to America, arriving in New York in early 1911. In the same year, back in Korea, Japan passed the Education Act which forced all Korean schools to close and within three years there were virtually no Korean schools left teaching in Korea.

---

[52] Picture: Carl Prinz von Hohenzollern, *Meine Erlebnisse wahrend des Russisch-Japanischen Krieges, 1904-1905*, Ernst Siegfried Mittler und Sohn, 1912

도산
Do-San

The 'Hungsadan'. Circa 1917

Whilst in America, Ahn Chang-Ho was elected chairman of the Korean National People's Association which negotiated with the United States Government. During this time he formed the '*Hungsadan*', a secret organization of patriots. The Hungsadan (Young Korean Academy) goal was *"laying the groundwork for the great undertaking of enlightening the people of Korea."*

The Hungsadan had a set of four fundamental principles, which were:
1. Seek the truth
2. Act upon the truth
3. Be loyal and trustworthy
4. Be courageous.

The Hungsadan also taught '5 Essential Teachings', these were:
1. Let us constantly strive to improve ourselves by seeking the truth, acting upon the truth, practicing loyalty and courage.
2. Let us love each other, be faithful to each other, and help each other.
3. Let us unite and work for the organisation, and devoting ourselves to the organisation.
4. Let us be honest in everything and fulfil our responsibilities.
5. Let us dedicate ourselves to the country and people with the spirit of service.

From Creation To Unification
The Complete Histories Behind The Ch'ang Hon (ITF) Patterns

The Hungsadan along with other organizations put pressure on the United States President (Woodrow Wilson) to speak on behalf of Korean autonomy at the Paris peace talks in 1918 (see Sam-Il chapter). On the 1st March, 1919 the Sam-Il demonstrations took place (See Eui-Am and Sam-Il chapters), as the Provisional Korean Government declared independence from Japan, calling for massive resistance from the Korean people. Though thousands were killed, arrested and tortured during unarmed demonstrations in Korea, in which the Japanese police fired into the unarmed crowds, Ahn Chang-Ho was not deterred and continued his work in the United States. Towards the end of March he travelled to Shanghai to help form part of a Provisional Korean Government and help draw up a Democratic Constitution for Korea along with future South Korean President Syngman Rhee and Kim Ku. Whilst there he even created a village in Manchuria for wandering Korean refugees, but after two years, he resigned his post after becoming disillusioned with the provisional Korean leaders and their in-fighting and returned to America.

In 1926, Ahn Chang-Ho returned to China and established the *Deagongjuue* (Great Public Spiritism or Korean Independence Party), providing the Provisional Korean Government with a political organization outside of Korea.

Whilst in Shanghai in 1932, Ahn Chang-Ho was arrested following bombings by Korean patriot Yoon Bong-Gil, which led to the Japanese police rounding up Korean independence activists. Ahn Chang-Ho was arrested on 29th April, as the police alleged he had something to do with the bombings and on 7th June, 1932 Ahn Chang-Ho was shipped back to Korea, under arrest. This was the first time he would have been back to Korea since 1910! After being returned to Seoul, Ahn Chang-Ho was sentenced to 4 years imprisonment, but was paroled after 2 years.

Yun Bong Gil, Shanghai, 1932

도산
Do-San

In 1937 Ahn Chang-Ho was arrested again due to the continuing political unrest and his Anti-Japanese activities, where, despite his age, he was imprisoned and tortured by the Japanese. However, due to having severe tuberculosis (a common illness in Korea at that time), as well as pleurisy and peritonitis, Ahn Chang-Ho was eventually released (on bail) to Kyungsung University hospital, in Seoul, where he passed away on 10th March, 1938 – a national hero.

It is the belief of many scholars, that if Ahn Chang-Ho had lived beyond Korea's liberation in 1945, there would be no divided Korea at all!

Ahn Chang-Ho's Prison Picture, 1937

Ahn Chang-Ho had five children - 3 boys and 2 girls. It was while in America the first time that Ahn Chang-Ho's wife, Lee Hae-Ryon, gave birth to their son Ahn Pil-Ip on 29th March, 1905. Born in California he was the first American citizen born of Korean parents in the USA. In school he developed a love for acting but as Korean actors were held in low esteem he was discouraged by his mother. At one point he was offered a role in a Douglas Fairbanks movie and when he excitedly told his mother, she forbade him from leaving the house for 3 days and he lost the role. However, in 1925 when his father was home from his many trips abroad, Pil-Ip had a discussion with his father about his love of acting and Ahn Chang-Ho actively encouraged him to pursue his career, encouraging him to be the best he could at what he loved as that would resonate to the world world his dream that non-Koreans would see Koreans as a proud and equal race.

Ahn Pil-Ip became known as Philip Ahn and his acting career would span 40 years in which he would feature in TV shows and films with some of Hollywood's greatest legends, however he is best remembered for

Philip Ahn as Master Kan

his famous role in the 1970's series *'Kung-Fu'* (starring David Carradine). Philip Ahn played Master Kan, the wise monk who was in charge of the Shaolin Temple and *'Grasshoppers'* mentor. As well as his acting, Philip Ahn was, for nearly 20 years, the honorary mayor of Panorama City, California. Philip Ahn passed away on 28th February, 1978. Philip Ahn's career is honoured by a star on Hollywood's Walk of Fame.

Ahn Chang Ho's 2nd son, Ahn Pil-Son was born on 5th July, 1912 and appeared in quite a few films as well, with his most notable appearance being in the television series *'Buck Rogers'* with Buster Crabbe, where he played Prince Tallen. Ahn Pil-Son's acting career stopped when he decided to pursue a career in engineering and went on to be one of the designers of the famous *'Spruce Goose'* airplane. Ahn Pil-Son passed away in May, 2001.

Ahn Pil-Son as Prince Tallen

On the 16th January, 1915 Ahn's first daughter was born. Ahn Su-San was his 3rd child and served in the US Army before opening the Moon-Gate restaurant, which she ran with her sister, Ahn Soo-Rah who was born on 27th May, 1917. The restaurant ran from the same location for over 40 years. Ahn Soo-Rah also became a social worker.

Sadly, Ahn Chang-Ho never got to see his youngest son, Ahn Phil-Young who was born on 26th September 1926, as Ahn Chang-Ho had left for China whilst his wife was pregnant and sadly never returned home again. Like his brothers, Phil-Young also became an actor with his screen name as Ralph Ahn. His acting career saw him feature in many films and television shows, amongst them the martial arts film *'The Perfect Weapon'* and Chuck Norris's *'Walker Texas Ranger'* series.

Originally, Ahn Chang-Ho was buried outside the capital city of Seoul, in Manuri Cemetery, by the Japanese, but in 1973 the Do-San

도산
Do-San

The last ever picture taken of Ahn Chang-Ho, 1938

Ahn Chang-Ho's Grave

Memorial Park was opened in Shinsa-dong, Seoul. It was built to mark the 95th anniversary of Ahn Chang-Ho's birth and Ahn Chang-Ho's body was exhumed from the hills outside Seoul and reburied within the park, laid to rest along side his wife, Lee Hae-Ryon.

The 24 movements of this pattern are said to represent Ahn Chang-Ho's entire life devoted to the education of Korea and its independence movement. However, as Ahn Chang-Ho's lifeline dates are given as 1876-1938, this means he was 62 (or more correctly, 60 – *see previous footnotes*) when he died, this can be a little confusing. Some feel the 24 movements are in reference to

Ahn Chang-Ho Memorial, Riverside, California, USA[53]

---

[53] Picture courtesy of the International Relations Council of Riverside, CA

From Creation To Unification
The Complete Histories Behind The Ch'ang Hon (ITF) Patterns

General Choi stating that the 24 patterns of Taekwon-do represent *'One day in the universe or an entire lifetime'*, which many now include in the short descriptions of Do-San tul, stating *'the 24 movements of this pattern represent his entire life which he devoted to furthering the education of Korea and its independence movement'*, however, when Do-San was formulated there were only 20 patterns of Taekwon-do and the added *'24 hours represent..'* (in reference to Do-San) was not included in any descriptions until around 1983 - so this cannot be the original reason. I feel (initially at least) the 24 movements were in reference to the age at which Ahn Chang-Ho became nationally recognized as a leader of his countrymen, something which occurred not in Korea, but actually in the United States of America.

A newspaper article about Ahn Chang-Ho, printed in 1976

원효
Won-Hyo

Won-Hyo was the noted monk who introduced Buddhism to the Silla Dynasty in the year 686 A.D.

Won-Hyo is the fourth pattern of Ch'ang Hon Taekwon-Do, usually taught at 6th Kup, Green belt. It has 28 moves and was developed in Malaysia between 1962 and 1964 with the help of Master Kim, Bok Man and Master Woo, Jae Lim.

The standard definition to this pattern is slightly misleading! Firstly, 686 AD is the year Won-Hyo passed away, not when Buddhism was introduced to the Silla Dynasty, as (secondly) Buddhism had already found its way to the Silla Dynasty, exactly 90 years before the birth of Won-Hyo[54], but it remained out of reach of the ordinary people and it was Won-Hyo who was solely instrumental in bringing it to the masses.

A sketched image of Won-Hyo [55]

Won-Hyo was born Sol-Sedang in 617 AD in Apnyang, now the modern city of Gyeongsan in Kyongsang Province. Won-Hyo was his penname, which was derived from his nickname *'sedak'* which means *'dawn'*, with Won-Hyo meaning *'break of dawn'*.

---

[54] King Beop-Heung tried to establish Buddhism as the official state religion in 527 AD but the decision wasn't popular with the Royal court and it was opposed. So, with the aid of some others, the king hatched a plan to convince the Royal Court of its worth and in 528 AD he executed a 22 year old monk by the name of Ichadon in order to make him a martyr. Stories of Ichadon's death said that his blood ran *'white as milk'* and this (whilst probably propaganda by the king) was seen as an omen, enabling the king to decree that everyone had the right to practice Buddhism.

[55] Courtesy of David A. Mason. *www.san-shin.org*. Reproduced with permission and thanks.

From Creation To Unification
The Complete Histories Behind The Ch'ang Hon (ITF) Patterns

'Sedak', Won-Hyo's nickname comes from the story of his birth. His mother and father were fortunate with their station in life, his father (Sol-Damnal) was a government official and they lived comfortably and had everything they wanted, except for a child. His mother prayed to Buddha every morning at dawn, in the hope that he would send her a child and one night, it is said she had a special dream in which the largest star in the sky sped down from heaven, like an arrow and pierced her bosom. This was considered a good omen and very soon after she was found to be pregnant.

Whilst pregnant, Won-Hyo's mother was passing the Chestnut Valley and fell into labour. With her labour, it was too hard to make it home and the day was getting late, so Sol-Damnal made a shelter, to protect her from the wind and cover her during labour, by removing his outer clothes and hanging them from the branches of a chestnut tree. Whilst the female attendants helped deliver the baby, Sol-Damnal stood close by praying for a safe delivery. It is said that just before Won-Hyo arrived, five clouds of brilliant light enveloped the shelter, whereby shortly afterwards Won-Hyo was born. He was named 'Sedang' and given the nickname '*Sedak*' as he was born at dawn. Won-Hyo, the pen-name he used years later would be derived from this nickname and means '*break of dawn*'. The chestnut tree (often referred to as a sal tree or sala tree) is significant in this story, as it is usually only found in stories or legends of extremely revered people!

Interestingly, the legend also has much in common with the birth of the Guatama Buddha (Buddishm being the path Won-Hyo was destined to follow), where by his mother, Queen Maha Maya also had a dream, that of a white elephant with six tusks that pierced her side, and then she became pregnant. Whilst travelling to her mother's house, Queen Maha Maya went into labour by a grove and gave birth under a sal tree with a sunbeam stretching down from Heaven!

Won-Hyo was a child prodigy, so gifted that he could *"infer ten things after learning one"*, he was also a skilled horse rider and javelin thrower and became a Hwa-Rang (See Hwa-Rang chapter). Civil war between the three kingdoms (Silla, Goguryo and Baekje) was rife in Korea at this time and legend has it that Won-Hyo, as a young man, took part in these civil wars and it was seeing many of his fellow Hwa-Rang and

원효
Won-Hyo

friends slaughtered that made him realize the briefness of human life and that drove him to become a monk. At just 15 years old, whilst still a Hwa-Rang, he turned his home into a temple and renounced the world and by the age of 20 he had turned his back on violence altogether and pursued his religious beliefs, taking on the penname *'Won-Hyo'*.

It is unknown exactly why Won-Hyo turned to Buddhism as his chosen religion, or who he studied under (or if he even had a single dedicated teacher at all – which would have been highly unusual at the time). One thought is that, although his family had a place in the 'society' of the time, he was in the lower kolp'um class and that made promotion prospects to a decent government position limited and it is thought that by becoming a Buddhist, members of the kolp'um class bypassed the hierarchical class system and raised themselves in societies eyes.

In 650 AD Won-Hyo and his friend and fellow Buddhist, Uisang travelled by sea to China in order to study under the famous Buddhist scholar Huan-Tchuang. At this time, Silla and (Tang) China were allies, but Silla and Goguryo were not. Goguryo was also in a state of alert, with heightened tension due to a recent Tang invasion and, as Won-Hyo's boat passed close to Goguryo, a Goguryo patrol boarded the boat and wrongly identified both Won-Hyo and Uisang as spies. After being detained for several weeks, they were released (some say escaped). It is thought, that though Won-Hyo was dismayed at not making it to China, what he witnessed while being detained, affected his Buddhist philosophies further.

In 661 AD Won-Hyo and Uisang again tried to travel to China. During their journey, a great storm broke out and in the darkness they sought shelter and found a cave to rest up in. Tired from the trip, they fell asleep in the dark cave and during the night Won-Hyo awoke and was thirsty. He fumbled around in the darkness and felt a vessel, which was filled with water from the rain. He picked it up and drank from it, quenching his thirst with the refreshing water. When he awoke the following morning he looked for the vessel, only to realize it was a rotten skull and on closer inspection was swarming with maggots – Won-Hyo fell down and vomited at the sight!

Looking around, they realized they were not in a cave, but in a burial chamber, but the storm remained fierce and they had no choice but to stay in the chamber another night. On the second night, now knowing where he was, Won-Hyo couldn't sleep, the sounds he found terrifying and he had visions of ghosts and it was because of all this that Won-Hyo had a *'sudden awakening!'* He realized, that when he thought it was simply a cave, he slept soundly and when he thought the vessel was simply a vessel full of rain water, it quenched his thirst, but when he realized he was sleeping in a burial chamber, he felt very uncomfortable and to know the vessel was a skull made him feel sick! From this he determined *'When a thought arises, all dharmas (phenomenon) arise, and when a thought disappears, the shelter and the tomb are as one'*. His *'awakening'* was the inner enlightenment that *'everything is created by the mind alone'*.

A picture depicting Won-Hyo's *'sudden awakening'* [56]

Upon this, Won-Hyo decided that there was no need for him to find a master, as he now understood *'life and death'* and considered there was no more to learn. Whilst Uisang continued to China, Won-Hyo

---

[56] Picture courtesy of Wonkeun Nam, Korean Buddhist Monk. Reproduced with permission and thanks.

원효
Won-Hyo

headed back towards Korea. His revelation changed his Buddhist philosophy. He developed the Chongto-Gyo or *'Pure Land'* sect. He believed that teaching by word of mouth, living with the public, enduring their same hardships and passing on the Buddha's teaching directly was a truer way of following Buddha's will. Before this, only members of the royal family or aristocracy would practice Buddhism as they were the only ones who could read, however, Won-Hyo's new philosophy didn't require long study of Chinese literature for the sect members, just diligent prayer and it made his branch of Buddhist philosophy easily accessible to the lower classes, thus making it popular among the entire population.

In 662 AD Won-Hyo left the priest hood altogether and travelled the country, spreading Buddhism to everyone, from beggars to princes and it is though this effort that eventually, the whole of Silla turned to Buddhism.

He held meetings for both ordinary citizens and royal family alike, in order to teach Buddhism to as many people as possible and at one such meeting, he encountered a Princess: the second daughter of King Muyeol (whose wife was the younger sister of General Kim, Yoo Sin – see Yoo-Sin chapter).

Won-Hyo teaching Buddhism to the masses [57]

Princess Yosok was a widower, her husband had been a Hwa-Rang but had been killed in battle and she sought comfort through Won-Hyo's words. In fact, his words had a profound effect on her and as she swirled them through her mind over and over, she became sick. A royal physician was summoned, but he could find nothing wrong with her. She was sick from love!

---

[57] Picture courtesy of Dale Quarrington. Reproduced with permission and thanks.

From Creation To Unification
The Complete Histories Behind The Ch'ang Hon (ITF) Patterns

Expressing a wish to see Won-Hyo again, a servant suggested she host one of Won-Hyo's meetings at the palace. Won Hyo held the meeting and as he was about to leave, a maid told him that Princess Yosok would like to serve him some rare tea before he left. He was escorted to the princesses chambers which were fragrant with the tea's aroma. Princess Yosok served him herself and he drank the tea. Finally, the Princess could not restrain herself any longer and confessed to the real reason she had invited him to the palace, telling him that she couldn't keep him out of her thoughts and that her wanting of him was making her sick! She begged Won-Hyo for help, saying that if he didn't help her, she would surely die!

Won-Hyo was embarrassed, but explained that he was a monk and as such, worldly love was forbidden and he must observe the Buddhist precepts. Princess Yosok responded by saying *"But Master, do the precepts not forbid you to leave me to die?"*

Won-Hyo closed his eyes and thought about the situation. He agreed with the princess, that leaving another to die was a great sin, but in order to fulfill the princesses wish, they must have the kings permission as in that era, widows were not permitted to remarry!

Won-Hyo left the palace and for many days meditated on the situation in search of an answer – a way to save the princesses life! He realized that although one must follow the precepts, sometimes they conflict and thus cannot be followed exactly and, as saving a life was a precept, the way he would do so, although a sin in itself, it would be considered compassionate and thus forgivable!

A few days later Won-Hyo appeared in the Palace grounds singing a song over and over, the word were:

> *"Who will lend me an axe that has lost its handle?*
> *I will cut down a beam that will serve as a pillar in Heaven."*

He returned day after day, singing the same song over and over again and word of his strange behaviour soon spread sound the palace. No one understood the meaning of the song, but eventually, as he had hoped, King Muyeol came to hear it and pondered the words and

원효
Won-Hyo

meaning for himself! The king eventually came to understand its meaning: The axe that had lost its handle is like a woman who had lost her husband and the pillars of heaven represented an heir to the Silla kingdom! And with that, the king proclaimed that Won-Hyo was to marry a princess and between them have a wise son. The king smiled and thought of his daughter, Princess Yosok.

Won-Hyo was secretly taken to the residence of Princess Yosok where they were married in a simple ceremony.

As the months passed by, Won-Hyo's conscience weighed heavy on him for what he had done, even though his intentions were pure. Eventually he made up his mind to return to his original path, travelling the land teaching. He told the princess of his decision and as the tears welled up in her eyes she asked if she would ever see him again? He replied that he hoped to see her in the Pure-Land of Happiness and that she should seek the path of Buddha and not him, as by doing so she will forget her sorrow and find enlightenment. And with that, Won-Hyo bowed, formed his hands in prayer and left the palace forever! A few months later the princess realized she was pregnant and gave birth to their son, Sol-Ch'ong[59], who himself became a great Confucian scholar of Silla.

Won-Hyo [58]

Though Won-Hyo travelled the land and lived apart from his wife and son, it is thought they remained in contact as Won-Hyo often stayed at the Hyol temple and his son's house which was close by. It was at the Hyol temple that Won-Hyo entered Nirvana.

---

[58] Picture courtesy of David A. Mason. Reproduced with permission and thanks.

[59] I have read variations on the birth date of Sol-Ch'ong with him being born in 650 AD, 660 AD or 666 AD (by one record stating he was 20 at the time of his Fathers death). Though it may be unimportant to Won-Hyo's main story, it has some bearing on when this event took place and whether it was before his '*sudden awakening*'! As well as the age that Won-Hyo felt forced to break one of the Buddhist precepts as he would have been either 33, 43 or even 50 years old!

From Creation To Unification
The Complete Histories Behind The Ch'ang Hon (ITF) Patterns

In his lifetime, Won-Hyo had seen the unification of Korea's three kingdoms (Silla, Goguryo and Baekje) in 668 AD and brought about magnificent changes in Korea through his Buddhist philosophy and teaching, which had far reaching effects, not only in Korea but in Japan and China as well.

In 686 AD Won-Hyo passed away, aged 70 and his body was laid to rest[60] by his son, Sol-Ch'ong, at Bumhwang-sa temple. Upon his grave stone it was inscribed:

*'He strove to master the principles of the universe,
and made his goal the most profound truth of all'*

Bumhwang-sa Temple

During his lifetime, Won-Hyo authored 86 works (writings) in 240 fascicles, of which around 23 still exist today and are being translated by scholars. Of all his works, which are highly regarded by leading

---

[60] I have also read that following his Fathers death, his son mixed his Fathers ashes with earth and made a small statue in his Fathers likeness. The statue was enshrined at Bumhwangsa Temple and Sol-Ch'ong went there regularly to pay his respects. On one visit it is said that the head of the statue turned towards him and that is why the statues head is turned to one side today! Sadly, I couldn't find a picture of the statue!

원효
Won-Hyo

Buddhist scholars in not just Korea, but China and Japan as well, his work, the *'Awakening of Faith'* is considered the most influential text in Korean tradition ever.

Though Buddhism had found its way to Silla 90 years before the birth of Won-Hyo, it had remained out of reach of the common people. Won-Hyo brought the teachings of the Buddha, from being reserved for the royal family and aristocracy, to every man, woman and child in a unified Korea, even creating songs to help teach the word of Buddha to the common man. Many temples were built because of him and monks from around the word travelled to Korea to learn from him. And most of all, he did this on his own, without a teacher to guide him and was one of the few (if not the only) Buddhist monk to have not had education in Buddhism in China, as so many others did!

A statue of Won-Hyo in Hyochang Park, Seoul [61]

There are many wondrous stories of Won-Hyo in various texts, most of which have miraculous things happen in them, which is testament to the far reaching effect Won-Hyo had. His life as a monk, may have seemed or sounded simple to most, but I'm sure, upon reading this, you can see the profound effect Won-Hyo had on both Korea and Buddhism alike!

---

[61] Picture courtesy of David A. Mason. Reproduced with permission and thanks.

"The best of prophets of the future is the past."

- Lord Byron

율곡
Yul-Gok

Yul-Gok is the pseudonym of a great philosopher and scholar Yi I (1536-1584) nicknamed the "Confucius of Korea" The 38 movements of this pattern refer to his birthplace on 38° latitude and the diagram represents "scholar".

Yul-Gok is the fifth pattern of Ch'ang Hon Taekwon-Do, usually taught at 5th Kup, Green belt. It has 38 moves and was developed in Malaysia between 1962 and 1964 with the help of Master Kim, Bok Man and Master Woo, Jae Lim.

Yul-Gok is named after Korea's great philosopher and scholar Yi I who was born in the Ojukheon House[62] in Kangwon Province on 26th December, 1536 during the Joseon Dynasty.[63] The Ojukheon House belonged to Yul-Gok's father and has been maintained throughout the years by his ancestors.

The Ojukheon House where Yul-Gok was born

Yul-Gok's father was a State Councillor and his mother was an accomplished calligraphist, poet and artist and as such, Yul-Gok was a child prodigy. It is said he learnt to read Chinese scripts by the time he was just 3 years old, and by the age of 7 he was writing his own poetry

---

[62] The name is derived from the black bamboo trees that surround the house. Built during the reign of King Jung-Jong (1506-1544), it is one of the oldest wooden residential buildings in Korea and is designated as a national treasure. Inside it today is the *'Mongryongsil'* (Yul-Gok Memorial Hall). The house has been maintained throughout the last 500 years by Yul-Gok's descendants.

[63] The Joeson (or Chosŏn) Dynasty lasted from 1392 to 1897. Often referred to as the Yi Dynasty, after its founder Yi Song-Gye.

From Creation To Unification
The Complete Histories Behind The Ch'ang Hon (ITF) Patterns

and had finished all his lessons of the Confucian classics. When he was 13 he passed the Civil Service literary examination.

Yul-Gok means *'Valley of Chestnuts'* and was the penname chosen by Yi I in his later years as he continued writing many revered texts and documents. Yul-Gok lived by how he preached and took sincerity very seriously. He felt *'A sincere man was a man that knew the realism of heaven'*. He wrote that harmony could not be maintained in a house unless every family member was sincere. He also felt that a man should carry out a *'deep reflection of their selves'* when they had been confronted by misfortune, in order to correct their own mistakes and lead a better life.

Yul-Gok

Yul-Gok's mother passed away in 1551, when he was just 16 years old and Yul-Gok withdrew from society and secluded himself to Mount Kumgang (Diamond Mountain), where he meditated and studied Buddhism for 3 years. Upon leaving the mountain he started to study Confucianism and two years later he got married.

The Diamond Mountains, Korea
(notice the tower in the middle)

율곡
Yul-Gok

A year after his marriage, Yul-Gok visited Yi-Hwang (See Toi-Gye chapter) and stayed with him for a while. Yi-Hwang was his elder and was considered a great scholar who also studied Confucianism. Yi-Hwang would have been around 58 years old at the time of Yul-Gok's visit, where as Yul-Gok was only 23. Both Yul-Gok and Toi-Gye developed Neo-Confucian[64] philosophies based on the teachings of Zhu-Xi, a 12th Century Confucian scholar from China, yet they differed slightly. The concept (Confucianism) is based on Li (reason) and Chi (vital force), which are directly responsible for how the universe works. Toi-Gye believed that Li was the main component and controlled the Chi, whereas Yul-Gok felt the opposite happened, and the Chi was the controlling factor of Li.

Yul-Gok's father passed away when he was 26 and following the traditional 3 years in mourning, at aged 29, Yul-Gok took and passed a Higher Civil Service exam with full marks, which was due to the thesis he wrote titled *'Ch'ondoch'aek'* (Book on the Way of Heaven). This thesis was impressive as it showed his impressive knowledge of history, his understanding of the Confucian philosophy of politics, as well as his deep knowledge of Taoism. It is regarded as a literary masterpiece. Following this exam he began to work for the government and continued passing exams. He passed 9 exams in a row with top honours, which led to him holding many important positions in the government, such as Korea's Minister of Personnel and War, Rector of the National Academy and Minister of Defence.

When Yul-Gok was 34 he authored the *Dongho Mundap* (Questions

---

[64] *Neo-Confucianism* was an attempt to create a more rationalist and secular form of Confucianism by rejecting superstitious and mystical elements of Taoism and Buddhism that had influenced Confucianism during and after the Han Dynasty. Although the Neo-Confucianists were critical of Taoism and Buddhism, the two did have an influence on the philosophy, and the Neo-Confucianists borrowed terms and concepts from both. However, unlike the Buddhists and Taoists, who saw metaphysics as a catalyst for spiritual development, religious enlightenment, and immortality, the Neo-Confucianists used metaphysics as a guide for developing a rationalist ethical philosophy. *Source: Wikipedia*

From Creation To Unification
The Complete Histories Behind The Ch'ang Hon (ITF) Patterns

and Answers at East Lake) which was a political piece, divided into eleven articles, which clarified his belief that a righteous government could be achieved.

By the time he was 40 years old, Yul-Gok had become a central figure in the politics of the kingdom. His vast experience in the various governmental offices gave him a wide view of what was needed for the kingdom and he was supported by the king, with many of his documents, such as the *'Memorial in Ten Thousand Words'* (a text about Confucian learning, self-cultivation and government administration) and *'The Essentials of the Studies of the Sages'* (a text about Confucian ethics, self-cultivation and statecraft), amongst others, being presented to the royal court. Some of his views centered around gaining a national consensus of the people as he felt that the opinion of the masses was directly related to the survival of the kingdom, rather than the government simply deciding everything without taking all classes of society into account, thus possibly leaving many unhappy with how the country was run. He also suggested the Taedong (Great Equity) System, in order to solve the poor financial state at the time, this system taxed land rather than houses, so the bigger the land, the larger the tax, but at the same time, the larger land meant more products could be grown, which would in turn be bought by the government from the taxes.

By 1576, political strife in the kingdom had escalated and Yul-Gok became disillusioned with it all, so he stepped down and returned home to devote his time to study. During this time he authored *'The Essentials of Confucianism'* which was a text that showed how to lead a good life based on Confucianism.

At the age of 45, Yul-Gok returned to the government but little had changed. He tried his best to reduce the political turmoil, writing many new works and documenting important historical events. At this time, the kingdom had basically been divided into two main

율곡
Yul-Gok

political parties[65], each bickering and undermining the other as they vied for power, making satisfactory and effective decisions by the King, with his non-committal attitude very unforthcoming and Yul-Gok found it harder and harder to remain in a neutral position.

Just before he left the government in 1583, Yul-Gok proposed that the government train and equip a 100,000 man Army Reserve Corp to reinforce the regular army against a Japanese attack. However, like many of Yul-Gok's ideas at the time, it was never implemented due to the East/West political conflicts within the government. This was highly unfortunate as just 9 years later, Korea was invaded and occupied by the Japanese as the Korean military forces failed to resist the army of Hideyoshi Toyotomi. Yul-Gok died one year later, in 1584.

Hideyoshi Toyotomi

Yul-Gok's beliefs in loyalty, sincerity and the improvement of the individual were displayed in his own actions throughout his whole life. As an example, Yul-Gok's stepmother enjoyed drinking wine, something which Yul-Gok never approved of. He never told her of his disapproval and every morning he brought her several cups of wine. Years later, she finally decided to stop drinking of her own accord, never knowing about Yul-Gok's displeasure. When Yul-Gok passed away, she clad herself in white and mourned him for 3 years, grateful for his dedication to her and his non-judgmental attitude regarding her drinking!

Even after his death in 1584, Yul-Gok's writings continued to have a deep effect on Korea and its government because of his dedication to

---

[65] Known as the *'East/West Divide'* – named due to the area of Seoul where their offices were located. As well as their political differences, each party also developed philosophical differences, which were ironically based on Neo-Confucianism, with those in the East following Yi-Hwang's version and those in the West following Yul-Gok's version!

From Creation To Unification
The Complete Histories Behind The Ch'ang Hon (ITF) Patterns

Confucianism and the theory of government. In total, Yul-Gok wrote 193 works, in 276 publications in 6 languages. Following his death *'Yul-Gok Chônjip'* (The Complete Works of Yul-Gok) was compiled.

Along with Toi-Gye (Yi-Hwang), Yul-Gok (Yi I) is remembered as one of the two Great Confucian Scholars of Korea. In Seoul there is a street (Yulgongno) named after him and he is featured on the Korean 5,000 won note.

중근
Joong-Gun

Joong-gun named after the patriot Ahn Joong-Gun who assassinated Hiro-Bumi Ito[66], the first Japanese governor-general of Korea, known as the man who played the leading part in the Korea-Japan merger. There are 32 movements in this pattern to represent Mr. Ahn's age when he was executed at Lui-Shung prison (1910).[67]

Joong-Gun is the sixth pattern of of Ch'ang Hon Taekwon-Do, usually taught at 4th Kup, Blue belt. It has 32 moves and was developed in Malaysia between 1962 and 1964 with the help of Master Kim, Bok Man and Master Woo, Jae Lim.

Ahn Joong-Gun was born in the town of Hae-Ju in the province of Hwang-Hae on 2nd September, 1879. As a youngster he learnt Chinese literature and western science but was more interested in martial arts and marksmanship. Sadly, most of his life was spent watching various nations vie for control of his country of birth – Korea – the nation he loved, fought and died for!

In 1894, when Joong-Gun was just a teenager, China and Japan began what became known as the Sino-Japanese[68] War, where they both fought to control Korea. Japan saw the control of Korea as part of its national security and ideally wanted it under Japanese control or at the

---

[66] 'Ito' was his surname. Although originally, when writing a Japanese name in English it followed the same conventions as both Korean and Chinese names, by putting the surname (family name) first, following the Meiji Restoration in Japan (1868 to 1912), as part of its efforts to westernize itself, names written in English started to use the westernized version of writing the surname last. Though some authors prefer the traditional, surname first method, as General Choi used the western method I have also follow suit with all Japanese names in this book.

[67] He was actually only 30 years old when he was executed.

[68] Sino' is a prefix used in reference to China. It comes from the Latin word 'sinae'

From Creation To Unification
The Complete Histories Behind The Ch'ang Hon (ITF) Patterns

very least, independent of anyone else's control, by allowing Korea to remain independent. Just prior to the war, the Donghak Peasant Revolution had broken out, which saw Korean peasants protesting against political corruption within the Korean Government. The government was unable to quell the rebellion

Japanese troops during the Sino-Japanese war

on its own and asked the Ming Dynasty of China for help. China duly sent 3000 Chinese troops into Korea and the rebellion was crushed. However, by doing so and not informing the Japanese, the Chinese had broken an earlier convention (The Tientsin Convention) which stated that neither country would send any troops into Korea without informing the other first. In response Japan sent a force of 8000 into Korea and took control of the Palace in Seoul, replacing the current government with a Pro-Japanese Government. The Pro-Japanese Government then granted the Japanese the right to forcefully expel the Chinese troops from the country and war ensued! However, due to failures to modernise its armies, the Chinese troops were easily beaten by the better equipped Japanese soldiers and Korea was taken by the Japanese. The Chinese troops retreated and the Japanese troops pushed forwards towards Manchuria capturing various towns along the way.

The Japanese Army lays siege to Pyongyang, defeating the Chinese by an attack from the rear

중근
Joong-Gun

Realizing Japans superiority at the time, China pushed for a Peace Treaty, which was signed in April, 1895. The Peace Treaty saw China recognize Korea as an independent national state, as well as succeed some of its territories (including Taiwan) and pay Japan enormous amounts of money! However, the treaty also forced Japan to give up Port Arthur, which was a strategic port in China, which China then leased to Russia, which infuriated the Japanese!

In the same year, in order to hide him from the Japanese, Ahn Joong-Gun's father took him to a catholic church in Korea, that was run by a French priest, where he hid for several months. Whilst there, Ahn Joong-Gun was baptized and given the baptismal name of Thomas, encouraged to read the bible and started learning French. Ahn Joong-Gun remained Catholic for the rest of his life.

In 1900, the Boxer Rebellion broke out in China which saw the Chinese population attacking foreigners in the area. Eight nations sent in their forces in order to protect their interests in the area, but the Russian's, despite having had a good relationship with China since 1689, saw it as an opportunity to expand into Manchuria and order troops to be stationed there. The Chinese and Manchu population in Manchuria rose up in support of the Boxers, attacking Russians in the area. In response, the Russian troops slaughtered thousands of the local population and stationed 200,000 troops in Manchuria.

Troops of the Eight nations alliance of 1900. Left to right: Britain, United States, Australian colonial, British India, Germany, France, Austria-Hungary, Italy and Japan

From Creation To Unification
The Complete Histories Behind The Ch'ang Hon (ITF) Patterns

Russian troops deployed during the Boxer Rebellion

Japan saw the Russian troops in Manchuria as a direct threat to its ownership of Korea and when the troops expanded into northern Korea, Japan demanded they leave Korean soil as the presence of Russian troops conflicted with the Japanese claim on Korea. Despite negotiations, the Russians refused to remove their troops and war broke out between Japan and Russia, when Japan attacked a Russian fleet stationed at Port Arthur. Though Japan officially declared war on Russia in February, 1904, they had attacked Port Arthur before *'officially'* declaring war, which was something that incensed the Russian Tsar, Nicholas II.

In April, 1904 the Japanese took control of Port Arthur after many bloody land battles and continued in military dominance over the Russian forces, both on land and by sea. The continual defeats shook Russia's confidence and the war became very unpopular with the Russian people. In September 1905 a Peace treaty was signed which effectively left Japan in control of Korea!

It was during this war that Ahn Joong-Gun, aged 25, had started his own coal business. He only ran it for a short while because, following the *Japan–Korea Protectorate Treaty* (Eulsa Treaty) in 1905, Ahn Joong-Gun dedicated himself to educating the Korean people by establishing private schools, such as the *Sam-Heung* (Three Success) School and

중근
Joong-Gun

others in northwest Korea. Running schools during this turbulent time was difficult with many many hardships under the Japanese rule.

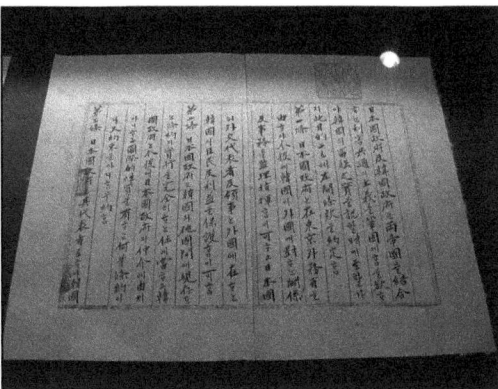

Hiro-Bumi Ito   *Japan–Korea Protectorate Treaty, 1905* [69]

One of Japans leading statesmen, Hiro-Bumi Ito, had travelled to Korea in November, 1905 with a letter from the Emperor of Japan. The letter requested that Emperor Gojong of Korea sign the *'Protectorate Treaty'*, which was part of Japans plan for the long term occupation of Korea. Hiro-Bumi Ito initially surrounded the Emperor's Imperial palace with Japanese troops in order to put pressure on Emperor Gojong to sign the treaty! Eight days later, Hiro-Bumi Ito entered the palace himself to make Emperor Gojong sign the treaty, yet the Emperor handed the decision over to his ministers. Ito pressured the weak ministers, threatening to beat them unless they signed the treaty. When the Korean Prime Minster, Han Gyu-Seol, continued to object, he was locked in a room and threatened with death if he didn't be quiet and the remaining ministers signed the treaty that day, giving Japan complete control over Korea by depriving it of its sovereignty, making it a protectorate of Japan.

Hiro-Bumi Ito was named the first Resident-General of Korea on 21st December 1905 and given total control of all the Japanese forces stationed in Korea, as well as all foreign relations and trade in Korea and was answerable only to the Japanese Emperor himself.

---

[69] Photo by Ryu Cheol. Cc-by-sa-3.0

From Creation To Unification
The Complete Histories Behind The Ch'ang Hon (ITF) Patterns

Remembrance photo taken after the signing of the Protectorate Treaty

Upon his return to Korea in March, 1906, Hiro-Bumi Ito ordered all foreign delegations to leave as he enforced the *'Protectorate Treaty'*. The treaty also gave the Japanese the right to buy the land from Korean citizens at cut price costs but even so, in many cases land was simply taken from them!

Despite the Treaty being signed, Emperor Gojong secretly appealed for help against the treaty and sent 17 personal letters to various kings or heads of state around the world, including Edward VII of England and Emperor Guang Xu of China, as well as letter to Russia, France, Germany, Austria, Italy and Belgium amongst others.

In March, 1907, the Japanese were getting worried by the various patriotic Korean organisations outside of Korea, especially in America, which could possibly invoke outside intervention. Japan sent a pro-Japanese American, D. W. Stevens, to distribute pro-Japanese propaganda in the US, but Stevens was assassinated by two Korean patriots whilst in San Francisco.

In June, 1907 Emperor Gojong secretly sent three emissaries to the Hague Peace Conference, but the other Countries refused to let them take part and when Hiro-Bumi Ito discovered this he forced Emperor

중근
Joong-Gun

Gojong to abdicate and replaced him with his son, Sunjong. Six days later, on 24th July 1907, a new agreement was forced on the Korean Government, which basically allowed Hiro-Bumi Ito to dismiss Korean Ministers and replace them with Japanese ones, as well as taking full control of both the Korean police and army. Emperor Gojong's abdication enraged the Korean people even further and rioting broke out, much of which was led by army units. Hiro-Bumi Ito's response was to disband both the police and the army, keeping only the palace guards as well as to take control of both the courts and prisons and put them under Japanese jurisdiction.

A photo of Emperor Gojong with his son, Sunjong

The Korean troops retaliated and although they were quickly defeated, the resistance continued and guerrilla groups formed to attack the Japanese forces. Anti-Japanese violence swept the country and the guerrilla forces were hunted down and defeated by the larger Japanese army. The unrest still continued and loyal Korean Government Ministers committed suicide, whilst those that had actually signed the treaty were assassinated by enraged Koreans and assassinations were attempted on prominent Japanese ministers as well! During the occupation, Ahn Joong-Gun exiled himself to Russia arriving in Vladivostok in 1907 where he joined a resistance group, rising to the rank of Lieutenant General.

Ahn Joong-Gun's resistance group had around 300 men (one of which was his brother), and they conducted raids against the Japanese along the borders of Manchuria, attacking Japanese troops stationed in northern Korea. His was one of many groups that operated out of Manchuria as it was close to the town of Kando in northern Korea.

From Creation To Unification
The Complete Histories Behind The Ch'ang Hon (ITF) Patterns

Kando itself was such a breeding ground for the guerrilla fighters that the Japanese placed a major military and police presence in the area in June 1909. However, Kando had a population of about 100,000 of which at least 20,000 were Chinese and when the Japanese cracked down on the area, the Chinese residents were caught up in the violence which caused considerable conflict between China and Japan.

With the increased Japanese presence in Kando, Ahn Joong-Gun's resistance group stepped up their attacks, resulting in many more Japanese deaths. The raids were planned and executed from within Manchuria which meant the Japanese could do little about it until an actual attack took place. To counter this, Japan made a deal with China and on 4th September, 1909 they signed a treaty that allowed the Japanese access to Manchuria via the Southern Manchurian Railway, allowing them to exploit the rich minerals in the region and in return, the Chinese received the *'territorial rights'* to Kando!

For many Korean patriots such as Ahn Joong-Gun this was *'the straw that broke the camels back'* as it incensed them that Japan could simply give away part of Korea, when it wasn't even theirs to begin with! Ahn Joong-Gun returned to Vladivostok to decide and plan his next move!

In March, 1909, Ahn Joong-Gun along with 11 others formed the Donguidanjihoe, a society of patriots whereby each member swore an oath to sacrifice themselves for *"The Restoration of Independence and Preservation of Peace in the East"* - cutting off the first joint of their ring finger to show their belief and faith in the cause.

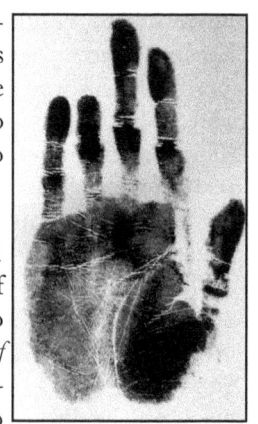

Ahn Joong-Gun's hand print [70]

---

[70] Pictures courtesy of Dr. George Vitale, VIII

중근
Joong-Gun

Due to the increased Japanese presence in Kando, Russia started to get nervous that Japan was setting its sights on Manchuria and arranged for Russia's Finance Minister, General Kokotseff, to meet with Hiro-Bumi Ito so they could calm the Russians fears. The meeting was arranged and Hiro-Bumi Ito was to meet General Kokotseff at Harbin in Manchuria on 26th October, 1909.

As Hiro-Bumi Ito arrived in Harbin, Ahn Joong-Gun was waiting; having slipped passed the Japanese guards, hiding a gun in his lunch box. As Hiro-Bumi Ito stepped off the train, Ahn Joong-Gun pulled out his pistol and shot Hiro-Bumi Ito three times. In the shooting Ahn Joong-Gun also shot and seriously injured 4 others, all Japanese ministers. As the shooting finished Ahn Joong-Gun shouted for Korean Independence in Russian, shouting *"Корея! Ура!"* whilst waving the Korean flag.

The gun and bullets used by Ahn Joong-Gun at Harbin station [71]

A picture depicting Ahn Joong-Gun shooting Hiro-Bumi Ito at Harbin station.

---

[71] Picture courtesy of Dr. George Vitale, VIII

From Creation To Unification
The Complete Histories Behind The Ch'ang Hon (ITF) Patterns

As he expected, Ahn Joong-Gun was immediately arrested by Russian guards, who held him for two days before they turned him over to the Japanese. When Joong-Gun found out he had actually killed Hiro-Bumi Ito, he made the sign of the cross in gratitude and said *"I have ventured to commit a serious crime, offering my life for my country. This is the behavior of a noble-minded patriot."*

Page from the Japan Advertiser Paper, 27.10.1909 [71]

Ahn Joong-Gun insisted on being called by his Catholic name, Thomas, by his captors. After being handed over to the Japanese he was imprisoned at Port Arthur. His incarceration lasted around 5 months, during which he was tortured but his spirit never broke. Ahn Joong-Gun went through six trials, all the time insisting that he should be treated as a prisoner of war, as a Lieutenant General of a Korean Resistance Army, as opposed to just a common criminal.

At one trial he gave a list of 15 reasons (crimes that Hiro-Bumi Ito committed) to explain why he decided to assassinate him. These were:

1. Assassinating the Korean Empress Myeong-Seong[73]
2. Dethroning the Emperor Gojong

---

[72] Picture courtesy of Dr. George Vitale, VIII

[73] Emperor Gojong's wife

중근
Joong-Gun

3. Forcing 14 unequal treaties on Korea
4. Massacring innocent Koreans
5. Usurping the authority of the Korean government by force
6. Plundering Korean railroads, mines, forests, and rivers.
7. Forcing the use of Japanese banknotes.
8. Disbanding the Korean armed forces.
9. Obstructing the education of Koreans.
10. Banning Koreans from studying abroad.
11. Confiscating and burning Korean textbooks.
12. Spreading a rumour around the world that Koreans wanted Japanese protection.
13. Deceiving the Japanese Emperor by saying that the relationship between Korea and Japan was peaceful when in truth it was full of hostility and conflicts.
14. Breaking the peace of Asia.
15. Assassinating the Emperor Komei[74]

Empress Myeong-Seong

At his sixth trial Ahn Joong-Gun was sentenced to death by hanging by the Japanese court. Though he expected to be executed, he was still angered by the decision as he wanted to be viewed as a prisoner of war, rather than an assassin and executed by firing squad!

On the day his sentence was announced, he was visited by his two brothers who relayed a message from his mother. The message said *"Your death is for the sake of your country, and don't ask for your life cowardly. Your brave death for justice is a final filial regards to your mother."*

Joong-Gun told his brothers *"After I die, you can bury me in Harbin. But when Korea wins back its independence, please move my bones and bury them in my country. Even in Heaven, I will always think about our independence. When you go back to Korea, give the people my message that they should unite and achieve our most important goal. When I hear the news of our independence, I'll celebrate it*

---

[74] The Japanese Emperor who unexpectedly died of (officially) smallpox, despite never having been ill before - there is a belief that he was actually poisoned!

in Heaven. It is my sincerest wish that Korea be liberated. I have no regrets about my death."

Despite all that had happened during his life, Ahn Joong-Gun felt that with the death of Hiro-Bumi Ito, that Japan and Korea could become friends due to their similar traditions, and along with China they could form a union and restore peace to the East. This was stated in an essay he wrote in prison whilst awaiting execution, it was titled *'On Peace in East Asia'*. In the essay, which he never got to complete he recommends a combined armed forces and the issuing of joint bank notes between the three countries.

Though not trained, Ahn Joong-Gun became renowned for calligraphy work which he did whilst in prison, he signed his work with his signature and hand print. His handprint shows his left hand, missing the last joint of his ring finger, which he had cut off as a show of his determination when he pledged to kill Hiro-Bumi Ito. Ahn Joong-Gun inspired many people with his righteousness, humanity and above all his spirit; this included lawyers and prosecutors, as well as many of his Japanese prison guards.

As he awaited his execution on 26th March, 1910, Joong-Gun did some calligraphy and wrote a final message to the Korean people. The message said:

"To My People: I worked hard abroad for three years to regain Korea's independence and maintain the peace in Asia. However, I have to die before achieving our common goal. If the twenty million Korean people work diligently to advance education and industry, and finally achieve our independence, I will be a happy soul in Heaven."

At 10am on 26th March, 1910, exactly 5 months to the minute that Hiro-Bumi Ito died[75], Ahn Joong-Gun was executed at

Ahn Joong-Gun
- Notice the missing finger!

---

[75] Hiro-Bumi Ito was shot at 9.30am on 26th October, 1910 and died half an hour later from his wounds.

중근
Joong-Gun

Lui-Shung prison, in Port Arthur, China. He was just 30 years old.

'The Best Rivers and Mountains'

The sacrifice Ahn Joong-Gun made, his attitude and that of his compatriots symbolized the loyalty and dedication of the Korean people to their country's independence and freedom from the Japanese. Ahn Joong-Gun was a patriot who loved his country, so much so that in the end, he gave his life for it. His love was captured forever in the calligraphy he wrote whilst awaiting his execution, which simply said *'The Best Rivers and Mountains'*, implying he felt his country to be the most beautiful place on earth, worth dying for. Some stories say that it was written on his cell wall, in his own blood!

Following the death of Hiro-Bumi Ito, Arasuke Sone took on the role of Resident-General of Korea before Masatake Terauchi succeeded him, becoming the 3rd Resident-General of Korea. Masatake Terauchi was to execute the Japan-Korea Annexation Treaty[76] in 1910 which actually made him the 1st Governor-General of Korea.

Arasuke Sone

Interestingly, Ahn Joong-Gun's cousin, Ahn Myeong-Gun tried to assassinate Masatake Terauchi, but failed and was imprisoned for 15 years. His brothers, another cousin and nephew joined the Provisional Government of the

Masatake Terauchi

---

[76] This treaty annexed Korea altogether, basically giving the Emperor of Japan sovereignty over the whole of Korea as opposed to being run under the *'guidance'* of a Japanese Resident-General.

From Creation To Unification
The Complete Histories Behind The Ch'ang Hon (ITF) Patterns

Republic of Korea in Shanghai, which was considered a Korean Government in exile at the time, and fought against the Japanese in Shanghai, whilst another nephew joined the National Revolutionary Army of China and also fought against Japan in Shanghai, before joining the Korean Liberation Army, later becoming a Lieutenant General in the Republic of Korea Army and a member of the National Assembly of South Korea.

Poor reporting of Hiro-Bumi Ito's assassination by the Hawaiian Gazette. 26th October, 1909 [77]

Ahn Joong-Gun went from being a teacher, to a guerrilla leader and freedom fighter but is forever remembered as a famous Korean patriot, who died for the love of his country.

In 1962 he was posthumously awarded the Order of Merit for National Foundation medal by the South Korean Government, an award reserved for those who contributed to the founding of the modern Republic of Korea. In 1970 memorial halls were built in Seoul to honour Ahn Joong-Gun and in 2006 the Chinese Government also built a memorial hall in his honour, at Harbin! In 2006 an American band called 'Scrabbel' released a track titled *'1909'* about the assassination of Hiro-Bumi Ito by Ahn Joong-Gun. The video features footage of the shooting from a film of the same name.

---

[77] Picture courtesy of Bert Edens

퇴계
Toi-Gye

Toi-Gye is the pen name of the noted scholar Yi Hwang (16th century), an authority on Neo-Confucianism.[78] **The 37 movements of the pattern refer to his birthplace on 37° latitude, the diagram represents "scholar".**

Toi-Gye is the seventh pattern of of Ch'ang Hon Taekwon-Do, usually taught at 3rd Kup, Blue belt. It has 37 moves and was developed in Malaysia between 1962 and 1964 with the help of Master Kim, Bok Man and Master Woo, Jae Lim.

Yi Hwang[79] was was born on 25th November, 1501 in On'gye-ri (now Tosan) in the province of Gyeongsang and was the youngest of 8 children. When Yi Hwang was only 12 years old his Uncle taught him the *Analects of Confucius*[80] and he started to write poetry after greatly admiring the work of Chinese poet, Tao Qian. His own poem, Yadang (Pond in the Wind), which he wrote when he was 18 is admired throughout the world, which is when he possibly first used his penname Toi-Gye, which means *returning stream*.

When he was 20, Yi Hwang studied the I Ching[81], immersing himself

---

[78] *Neo* means 'new' and is derived from the Greek word *neos*.

[79] If using the Revised Romanization of Korean translation, as I have in the rest of this book, his name should actually read I-Hwang; however, as most students know him as Yi-Hwang, I have used that pronunciation throughout the chapter to avoid confusion.

[80] The *Analects of Confucius* is collection of ideas and sayings from the Chinese Philosopher Confucius.

[81] The *I Ching* or *Book of Changes* is one of the oldest classical Chinese text, thought to be written around 221 BC and is based on the 8 Trigrams.

From Creation To Unification
The Complete Histories Behind The Ch'ang Hon (ITF) Patterns

in the works, while at the same time studying Neo-Confucianism.[82] When he was 23 he travelled to Seoul to enter the National Academy, which was the foremost educational institute of its day. At 27 years old he passed the preliminary exams required to become a government official, however, he returned to the National Academy when he was 33 to continue his education and in the same year (1534) he passed the Civil Service examinations with the highest of honours, which led him to be highly regarded by his contemporaries, more so as the exams were usually only passed by those much older than Yi Hwang was.

Whilst working for the government, Yi Hwang continued his scholarly studies but returned to his childhood home, following the death of his mother when he was 37, whom he mourned for 3 years. He held multiple positions within the Government, including the role of Secret Royal Inspector[83], which was a position directly appointed by the King which, due to his integrity, allowed him to relentlessly route out corrupt officials.

A court document written by Yi Hwang

In his spare time, Yi Hwang wrote poetry, often about rivers and mountains as he loved nature and they were his favourite natural beauties. To increase his self-discipline and concentration he also played a game called 'tuhu' (arrow throwing), which involved throwing arrows by hand, into a jar with a small top from about 2 metre's away.

A game of tuhu

---

[82] See Yul-Gok chapter, page 71, footnote 64 for a full explanation of Neo-Confucianism.

[83] A Secret Royal Inspector was appointed directly by the King and travelled to the local provinces and secretly monitored the officials.

퇴계
Toi-Gye

Eventually, Yi Hwang became disillusioned due to the continuous power struggles within the government and stepped down from office and retired. However, though he was no longer active within the Royal Court, he was brought out of retirement to become Governor of Danyang when he was 48, after which he became Governor of Punji where he redeveloped the *Baekundong Seowon*, a private Neo-Confucian Academy built by his predecessor, Ju Se-Bung.

In 1552, Yi Hwang was named Head Instructor of the National Academy at age 50, but turned down other prominent positions later on. Yi Hwang's Neo-Confucianism became very popular both with scholars and government officials who supported the building of schools devoted to Neo-Confucianism and its teachings and Yi Hwang capitalised on this and founded the *Dosan Seodang* (Dosan private school) where he continued teaching his students, as well as investing his time into his own meditation and study.

'Seodang' drawn by Kim Hongdo in the late 18th century

The school prospered, not least because of Yi Hwang's royal connections, which allowed the school to run for free, as well as affording it numerous donations (books, land, cattle etc.) from the king.

Buddhism went into decline as the Neo-Confucian philosophies of both Yi Hwang and his younger contemporary, Yi I (Yul-Gok) became popular amongst the government. However, their philosophies differed slightly which resulted in the East/West government divide (see See Yul-Gok chapter, page 73, footnote 65), which meant the officials spent more time arguing, fighting and undermining

From Creation To Unification
The Complete Histories Behind The Ch'ang Hon (ITF) Patterns

each other, with few crucial decisions being made, which eventually enabled the Japanese to invade and occupy Korea under the command of Hideyoshi Toyotomi in 1583.

An older Yi Hwang

King Myeong-Jong tried to entice him back to the government, but Yi Hwang continually refused, preferring to continue his private studies. He did return to government once more however, at the request of the king, when envoys from the Ming Dynasty of China travelled to Seoul – he was 67 at the time. When King Myeong-Jong suddenly died, his successor, King Seonjo appointed Yi Hwang as Minister of Rites, but he turned down the position and resumed his studies. However, King Seonjo was insistent that Yi Hwang return to government and eventually he resumed office when he was 68, writing advisory documents and giving lectures on his philosophies, the I Ching and other Confucian scripts he had studied.

Yi Hwang died in 1570, aged 70, having been in public service for 40 years, in which time he had served 4 kings[84], held 29 different government positions and developed his Neo-Confucianist philosophies. Following his death, King Sonjo posthumously promoted Yi Hwang to the highest ministerial rank and the Dosan Seodang, which Yi Hwang originally founded

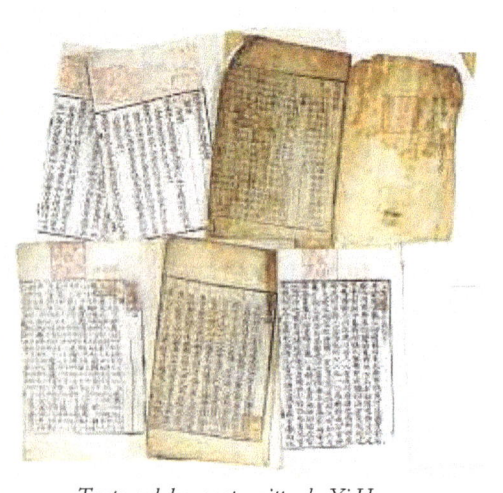

Texts and documents written by Yi Hwang

---

[84] King's Jung-Jong, In-Jong, Myeong-Jong and Seonjo.

퇴계
Toi-Gye

Dosan Seowon

and built was reformed 4 years after his death, into what is now known as the *Dosan Seowon*, which, while retaining its areas for study also became a shrine to Toi-Gye.

Of his poems, there is a collection called *'The Twelve Songs of Tosan'* which were recorded on four wooden blocks and are still preserved at his shrine, the *Dosan Seowon*. It is believed the blocks were carved from Toi-Gyes own hand writing in 1565 and are considered the oldest existing written version of any traditional Korean poetry or sijo. The poem is about the beauty of nature and the essence of being human. Originally written in Hangul, it translates as:

Some say I ought to live this way;
some say I ought to live that way.
Others call me a bumpkin,
a hayseed, a country hick.
Must I forsake my lifelong love
of nature's rocks and ageless springs?

The old teacher never saw me;
he lived long before my time.
Though I may never meet him,
I can see the road he travelled.
With his wise road before me,
what reason for me to stray?

From Creation To Unification
The Complete Histories Behind The Ch'ang Hon (ITF) Patterns

Gentle mist and haze caress my home;
    wind and moon are my friends.
The land around is peaceful now,
    and I count my final years.
Life, old mate, I hope to give you back
    a true and shameless soul.

Fragrant orchids in the valley
    lend enchantment to the air;
those puffy clouds over the mountain
    are also delightful.
Amid pleasures such as these,
    I still long for my dear one.[85]

In the pattern definition, the reason for the 37 movements is stated as due to "to his birthplace on 37° latitude". However, as a latitude line runs all the way around the earth, this could (in theory) be anywhere along that line, as there is no longitude measurement given to give a correct coordinate. It is also well known that Toi-Gye was born in On'gye-ri, making this explanation of the 37 movements within the pattern rather nonchalant. What is interesting however is that Yi Hwang became a prominent government figure at the age of 33 and continued in that mode until his death, aged 70, which meant he was one of the most influential government figures, held in the highest esteem by the kings and courts of Korea for 37 years!

Yi-Hwang is considered one of the two great Confucian Scholars of Korea and also (like Yul-Gok) has a street in Seoul named after him (Toegyero) and he is featured on the Korean 1,000 won note, with the Dosan Seowon on the reverse. Various institutes devoted to Toi-Gye's philosophies were formed after his death and still continue today, not just in Korea, but aslo in Japan, Taiwan, Germany and the United States and commemorative services to Toi-Gye are still held twice a year at the Dosan Seowon.

---

[85] The last word in the poem, when translated from its original Hangul, is 'Nim', which many Taekwon-Do students will recognise. In this context it can alternatively be translated as lord, lover, king or god.

화랑
Hwa-Rang

Hwa-Rang is named after the Hwa-Rang youth group, which originated in the Silla Dynasty in the early 7th century. The 29 movements refer to the 29th Infantry Division, where Taekwon-Do developed into maturity.

Hwa-Rang is the eighth pattern of Ch'ang Hon Taekwon-Do, usually taught at 2nd Kup, Red belt. It has 29 moves and was developed in Korea in 1955 with the help of Colonel Nam, Tae Hi. And (then) Sergeant Han, Cha Kyo Though it is the eighth pattern practiced by students, it was the first pattern for Ch'ang Hon Taekwon-Do ever developed.

The Hwa-Rang (meaning Flower Boys or Flowering Youth) were an elite group of warriors from the Silla Dynasty of ancient Korea in the late 6th and early 7th Century BC and are often seen as the Korean

From Creation To Unification
The Complete Histories Behind The Ch'ang Hon (ITF) Patterns

A picture depicting Hwa-Rang warriors in training

equivalent of the Japanese Samurai, but the Hwa-Rang pre-date the Samurai by some 500 years, dying out (in the 10th Century BC, when Silla fell) before the Samurai and their code of Bushido even came to exist in Japan (around the 12th Century).

The Hwa-Rang beginnings were not as many presume; as legendary warrior knights groomed for the battlefield, with extremely high ethics and moral codes. In fact, in the beginning they were not warriors at all, they were not even male!

According to the text *'Samguk Sagi'* (History of the Three Kingdoms) and *'Samguk Yusa'* (Memorabilia of the Three Kingdoms)[86], what we now know as the Hwa-Rang warriors were originally formed by King Jin-Heung (540-576 AD), as two groups of beautiful women. These groups of woman were called *'Won-Hwa'* (Original Flowers) and though it isn't totally clear as to their original role, some believe they

---

[86] Samguk Sagi (1145) is a historical book and Samguk Yusa (1285) is a collection of folktales, legends and historical accounts of the era. Both books, along with Haedong Goseungjeon (Lives of Eminent Korean Monks, 1215), contain information on the Hwa-Rang, though they cite former sources that are no longer in existence for their information.

화랑
Hwa-Rang

A picture of Hwa-Rang warriors escorting Queen Seondeok from the 2009 Korean historical drama 'Queen Seondeok of Silla'

were simply court beauties or courtesans as a better term. If you consider they were also trained in ethics, sincerity, loyalty, filial piety and fraternal piety, plus the fact that women had a much more prominent role in the Silla dynasty (which included three queens)[87] - quite different from the Chinese male dominated type roles of that era, 'courtesans' may be a rather fatherly simplistic historical view. The leaders of these two groups were named Nam-Mo and Jun-Jeong, but they grew jealous and bitter towards each other which resulted in Jun-Jeong murdering her rival Nam-Mo, which led to the Won-Hwa being disbanded, as well as Jun-Jeongs execution.

Some years afterwards, according to the Samguk Yusa, the King of Silla was *"concerned about the strengthening of the country"* and issued a decree to choose young boys of good moral character, from good families (often thought of as from the aristocracies families) and created the first *'Hwa-Rang'*. However, in the Samguk Yusa, it was

---

[87] One of the queens was Queen Sun-Duk (632-647AD) who has a pattern by the GTF named after her.

From Creation To Unification
The Complete Histories Behind The Ch'ang Hon (ITF) Patterns

written as *Hwanang* which meant 'Flower Girls'! This could mean that the Hwa-Rang were not originally set up to be warriors, but rather a group to educate the young men of Korea to be better for their country by following strict moral codes, for the well being and unity of the kingdom.

Prior to this, in 520 AD, King Beop-Heung had instituted the Bone Rank System)[88] and in 527AD Silla had adopted Buddhism as its main religion. The Hwa-Rang utilised the Bone Rank System, coupled with Buddhism and really came to fruition as they adopted their code of chivalry, which was taught to them as the *'Five Commandments for Secular Life'* by a monk called Won Gwang, after two young Hwa-Rang sought him out for spiritual guidance. This later became known as the 'Code of the Hwa-Rang' and the five commandments (Se Sok O Gye) which are as follows:

1. Loyalty to one's king
2. Love and respect your parents and teachers
3. Trust among friends
4. Never retreat in battle
5. Never take a life without a just cause

Hwa-Rang warriors also lived by the 9 Virtues (Kyo Hoon), these are: Humility, Justice, Courtesy, Wisdom, Trustworthiness, Goodness, Virtue, Loyalty and Courage.

As Silla expanded its territories, hostilities grew with other Kingdoms and the royal court took a more interested role in the Hwa-Rang, which up until this time had mainly been groups led by young men from the aristocracy and overseen by an appointed high official. The groups learned military skills such as swordsmanship, archery, horsemanship, chariot driving, javelin and military strategy and grew in numbers to hundreds of groups, comprising of between 500 to 5000 men; lead by a commander or Kuk-son. Training could take up to 10 years before the title of 'Hwa-Rang' was even attained! The first ever Kuk-son is recorded to be a warrior named Sul Won-Nang.

---

[88] The Bone Rank System was a system used to separate the aristocracy of the Silla Kingdom, into their hierarchical levels.

화랑
Hwa-Rang

Hwa-Rang warriors riding into battle

It is thought that the unarmed combat portion of the Hwa-Rang's training came from the neighbouring kingdom of Goguryeo via King Kwang-Gae the Great, who assisted Silla when it was invaded by the other dominant kingdom of the era, Baekje. He sent his armies to assist Silla, which included his own elite warriors called the *Sunbae* (meaning literally *elders*, but also translates as *'a man of virtue who never retreats from a fight'*), who were trained in a similar fashion to the Hwa-Rang, but also learnt Su-Bak, an unarmed martial art developed for the Goguryeo military from Chinese roots. Su-Bak consisted primarily of upper body techniques, whereas a traditional fighting folk dance of the era, that consisted of lower body techniques (i.e. leg techniques), was known as Taek-Kyon. It is thought that Su-Bak and Taek-Kyon were used as the unarmed portion of the Hwa-Rang warriors training and though they were two separate arts, years later they merged and the term Su-Bak was dropped and it all became known as Taek-Kyon.

Ironically, the Hwa-Rang Warriors would later play a major part in the fall of Goguryeo which led to the unification of Silla or the end of the Three Kingdoms Era, as it is known. Also rather ironically, it was a Silla and Tang (Chinese) alliance that allowed Silla to defeat both Goguryeo and Baekje to form the Unified Silla in 668 AD, but by 674

From Creation To Unification
The Complete Histories Behind The Ch'ang Hon (ITF) Patterns

AD Silla and the Tang were at war because the Tang tried to exert control over its ally, even placing a Protectorate General's office in Silla, similar to what the Japanese would do many years later (see Joong-Gun chapter).

Hwa-Rang students learned the Five Cardinal Confucian Virtues (kindness, justice, courtesy, intelligence and faith), the Six Arts, the Three Scholarly Occupations (royal tutor, instructor and teacher) and the Six Ways of Government Service (holy minister, good minister, loyal minister, wise minister, virtuous minister and honest minister). According to the historical text *"...able ministers and loyal subjects are chosen from them, and good generals and brave soldiers are born there from."*. Indeed, many of the greatest generals of Silla and its kings had served as Hwa-Rang, such as General Kim Yoo Sin (of whom the 3rd degree pattern is named after), even monks such as Won-Hyo were once Hwa-Rang as well!

Hwa-Rang planning their next battle

There was a book called *Hwarang-Segi* that was said to have contained records of the lives of over 200 individual Hwa-Rang warriors, but sadly it was lost or destroyed during the Japanese occupation of Korea. However, some stories of the exploits of the Hwa-Rang warriors remain such as the story of the bravery of Hwa-rang warrior

화랑
Hwa-Rang

Kwan Chan (as detailed in the Ge-Baek chapter), as well as one about two Hwa-Rang (Gwisan and Chwi-Hang); the two Hwa-Rang who originally asked monk Won Gwang for spiritual guidance (receiving the *Five Commandments for Secular Life*), who, during an ambush, witnessed their Commander fall from his horse, whereby they attacked the enemy shouting *"Now is the time to follow the commandment to not retreat in battle"*, rescued their Commander and gave him one of their horses and defended his escape, killing many of the enemy as they did so, before finally being killed themselves, *"dying from a thousand cuts"*!

Undoubtedly, the most famous Hwa-Rang warrior was General Kim Yoo-Sin (who's exploits you will read about in the Yoo-Sin chapter), but the first recorded instance of a heroic victory by a Hwa-Rang warrior is said to be that of Sa Da-Ham - It is written that in 562 AD, when he was only 15 years old, he raised a 1,000 man strong army all by himself, in order to support Silla in its war against its neighbour, the Gaya Confederacy. His army was charged with supporting the Silla forces in attacking a main Gaya fort and Sa Da-Ham requested to lead the first charge.

Though he was only young, King Jin-Heung was impressed and allowed him the honour and it is said he was the first person to breach the forts walls, with victory following soon after. The king praised his deeds and offered Sa Da-Ham 300 slaves and a considerable amount of land as a reward for his courage and bravery. However, Sa Da-Ham said he did not wish to receive personal rewards for his actions, which he did for his king and country and thus freed the slaves and accepted just a small bit of land, so as not to offend the king.

As a child, Sa Da-Ham had made a death pact with his best friend Moo Kwan-Rang; should either of them ever died in battle the other would kill himself as well. After his heroic victory at the Gaya fort, Sa Da-Ham received news that Moo Kwan-Rang had been killed in another battle and was inconsolable in his grief. Sa Da-Ham showed his loyalty to his friend and refused to eat or drink as he mourned. On the 7th day he died, fulfilling his sworn oath to his best friend.

Another story, which shows the loyalty the Hwa-Rang had to one

From Creation To Unification
The Complete Histories Behind The Ch'ang Hon (ITF) Patterns

another concerns a Kuk-son named Bi Yeng-Ja, whom General Kim Yoo-Sin had asked to lead an attack against a large force of Tang (Chinese) soldiers, that was almost certainly a suicide mission. Bi Yeng-Ja accepted the mission by saying *"You have given me a great honor to show loyalty to my king and country"*, but also asked General Kim to look after his only son, so as to prevent him following his father into battle, so his family would survive for another generation. The General agreed to the request and Bi Yeng-Ja rode into battle.

Unfortunately Bi Yeng-Ja was killed and before General Kim could stop him, Bi Yeng-Ja's son had jumped on a horse and rode into the battle, but was also killed. Two servants of Bi Yeng-Ja also entered the battle, such was their loyalty and they were also killed. These acts of courage, loyalty and bravery were witnessed by the remaining Silla soldiers, who deeply moved by what they had witnessed and in recognition charged into battle to avenge their deaths and in doing so, defeated the entire Tang forces and won the battle.

The Hwa-Rang also had what you could consider its own Special Forces unit, akin to the famous Ninja of Japan. They were known as the *'Sulsa'* (Knights of the Night) and specialised in intelligence gathering and assassinations. The Sulsa were trained in survival tactics, tracking, trailing, camouflage and concealment, as well as healing techniques and herbal medicines. There were two sides to the Sulsa training; Jung-Do or *'way of the true sword'* where a Sulsa would fight openly, with honour and Am-Ja or *'way of darkness'* which taught them trickery and deceit to accomplish their task by whatever means were necessary.

A Sulsa

The Sulsa were highly trained warrior athletes, able to do seemingly supernatural things if witnessed by the average man. Stories of them flying, falling from great heights and walking on water, were all told

화랑
Hwa-Rang

about them, when in fact they were either just tricks, feats aided by the tools of their trade or simply their extreme athletic abilities in action.

As they were Hwa-Rang, they too followed the codes and did not kill indiscriminately, as their high level of training usually allowed them to kill only the intended target and slip out before anyone noticed.

A well known story of a Sulsa was that of Kwan Chan, who you will read more about in the Ge-Baek chapter. When he was 15 years old, yet still a highly accomplished Hwa-Rang, the King of Silla asked him to kill a baekje General called Jua Jang-Gun. The only way to get close to the general was by way of infiltration, which Kwan Chan did by moving into a Baekje town in order to work his way up Baekje society. Kwan chan was an accomplished dancer and he showed his dancing around the town and became admired for his skills. News of his skills soon reached the King (Ui-ja), who invited him to perform in front of his royal court.

Seizing the opportunity, Kwan Chan went to the court and performed a dance, which was basically a modified version of a pattern, known as Sang Gum Sul, in which two swords were used. The king and the court enjoyed the dance and as he came to finish he stabbed General Jua Jang-Gun with one of the swords, killing him instantly before escaping. Sang Gum Sul pattern (hyung) was turned into a folk dance called 'Sang Gum Moo' and is still practiced in Korea to this day.

Hwa-Rang's 29 movements represent the 29th Infantry Division, where Taekwon-Do developed into maturity. According to his own memoirs, when the Korean War finished and Korea was reforming its armed forces, General Choi was offered command of the 28th Infantry division, which had already been formed. The General asked if the 28th was the last division to be formed to which he was told that they had one more division planned, which hadn't been formed yet. General Choi asked to take control of that Division, explaining that as he was promoted later than others, who were already anxious to take control of a Division, he would rather take control of the last one and make it into the best unit possible.

From Creation To Unification
The Complete Histories Behind The Ch'ang Hon (ITF) Patterns

The 29th Infantry Division was formed in September, 1953 on Je-Ju Island, which General Choi made his base for training. In his memoirs he says he did his best to make the unit *'the most righteous and desirable in the army'*. The unit's emblem is the Generals clenched fist, originally drawn by his own wife, but later drawn by an artist to create a 'forceful' emblem. The divisions name was 'ICK' which, according to General Choi, is the sound when you pronounce 29th in Korean quickly; however, General Choi says he chose it due to Korean resistance fighter Shin, Ik-Hee with both the number 9 (of 29th) and the picture representing his own fist. The 2 is said to represent a divided Korea (North and South), as well as the units emblem having a shape that represents Korea, so the fist over the (shape) of Korea and the 2 and the 9 represent General Choi destroying the 38th parallel that divides Korea and reuniting it into one country again. The unit was also known as the *'Fist Division'*. It is interesting that the ITF emblem also features General Choi's fist!

The ICK patch [89]

It was whilst in charge of the 29th Infantry division that soldiers trained in Karate (Kong Soo Do) which General Choi later developed into Taekwon-Do. Another thing of note is that according to General Choi, during the daytime the soldiers of the 29th practiced combat training, but at night time were schooled in literacy which is very similar to the Hwa-Rang! The 29th Infantry division was also where the Oh Do Kwan was founded. The Oh Do Kwan was the martial school of General Choi within the Korean military and means 'Gym of My Way'. In Korean 'Oh' translates as 'My, Mine or Our', whilst 'Do' translates as 'Way' and 'Kwan' as school or gym. In his memoirs, General Choi said he chose the name due to a saying by Confucius *'Oh Do Il Kwan Zi'* meaning *'My principle is to master one thing'*, which represented General Choi's ambition of creating Taekwon-Do and spreading it throughout the world with the help of his instructors – those who had mastered the 'One thing'!

---

[89] Recreation of the ICK emblem patch. Picture courtesy of Master Doug Nowling VII, *Kido Kwan Martial Arts International*. Reproduced with permission and thanks.

화랑
Hwa-Rang

A monument was erected by General Choi on Jeju Island, to commemorate the formation of the 29th Infantry Division. The stone on top features the 'Fist' emblem of the division, which also adorned their patches and division flags.

The Jeju Island Monument, with the 'Fist' stone (inset) [89]

The pillar is triangular in shape, with a square base and the Hanja (text) that adorns every side was designed by General Choi himself.

---

[90] Jeju Island Monument photographs courtesy of Dr. George Vitale, VIII

From Creation To Unification
The Complete Histories Behind The Ch'ang Hon (ITF) Patterns

The monument was knocked down and buried by Jeju Island locals, who were afraid of reprisals by the military dictator Chun Doo Hwan[91], (whom General Choi was also very critical of) following a visit to the island by his brother. It was only restored in the early 21st century when locals remembered it, dug it up and restored it.

Though the Hanja[92] on the base pieces represent the names of the various military officers at the time; there are two of them that relate directly to General Choi.

The larger centre text says '29th Infantry Division Founding Location', with the smaller Hanja on the right reading 'Infantry Division Captain - Major General Choi Hong Hi'

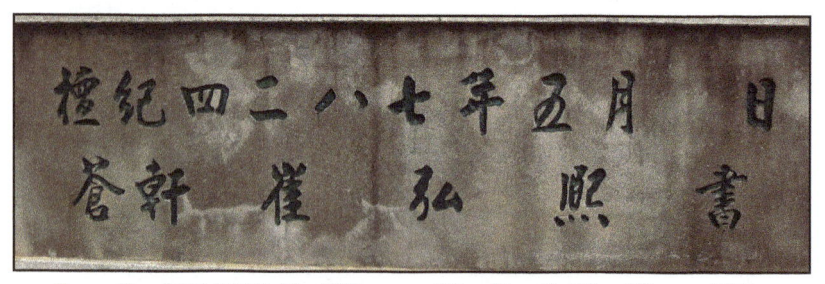

Korean Year 4287 (1954) May ?? Day   Ch'ang Hon Choi Hong Hi   Written

---

[91] Chun Doo Hwan was the brutal military dictator that succeeded the former South Korean President, Park Chung Hee, after he was assassinated in 1979. He was later convicted and sentenced to death for his crimes against the people, once a democratically elected civilian leadership was voted in.

[92] Many thanks to Grandmaster Phap Lu, Mr. Minh Luong, Instructor Jerry Potts and Dr. George Vitale for help with the translations of the monument.

화랑
Hwa-Rang

The Hanja written on the columns were to inspire the men of the unit and show everyone else what a strong unit they were!

Cultivating Physical Strength   *Strengthening Fighting Spirit*   *Absolutely Devoted to Training and Cultivation*

For me, it is obvious that General Choi modelled the 29th Infantry division on the Hwa-Rang warriors of ancient Silla, as General Choi must have seen his unit as similar in mode to the Hwa-Rang of old; as a military fighting force known for their courage and skills, but with morals and aims of well being and unity of the country he loved.

"Some say that the age of chivalry is past, that the spirit of romance is dead. The age of chivalry is never past so long as there is a wrong left unredressed on earth."

- Charles Kingsley

충무
Choong-Moo

Choong-Moo was the name given to the great Admiral Yi Soon-Sin of the Yi Dynasty. He was reputed to have invented the first armoured battleship (Kobukson) in 1592, which is said to be the precursor of the present day submarine. The reason why this pattern ends with a left hand attack is to symbolize his regrettable death, having no chance to show his unrestrained potentiality, checked by the forced reservation of his loyalty to the king.

Choong-Moo is the ninth pattern of Ch'ang Hon Taekwon-Do, usually taught at 1st Kup, Red belt. It has 30 moves and was developed in Korea in 1955 with the help of Colonel Nam, Tae Hi. Though it is the ninth pattern practiced by students, it was the second pattern for Ch'ang Hon Taekwon-Do ever developed.

Choong-Moo is named after the great Admiral Yi Soon-Sin of the Yi Dynasty.[93] Admiral Yi was born on the 28th April, 1545 in Geoncheon-dong Street of Hanseong (then the capital, which is now a district of Seoul). When he was young, Yi Soon-Sin was proficient in reading and writing Chinese and enjoyed playing war games with his friends, making his own bows and arrows.

Yi Soon-Sin

At around 31 years of age (1576) Yi Soon-Sin first failed, then passed the military exam. In the first exam he impressed the judges with his

---

[93] Though often referred to as the Yi Dynasty, after its founder Yi Song-Gye, it is better known as the Joseon (or Chosŏn) Dynasty and it lasted from 1392 to 1897

From Creation To Unification
The Complete Histories Behind The Ch'ang Hon (ITF) Patterns

swordsmanship and archery skills, but unfortunately he broke his leg during the cavalry assessment phase. However, once it healed, he re-entered and passed whereby he was posted to *Bukbyeong* (Northern Frontier Army) in Hamgyeong province. Now 32, he was the oldest junior officer and spent his time defending the border villages against the Manchu's (though in Yi's time they were known as Jurchen people), where he showed great tactical, strategic and leadership skills. In 1589 he managed to capture the Jurchens chief, Mu Pai Na, who he executed immediately.

Following his father's death, Yi spent 3 years away from the army in mourning (a tradition at the time), after which he returned to continue his fight against the Jurchens and led many successful campaigns against them.

With his career flourishing so early on, some of his seniors became jealous of his accomplishments and falsely accused him of desertion from the battlefield, with the conspiracy led by General Yi Il (who later failed to defend against the Japanese invasion at the Battle of Sangju – one of the first land battles of the Imjin War).[94]

Yi Soon-Sin overseeing the training of his troops.
Painted by the artist Jung, Chang Sub, 1978

---

[94] The Imjin War, also known as the 'Seven Year War'. See page 23, footnote 17 for more details.

충무
Choong-Moo

Following the accusations, Yi Soon-Sin was stripped of his rank, imprisoned and tortured. Eventually he was released and allowed to fight as a simple enlisted soldier. However, it wasn't long before he once again rose through the ranks and was soon appointed Commander of the Seoul *Hunryeonwon* (a military training center).

Yi Soon-Sin's accomplishments did not go unnoticed and in 1590, within the span of a few months, Yi Soon-Sin had received four military appointments in quick succession, each giving a greater role than the previous. These were: Commander of the Kosarijin Garrison (Pyeongan province), then Commander of the Manpo Garrison (also Pyeongan province), then Commander of the Wando Garrison (Jeolla province) and finally as Commander of the Left Jeolla Naval District.

In 1591, as war loomed with Japan, and the Jurchens gaining strength under new leadership, the royal court was unsure of a course of action to deal with the growing threat. Yi Soon-Sin took up his new post as Commander of the Left Jeolla Naval District and started to build up the Navy through a series of reforms, one of which led to the construction of the famous Kobukson (Turtle Boat).

The main ships of the Joseon navy in that era were called 'Panokseon' (meaning Board Roofed Ship), which in many ways were superior to those within the Japanese fleets, as they had very strong hulls and a flat keel due to Koreas coastal waters, so the ships could actually sit on the tide planes when the tides were out - it also made them much

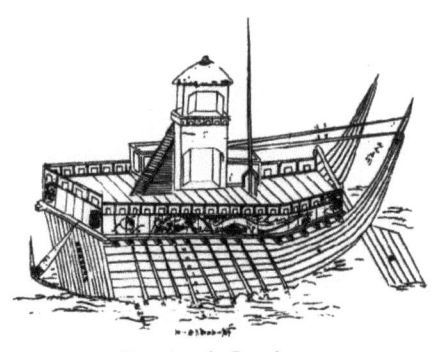

Drawing of a Panokseon

more manoeuvrable in shallow waters. The 'Panokseon' could carry up to 20 cannons, compared to the Japanese ships that only carried 1 or 2 cannons. However, the development of cannons had been sorely neglected by the Joseon Government, but Admiral Yi made it his priority to develop cannons for his fleet, ending up with ones called

From Creation To Unification
The Complete Histories Behind The Ch'ang Hon (ITF) Patterns

Heaven, Earth, Black and Yellow.[95] The lack of cannons on the Japanese ships was because their favourite tactic was to not to slug it out with cannons in the open sea's, but to catch and board the enemies ships and engage in hand to hand combat to destroy all on board - and in this this area, the Japanese ships were superior to the Joseon Panokseon, as they were faster.

Hideyoshi Toyotomi

In 1592, Hideyoshi Toyotomi ordered Japan to invade Korea in order to use it as a base of operations to invade the Ming Dynasty of China. Toyotomi had unsuccessfully tried to secure two Spanish Galleons to support his fleet, but when that had failed, he increased his fleet to 1,700 ships with the thought that with so many ships, he would easily overwhelm the Joseon navy. With his massive fleet ready, Toyotomi ordered it to first secure the Korean port of Busan, in the South of the country which was to become his base of operations.

The Japanese Landing at Busan

Though Yi Soon-Sin had never commanded a navy before, he engaged the Japanese fleet in battle at Goeja Island, known as the Battle of Okpo (as it was fought over 2 days, around Okpo harbour).

---

[95] Heaven was the largest cannon and fired an arrow shaped like a rocket, to a range of 500m, as well as standard 'cannon shot', up to 1 Km.. Earth was slightly smaller, with Black and Yellow being smaller still.

충무
Choong-Moo

A painting depicting the Battle of Okpo, painted by the artist Moon Hak Jung, 1978

This was not only Yi Soon-Sin's first naval battle, it was the first battle of the Imjim war and also Yi Soon-Sin's first victory. Following this battle, Yi Soon-Sin was promoted to Commander of the Three Provinces by King Seonjo, which gave him command over 5 navies.[96] The modern day equivalent to this rank is Admiral.

Soon after the Battle of Okpo, Admiral Yi received reports from Admiral Won Gyun, that Japanese ships had been sighted at Sacheon and on the 29th May, 1592 Admiral Yi's fleet sailed to meet them at what was to be his second battle.

Arriving at Sacheon, Admiral Yi surveyed the area and saw 12 very large Japanese battleships in the harbor, with numerous other smaller boats, all overlooked by a cliff top, meaning he couldn't attack as he did at Okpo, as soldiers would counter-attack from the cliff tops with guns, raining bullets down on his ships.

Yi Soon-Sin was a great strategist and knowing that the Japanese were over-confident and boastful, he devised a plan to lure the Japanese

---

[96] Jeolla Right and Left Navies, the Gyeongsang Right and Left Navies and the Chungcheong Navy.

From Creation To Unification
The Complete Histories Behind The Ch'ang Hon (ITF) Patterns

A reconstruction of the Kobukson found at Yi-Soon Sin Shrine, in Asan.

fleet out to sea, where he had more room to manoeuvre and fight them.

Knowing his fleet would have been watched by the Japanese; Admiral Yi suddenly turned all his ships around and retreated! Or so it looked to the Japanese Commander who immediately ordered part of his fleet to pursue and destroy them.

It was during this battle that Admiral Yi first used the famous Kobukson or Turtle boat.[97] As the Japanese fleet slowly caught up with Admiral Yi it was nearly dark and the Admiral ordered all his ships to quickly turn and face the enemy, unleashing a hail of cannon balls and fire arrows, which, catching the Japanese by surprise, inflicted heavy damage to them.

By all accounts, the Japanese fared much better than in their previous

---

[97] Kobukson or turtle boat, which, contrary to popular belief wasn't invented by Admiral Yi, but rather brought back and improved from an earlier design to make it the ship it became. It was a battleship with an iron spiked roof to prevent boarding from the higher Japanese ships. At its stern it had a dragon's head which emitted smoke, as well as having 4 cannons within it. It also had 11 cannons along each side, two more at the stern and two at the rear (bow). It also had smaller holes from which arrows, guns and mortars could be fired. It was powered by two masts and sails, but could also be powered by its 20 oars pulled by 2 men per oar or 5 men per oar for faster manoeuvrability in battles.

충무
Choong-Moo

Admiral Yi and the famous Kobukson in the heat of battle!

battle, standing their ground and returning fire with their arquebuses, however it was not enough, as Admiral Yi's tactics prevented the Japanese from boarding any Korean ships as his fleets concentrated cannon fire prevented any ships getting too close.

As the enemies were worn down, Admiral Yi sent the Kobukson directly into the Japanese lines, causing fear and panic amongst the enemy fleet, destroying every Japanese ship to finish the battle. Things could have been much different however, as it was during this battle that Admiral Yi was shot, though luckily for the Korean fleet it was a minor injury, only puncturing the skin on his left arm.

After the Battle of Sacheon, Admiral Yi sent a letter to King Seonjo telling him about the Kobukson and how it had faired in the battle. It read: *"Several years ago, I already predicted the Japanese invasion. I have built the new war ships for the war. The ship looks like the turtle. I put the dragon head in front of the ship to fire the artilleries from its mouth. On the roof, there are long spikes which prevented the invaders from boarding it. The sides are covered with the boards which have the port holes. The holes are designed that we can see outside, but the enemy could not see inside. It can rush into the center of the enemy fleets and fire the artilleries to four directions. In this battle, the turtle ships carried out dramatically their mission as the vanguards when I faced the enemies. They were really successful."*

From Creation To Unification
The Complete Histories Behind The Ch'ang Hon (ITF) Patterns

On 14th August, 1592, Admiral Yi was involved in the Battle of Hansan Island, which was to become one of his most famous victories as it became a turning point in the war. At the Battle of Hansan, Admiral Yi's fleet destroyed over 47 Japanese ships, captured at least 12 and killed over 8,000 Japanese sailors and marines.

A Korean stamp depicting the Battle of Hansan island

The Battle of Hansan Island began after the Japanese realized that without control of the seas, its supply lines to its troops were under threat and so, Hideyoshi Toyotomi ordered one of his Commanders (Yasuharu Wakizaka), to combine his fleet with two other Japanese fleets and hunt down the Korean fleet and destroy them once and for all.

However, being impatient and knowing he had probably the best ships on the seas at that time, Commander Wakizaka set out alone with his 73 ships, to face Admiral Yi's fleet.

As Commander Wakizaka's fleet was anchored near the Gyeonnaeryang Strait, which was a narrow channel and thus a safe place to rest a fleet, Admiral Yi sent six of his ships into the channel to lure Wakizaka's fleet out. Wakizaka took the bait and gave chase, only to exit the channel to find the rest of Admiral Yi's fleet facing them.

Commander Wakizaka pressed forwards and engaged, but Admiral Yi had been working on a *'crane wing'* formation for his fleet, a common tactic in land battles, but not one used with ships.

Yasuharu Wakizaka was a legendary Japanese Commander himself, but he was highly aggressive. He not only ordered his entire fleet to chase the decoy ships, but continued into the middle of the crane wing, exposing his flank and eventually becoming totally engulfed and

충무
Choong-Moo

surrounded, as he tried the favoured Japanese naval tactic of getting as close as possible to the enemy ships and boarding them – however, the crane wing formation and long range firepower of Admiral Yi's fleet put paid to that.

A scene from the historical drama 'Immortal Admiral Yi Sun-Sin', showing the Crane Wing formation [98]

The battle continued for around 6 hours, before Commander Wakizaka abandoned his flag ship and escaped on a faster vessel. Other Japanese commanders were killed in the battle, with one committing seppuku on his ship as it burnt and sank. In the actual battle, Wakizaka lost 59 ships and though 14 escaped, most of them were so badly damaged they had to be abandoned on the way back. Very few ships ever made it back to Busan harbor, Japans main port during their occupation.

This victory is considered the most important of the war, as it effectively stopped Japan supplying its troops by sea, and slowed down the land advance so much that the Japanese troops got no further than Pyongyang (North Korea) and never really made it into China, which was the main plan of the invasion in the first place!

On 16th August, 1592 around the time Admiral Yi was attacking Japanese vessels anchored in Angolpo harbor, he wrote a famous poem, which reads:

> *When luminous moonbeams flash upon Hansan Isle*
> *Myself 'n solitude sit on watch-tower awhile,*
> *At a moment in deep tormenting anguish*
> *With a scepter sword around on my side,*
> *A lute tune out from nowhere renders*
> *But such gut-wrenching sorrows.*

---

[98] The crane wing formation was designed to defeat the enemy without losing men themselves, sinking their ships without allowing others to escape. It was like a 'U' shape, with the heaviest battleships at the centre, other ships to the side and still more ships at the rear to fill out the wing as it expanded to engulf the enemy.

From Creation To Unification
The Complete Histories Behind The Ch'ang Hon (ITF) Patterns

On 15th September, 1592, Admiral Yi attacked the Japanese fleet at their own base of operations at Busan, sinking 115 Japanese ships before withdrawing as he had no land forces to continue the battle with. Yi Soon-Sin reported the battle to King Seonjo; the report read as follows: *"So far, I have made the four movements which had about 10 battles. I won all of them. My men did their best in all sea battles. Especially, I have never seen the battles in which my men were more serious than the Busan Battle. I think they are worth receiving honors from Your Majesty..." "...Before I just faced not more than about 70 ships of invaders. But in this battle, I fought about 500 ships in the Busan port, the Japanese main headquarter, for all day. I finally destroyed and sank about 100 ships. Though I could not exterminate the soldiers on land, I believe this battle made them scared enough. And the achievements my men made in this battle is much bigger than those they did in any other battle."*

In 1597, Admiral Yi was once again relieved of his command following a plot by the Japanese, which used the dynasties bickering internal politics to rid themselves of whom they considered one of their greatest opponents to victory – Admiral Yi Soon-Sin. The plot involved a Japanese agent befriending a Korean General and convincing him he would spy on Japanese operations for him.

Eventually, General Kim Gyeong-Seo believed everything he was told and one day the spy informed the Korean General that the Japanese General Kato Kiyomasa, would soon be arriving with a great fleet of ships and that he should send Admiral Yi to ambush them. The news was relayed to King Seonjo who agreed to the operation, but when General Kim informed Admiral Yi, the Admiral refused, as he knew the area to be full of hidden, sunken rocks and he didn't trust information given by spies.

When the King was told of the Admirals refusal, his enemies at the court insisted he be replaced by General Won Gyun and Admiral Yi be arrested. Admiral Yi was

King Seonjo

충무
Choong-Moo

relieved of command and arrested, imprisoned and tortured to the point of death.

King Seonjo had become so convinced of Yi Soon-Sin's treachery that he wanted him executed, but Minister Jeong Tak and others that supported Admiral Yi convinced the king to spare him due to his past military record, though surprisingly the Prime Minister, Yu Seong-ryong, a childhood friend of Yi and his main supporter, remained quiet throughout the hearing!

Again, Yi Soon-Sin was released and demoted to become an infantry soldier under the command of General Gwon Yul. For many, this would have been worse than death itself, but Yi took it with humility, seeing himself simply as a loyal subject and went about following the orders given to him. Despite his now low position, many officers still treated him with respect due to his past and the knowledge that they knew he had done nothing wrong.

Admiral Yi's replacement, Won Gyun was nowhere near as competent as Yi. He (Won Gyun) failed to respond to reports of a fleet of Japanese ships quickly enough and allowed 1000 ships to land 140,000 Japanese reinforcements, but luckily the Chinese had also reinforced the Korean land troops so they were able to push the Japanese assault back to the South. If Admiral Yi were still in charge, the Japanese wouldn't have even attempted such a feat in the first place.

Won Gyun

Eventually, on 28th August, 1597, Won Gyun took the entire Joseon navy that Admiral Yi had built up and trained, consisting of 150 warships and 30,000 men, and attacked the Japanese navy with little forethought or preparation and he was slaughtered. In this battle, known as the Battle of Chilchonryang, Won Gyun had allowed the Japanese navy to close in and board his ships, slaughtering their crews. The same type of battle that Admiral Yi carefully planned against and avoided in his victories. All but 12 ships were destroyed, and despite

From Creation To Unification
The Complete Histories Behind The Ch'ang Hon (ITF) Patterns

escaping to a nearby island with a few other survivors, Won Gyun was captured and executed by soldiers from a nearby Japanese fort. This was to be the only sea battle the Joseon navy lost throughout the war with Japan and following this news, King Seonjo quickly reassigned Admiral Yi to his former post.

All in all, during four campaigns, Admiral Yi Soon-Sin had twenty three victories, but the most famous battle of all is considered to be the Battle of Myeongnyang, which took place on 26th October, 1597. In this battle Admiral Yi engaged a Japanese fleet of 333 ships (of which at least 133 were warships) with only 13 ships of his own.

Following the earlier battle, in which Admiral Won Gyun had been killed and lost virtually the whole of the Korean Navy, except for 12 ships that were saved by an officer called Bae Seol (who had left before the battle even began, as he knew what the outcome would be), Admiral Yi re-commandeered the ships and rallied the remaining crews, thought to be as little as 200 sailors and added his own flagship, making a total of 13. At the same time King Seonjo considered the navy a lost cause and decided to disband it. He sent a letter calling for the navy to disband and join its ground forces, whereby Admiral Yi replied in his own letter *"...I still have twelve battle ships...and I am still alive, the enemy shall never be safe in the Western Sea."*

An Older Yi Soon-Sin

With his tiny fleet of 13 ships (none of which were Kobukson) Admiral Yi took what was considered a last stand against the massive Japanese fleet of 133 battleships (though it was 333 altogether, if the support ships are included). Choosing a narrow straight where he could protect his flank, use the tides (which changed direction every 3

충무
Choong-Moo

A painting by Korean artist Kim, Yong Hwan depicting the Battle of Myeongnyang with its dangerous tides

hours) to his advantage and also tighten steel wire across the width of it, he sent a solitary ship to draw out the Japanese fleet.

To Admiral Yi's advantage it was a foggy day and the Japanese fleet took the bait and chased the Korean ship into the straight – waiting at the other end, hidden by the fog, was Admiral Yi's small fleet, which opened fire with cannon volleys, severely damaging the first group of Japanese ships. As this happened, on the shores, Admiral Yi's sailors tightened the steel wire between the other groups of Japanese ships, hampering their movements and allowing them to be better targeted, as well as taking away their advantage of numbers. All the while Admiral Yi's ships were obscured in the hillside shadows, hiding them from the enemy and making them difficult to hit.

As the battle waged a body was pulled from the water dressed in ornate Japanese armor. It was the body of Michifusa Kurushima, the commander of the Japanese fleet, whose brother Admiral Yi had killed at an earlier battle. Admiral Yi ordered that Kurushima's head be cut off and placed on the mast of his flagship, the sight of which caused

From Creation To Unification
The Complete Histories Behind The Ch'ang Hon (ITF) Patterns

the Japanese morale to drop considerably.

As the tides changed unexpectedly, the Japanese ships began drifting into one another, damaging them even further and during this confusion; Admiral Yi ordered his advance and attacked the remaining Japanese ships, which were packed tightly together due to the tides, making them easy pickings for the Korean cannon fire. With 30 ships destroyed and many more ships damaged, the Japanese fleet retreated.

This victory again, put paid to any idea of the Japanese supplying their land troops via sea, as the Korean navy was now in full charge of the Yellow Sea, the main supply route to Korea. With this, the Japanese army realized victory was impossible without supplies and reinforcements and began a full retreat. In the time it would take the Japanese to rebuild their fleet, Korea would also have time to rebuild theirs and gain additional ships from the Chinese, who so far had been keeping their own navy to protect their important ports, but, inspired by this battle, relaxed their protection and allowed Chinese ships to reinforce the Korean navy.

However, whilst the people of Korea celebrated Admiral Yi's great victory at the Battle of Myeongnyang, the defeated Japanese secretly sent 50 soldiers to Yi Soon-Sin's home village in Asan for revenge, where they burned down houses looking for Yi's family. Though many of his family managed to escape to the nearby mountains, his 3rd son Yi Myon-Shin remained, armed with a bow and a sword, to fight off the invaders. Yi Myon-Shin managed to kill 3 of the Japanese soldiers before he was killed himself - he was only 21 years old.

News of his sons death broke the Admirals heart but he felt unable to show his sorrow in front of his men so he sought the privacy of a friends house and wept. He expresses his sorrow for the loss of his son in his diary, writing: *'How could the heavens be so merciless. It is as if my heart is being burned and torn to pieces. Proper, by nature, it is I who should have died and it is you who should have lived. Yet since you are dead and I alive, how contrary to nature, how improper is it. The heavens and the earth are dark, and even the sun has lost its colour. Ah, how sad! My son, where are you now, having deserted me? Is it because you are such an outstanding figure that the heavens are*

충무
Choong-Moo

unwilling to leave you in this world, or is it because of my sin, that this great misfortune has befallen you. Even if I hold out in this world, now on whom can I lean my heart? I wish to follow you to the grave, to stay and weep with you together under the ground, but if I do, your brothers, sisters and your mother will have no one to lean their hearts on. Thus I endure, but my mind that wails is already dead, soulless. Passing a night now seems like waiting for a year to go by."* (War Diary, 14th October, 1597)

On 15th December, 1598 a massive Japanese fleet gathered in Sachon Bay (South Korea) in the Noryang straits, to break an allied blockade of one of their fleets, with the aim of merging them and sailing safely back to Japan.

Admiral Yi had been following reports of the occurring events and gathered his fleet of 85 ships (three of which were Kobukson) and 8,000 soldiers, along with the allied Ming fleet, led by Chen Lin, of 8 warships and 57 smaller ships, 5,000 Ming soldiers and 2,600 Ming marines and headed towards the massive Japanese fleet.

On 16th December, 1598, at 2 am, the Battle of Noryang began and as with his previous battles, Admiral Yi's tactics proved extremely effective at keeping the Japanese at bay and not allowing them to use their favoured tactic of boarding ships and soon saw them in full retreat.

Admiral Yi ordered his fleets to pursue and as they did so, a stray bullet struck the Admiral near his left armpit. Sensing it was a fatal wound the Admiral famously ordered one of his officers to impersonate him so as not to demoralise his men, by saying *"The war is at its height, wear my armor and beat my war drums. Do*

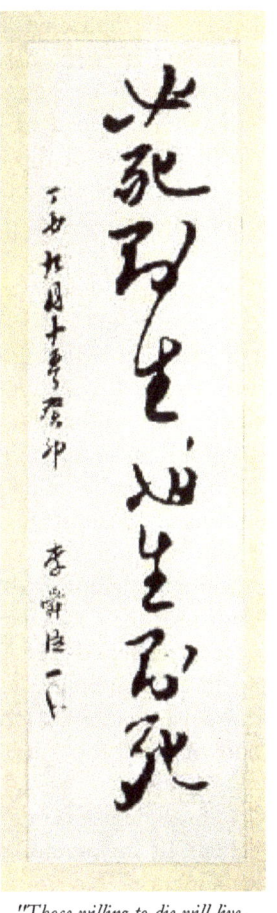

"Those willing to die will live, and those willing to live will die." - Calligraphy by Admiral Yi Soon-Sin

From Creation To Unification
The Complete Histories Behind The Ch'ang Hon (ITF) Patterns

not announce my death". Admiral Yi Soon-Sin died moments later.

Only two people had witnessed the Admirals death; Yi Hoe (the Admirals eldest son) and Yi Wan, (his nephew). Before anyone else could see the tragedy, they carried his body to his cabin and Yi Wan wore his uncles armour and beat the war drums until the end of the battle, just as the Admiral had asked.

During the battle, Admiral Yi's ship had rescued Chen Lin's many times and after the battle, when he came to thank him for coming to his aid, upon hearing the news of Admiral Yi's death, it is said that Chen Lin dropped to the floor three times, sobbing and beating his chest. The rest of the fleet, both Joseon and Ming, sobbed in grief at the news, once they heard as well. Admiral Yi's body was buried next to his father in Asan.

Throughout the invasion, Yi Soon-Sin's fleet was mostly cut off from the government and effectively had to fend for itself, leaving it up to the Admiral to supply all his men. Yi Soon-Sin was not just responsible for leading his men in battle, but also farming to feed them, salt production to raise money, military supplies, provisions, weapons and ammunition manufacture, as well as their distribution, caring for the wounded sailors and ship building. In 1593 there was a serious food shortage at the Navy base in Hansan which led to the death of over 600 sailors from starvation, leaving the remainder extremely malnourished and at risk from serious illness. Yi Soon-Sin expressed his concerns about his own troops lack of food, whilst the enemy remained well supplied, as well as his concerns about always being outnumbered, in his war diary (Nanjung Ilgi).[99] It is through these war diaries and communications sent to the king, that so much is known about the Admiral.

All through his career, whether as an Admiral or a lowly conscript soldier, he maintained the respect of both his own troops and many of his superiors. He treated everyone with respect and was considered an

---

[99] The original *Nanjung Ilgi* (War Diary) of Yi Soon-Sin consisted of 205 folio pages bound into 7 separate volumes. It has since been translated, along with his *Memorials to Court* and released as a book - *see Bibliography*.

충무
Choong-Moo

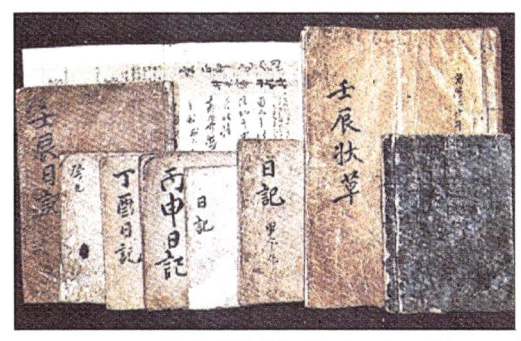

Admiral Yi's War Diaries, along with a sample of his handwriting.

extremely charismatic leader, often fighting alongside his own troops in the most dangerous of circumstances and was able to keep their morale up despite food shortages and news of continuous Korean losses in the ground war. The people loved him because of this and often supplied him with intelligence reports at great risk to themselves.

Yi Soon-Sin wrote down the values he believed a warrior must have, writing that a warrior must master 3 roads; knowledge of the world, understanding of things as they are and wisdom toward humanity. That a warrior should undertake 4 obligations; to provide national security at minimal cost, to lead others unselfishly, to suffer adversity without fear and to offer solutions without laying blame. That a warrior should practice and hone 5 skills; to be flexible without weakness, to be strong without arrogance, to be kind without vulnerability, to be trusting without naivety and to have invincible courage. Finally, he wrote that for security there are 10 keys; purity of purpose, sound strategy, integrity, clarity, lack of covetousness, lack of addiction, a reserved tongue, assertiveness without

Portrait of Admiral Yi, drawn in 1952

aggression, being firm and fair, and patience. Yi Soon-Sin was the epitome of what he wrote and believed in and lived his life accordingly.

Sadly, during King Seonjo reign, the kings view of Admiral Yi was manipulated so much, that even when he died the king is said to have shown no sadness or grief and simply held a 'blank expression'.[100] Following his death, the Joseon Government did not continue his navy reforms and the Joseon Navy, along with the Kobukson disappeared into the annals of history, with the entire Joseon military being reduced later on.

However, Yi Soon-Sin's legacy inspired generations of his family line, with over 200 of his direct male descendants passing military exams and pursuing careers in the military.

In 1643, Admiral Yi Soon-Sin was posthumously awarded the title Chungmugong meaning Duke of Loyalty and Warfare. Choong-Moo stands for Loyalty and Chivalry. He is revered throughout Korea and considered one of its greatest heroes of all time. He is famed, not only for the Kobukson, but for his courage, self-sacrifice and unerring loyalty to his country, despite the way he was treated and also for his famous last words.

As an Admiral, his skills as a tactician are also revered throughout the world's navies. In the book 'The Influence of the Sea on the Political History of

A statue of Admiral Yi Soon-Sin in Seoul, SK.

---

[100] According to a recent *Choson Ilbo* historical article.

충무
Choong-Moo

Japan' by George Alexander Ballard (1862–1948), a Vice-Admiral of the British Royal Navy he wrote *"This was the great Korean admiral's crowning exploit. In the short space of six weeks*[101] *he had achieved a series of successes unsurpassed in the whole annals of maritime war, destroying the enemy's battle fleets, cutting his lines of communication, sweeping up his convoys, imperiling the situation of his victorious armies in the field, and bringing his ambitious schemes to utter ruin. Not even Nelson, Blake, or Jean Bart could have done more than this scarcely known representative of a small and cruelly oppressed nation; and it is to be regretted that his memory lingers nowhere outside his native land, for no impartial judge could deny him the right to be accounted among the born leaders of men."*

In the same book, George Alexander Ballard also wrote *"It is always difficult for Englishmen to admit that Nelson ever had an equal in his profession, but if any man is entitled to be so regarded, it should be this great naval commander of Asiatic race who never knew defeat and died in the presence of the enemy; of whose movements a track-chart might be compiled from the wrecks of hundreds of Japanese ships lying with their valiant crews at the bottom of the sea, off the coasts of the Korean peninsula... and it seems, in truth, no exaggeration to assert that from first to last he never made a mistake, for his work was so complete under each variety of circumstances as to defy criticism... His whole career might be summarized by saying that, although he had no lessons from past history to serve as a guide, he waged war on the sea as it should be waged if it is to produce definite results, and ended by making the supreme sacrifice of a defender of his country."*

Admiral Heihachiro Togo (a 19th Century Japanese Admiral), took exception to Admiral Yi being mentioned in part of a speech in his honour and said *"It may be proper to compare me with Nelson, but not with Korea's Yi Soon-Sin, for he has no equal."*

Yi, Soon-Sin is featured on the Korean 100 won coin, whilst the Kobukson is featured on the 5 won coin.

A few films have been made about the life of Yi Soon-

---

[101] It was actually around 9 weeks

From Creation To Unification
The Complete Histories Behind The Ch'ang Hon (ITF) Patterns

Sin, but in 2004 a 104 episode Korean drama first aired on Korean television and later in the same year aired in the US. Which, despite having some 'artistic' inaccuracies, is held to high praise.

Though the reason for the pattern Choong-Moo having 30 movements is not mentioned in any of General Choi's books, it is possible that the 30 moves refer to the amount of ships destroyed by Admiral Yi's small force of 13 ships (against 133) at the Battle of Myeongnyang, his most famous battle of all.

"...In sea battle, all the sailors take one boat, and they cannot run away at the sight of the enemy vessels even though they wish to do so, because the supervising officers wave flags and beat the drum to row fast and charge into the enemy position, and kill them outright if they disobey the order. There is no alternative. The sailors must fight with their whole might – much more, the Turtle Ship dashes in front and the board-roofed ships follow after, shooting cannons marked "Earth" and "Black", and pouring down fire-balls and mortal arrows like rain and hailstones until the enemy loses his morale and his bleeding warriors drop into the water like falling leaves in the autumn wind."

- *Admiral Yi Soon-Sin*

Above: Posters for the 104 episode TV series *'The Immortal Yi Sun-Sin'*

광개
Kwang-Gae

Kwang-Gae is named after the famous Kwang-Gae-Toh-Wang, the 19th King of the Koguryo Dynasty, who regained all the lost territories including the greater part of Manchuria. The diagram represents the expansion and recovery of lost territory. The 39 movements refer to the first two figures of 391 A.D., the year he came to the throne.

Kwang-Gae is the tenth pattern of of Ch'ang Hon Taekwon-Do, usually taught at 1st Degree Black belt. It has 39 moves and was developed in Malaysia between 1962 and 1964 with the help of Master Kim, Bok Man and Master Woo, Jae Lim.

As the pattern definition says, Kwang-Gae is named after the 19th King of the Goguryo Dynasty. His full title, which was posthumously given to him, is *Kwang Gae Toh Wang*[102] which means roughly *"Very Greatest King, Broad Expander of Territory"*. His 'era name'[103] was *Yeongnak* and he was known as *Emperor Yeongnak the Great* during his reign.

Prior to Kwang-Gae's birth in 374 AD, the once great kingdom of Goguryo had lost much of its power following a major defeat by Baekje, which killed its reigning emperor at the time, Emperor Goguk-Won (who had reigned for forty years until his death in 371 AD). Emperor Goguk-Won was then succeeded by Emperor Sosurim who isolated the kingdom in order to rebuild it from its weakened state. Emperor Sosurim ruled for thirteen years until his death in 384 AD

---

[102] *Toh* defines a ruling title, with *Wang* meaning King

[103] An era name or reign name is a name chosen to be used by a monarch once they come to the throne and is different to the name they had as a prince. It was a medieval practice, especially in Asia. Posthumous names were sometimes accorded to a deceased monarch as well.

From Creation To Unification
The Complete Histories Behind The Ch'ang Hon (ITF) Patterns

and he was then succeeded by Kwang-Gae's father, Emperor Goguk-Yang.

Emperor Goguk-Yang ruled for only 8 years and died in 391 AD to be succeeded by Kwang-Gae. During his reign however, Emperor Goguk-Yang continued the isolation policies of the former Emperor, in order to rehabilitate and remobilize Goguryo's armies, eventually attacking Baekje in 386 AD (after allying with Silla). Baekje had become a dominant power, not just in Korea but in South East Asia and surrounded Goguryo in the South and West, which remained a constant threat to the kingdom.

Following his father's death, Kwang-Gae was crowned Emperor and gave himself the title 'Supreme King Yeongnak' to show he was the equal of other rulers of Asia, as well as the Emperor of Goguryo. Kwang-Gae continued to rebuild the army, as well as cavalry units and the navy and in 392 AD he also attacked Baekje.

Taking personal command, Kwang-Gae attacked Baekje using the 50,000 cavalry units he had built up, taking 10 walled cities (castles) along the kingdoms border. Baekje was furious and its King (Asin)

A Picture Of Kwang-Gae Overseeing A Battle

광개
Kwang-Gae

started a counter offensive but it was defeated as soon as it began, when the invasion force Baekje sent was defeated by Goguryo in 393 AD King Asin attacked again in 394 AD and was once again defeated by Goguryo.

With Baekje's continual defeats King Asin's leadership came under doubt and the kingdom began to crumble internally. In 395 AD, Goguryo defeated Baekje once again, gaining Goguryo more land for its kingdom.

In 396 AD, Kwang-Gae attacked Baekje once again. King Asin was expecting a land assault, but Kwang-Gae cleverly attacked by sea, catching King Asin with his defences down or deployed elsewhere. Kwang-Gae's troops burnt 58 of Baekje's walled fortresses as they defeated King Asin's troops. King Asin surrendered and handed his brother to Kwang-Gae as a captive on the condition that he may maintain his own rule of Baekje. Under Kwang-Gae, Goguryo had finally gained superiority over its long time rival, Baekje.

Kwang Gae Toh Wang

In 395 AD, in the North of Korea, Kwang-Gae led an attack himself and gained land in Manchuria, after defeating part of the Khitan tribe[104] located there.

Five years later, in 400 AD, the 'Later Yan'[105] (similar in nature to the Khitan), attacked and seized Goguryo territories. Kwang-Gae responded swiftly and regained most of them, driving them from Goguryo. Then, two years later (402 AD) he launched his own attack on 'Later Yan', seizing some of their border fortresses in order to

---

[104] The Khitan tribe were nomads located in Manchuria and similar in nature to the Mongols.

[105] The Later Yan was a state in North East China, founded by the Murang clans of the Xianbei tribe. The Xianbei were originally one tribe that split into various smaller tribes such as Murang, Tuoba, Khitan, Shiwei and Rouran establishing their own kingdoms.

From Creation To Unification
The Complete Histories Behind The Ch'ang Hon (ITF) Patterns

protect Goguryo from future attacks and just two years later he took the entire peninsula.

At the same time in 400 AD, Silla requested Goguryo's help in the South, to help in defending against a joint Japanese, Baekje and Gaya Confederacy[106] attack. Kwang-Gae sent 50,000 troops, defeating both the Japanese and Gaya Confederacy Calvary units. As a result, both Silla and the Gaya Confederacy were forced to submit to Kwang-Gae's authority, although 2 years later he returned Silla's King (Sil-Seong) to Silla to establish peaceful relations so he could continue his Northern conquests.

The rest of the Xianbei tribe kingdoms had not sat idly by when Kwang-Gae took over the 'Later Yan's' lands in 402 AD, and they responded by attacking Goguryo in 405 AD, but were defeated by Kwang-Gae. A year later the Xianbei tribe invaded again, but again Kwang-Gae defeated them. Following several more campaigns against the Xianbei tribe, as well as some against the Khitan tribes, Kwang-Gae was able to bring most of Manchuria under his control.

In 408 AD Kwang-Gae sent a peace delegate to meet with Gao Yun, the new leader of 'Later Yan', in order to broker a settlement between the two dynasties. Gao Yun was a descendent from the Goguryo Royal House, as his ancestors had been captured by the 'Former Yan', forerunners to the 'Later Yan'. Goguryo's power in the region remained strong for hundreds of years until the Tang Dynasty of China seized a large part of it during a war with Goguryo in the late 7th century.

In 410 AD Kwang-Gae began a conquest of the Kingdom of Dongbuyeo, a former tributary state of Goguryo that had fallen due to internal conflict, but had been revived in 285 AD by refugees from Buyeo (a Manchurian Kingdom). This small kingdom was no match

---

[106] The Gaya Confederacy was in essence a small kingdom made up of smaller territories but with an overseeing government. It lasted from 42 AD to 532 AD before finally being absorbed into Goguryo (whose authority it had submitted to since its defeat in 400 AD). Interestingly enough; Gaya existed in the early part of the famous 'Three Kingdoms' period of Korea, but although it covered quite a reasonable part of Korea (around half the size of Silla) it is not recognised as one of the three kingdoms at all, possibly due to it being a 'collective of territories' as opposed to one area of land, with one rule.

광개
Kwang-Gae

for Kwang-Gae's forces and suffered many defeats before finally surrendering. During the campaign Kwang-Gae's forces took 64 walled cities and conquered more than 1,400 villages. Kwang-Gae also attacked other Northern tribes, bringing them under his control and thus, gaining even more territory for Goguryo.

In 413 AD Supreme King Yeongnak (Kwang-Gae) died of unknown diseases, aged just 39. His rule lasted 22 years and in that time he accomplished a great deal for the Kingdom of Goguryo, as no Korean kingdom had ever ruled such vast territories before. Under Kwang-Gae's reign Goguryo once again became a major power amongst the Three Kingdoms. Kwang-Gae is also noted for using the first 'era name', that Goguryo kings used thereafter, as a way of showing Korean kings were the equals of their Chinese counterparts.

Only two kings of Korea have ever been bestowed with the additional title 'the Great'. Kwang-Gae is one and the other was King Se-Jong the Great, of the Joseon Dynasty – who invented the Korean alphabet and whom the 5th Dan pattern is named after.

In 1875 a Chinese scholar discovered a monument in Manchuria, which was built in 414 AD by King Jangsu (Kwang-Gae's son and successor to the throne). It is known as the Kwang-Gae-Toh Stele[107] and is 6 metres high. The stele contains a lot of information about

Janggunchong (Tomb of the General)

---

[107] A Stele is a stone slab erected for funerals or commemorative purposes and is usually taller than its width and is often inscribed or decorated with the names of the deceased (or sometimes living) and their deeds.

From Creation To Unification
The Complete Histories Behind The Ch'ang Hon (ITF) Patterns

Kwang-Gae's reign which covers much of what's been included in this chapter.

However, some of the information on the stele (known as the *sinmyo passage*) has also created some controversy as it seems to celebrate an event that has nothing to do with either Kwang-Gae or Goguryo, and seems to imply that Japan conquered Baekje and Silla in 391 AD Korean scholars don't believe this happened at all, as not one, of all the historical Korean documents, from any of the kingdoms, has any record of it whatsoever. They further go to say that technological differences at the time (with Koreans being the more superior) would have made it almost impossible for Japan to have subjugated them over an ocean barrier. And last of all, it makes no sense that a shrine dedicated to a great Goguryo King would list an achievement of Japan at all, more so if it was unrelated to Goguryo!

Kwang-Gae-Toh Stele [108]

On the Stele, the *sinmyo passage* has had many characters defaced or scratched out, so the passage reads:

- *Japan crossed the sea in 391 AD and defeated both Baekje and Silla, making them their subjects.*

This is dismissed by Korean Scholars, who instead feel that it may have been intentionally damaged by the Imperial Japanese Army to give precedent for their occupation of Korea in the 20th century, something they did with other historical records in the same era.

---

[108] Picture courtesy of Myung Han. Reproduced with permission and thanks.

광개
Kwang-Gae

Inscriptions on the Stele and a rubbing[109] of part of the sinmyo passage, showing the parts that have been erased

Instead, the Korean scholars believe it should have read:

- *Japan crossed the sea in 391 AD and was defeated by Goguryo along with Baekje and Silla making them (along with Gaya) their subjects.*

In 2011, Korean television aired a historical drama based on Kwang-Gae's life, from birth to the middle of his reign. It was hugely popular due to its CGI effects and its high profile lead actor, *Bae Yong-Joon* and was also aired all over Asia. However, it was banned in China because of its portrayal of Korean and Chinese history which conflicts with the Peoples Republic of China's *'One China'* idea, that they promote to their people!

---

[109] Photo by Brionies. Cc-by-sa-3.0

From Creation To Unification
The Complete Histories Behind The Ch'ang Hon (ITF) Patterns

Although General Choi has already stated in his pattern definition that the 39 moves are representative of the year 391 AD, the year Kwang-Gae ascended to the throne, interestingly Kwang-Gae was also 39 years old when he died, so the movements could also represent that!

포은
Po-Eun

Po-Eun is the pseudonym of a loyal subject Chong-Mong-Chu (1400)[110] **who was a famous poet and whose poem "I would not serve a second master though I might be crucified a hundred times" is known to every Korean. He was also a pioneer in the field of physics. The diagram represents his unerring loyalty to the king and country towards the end of the Koryo Dynasty.**

Po-Eun is the eleventh pattern of of Ch'ang Hon Taekwon-Do, usually taught at 1st Degree Black belt. It has 36 moves and was developed in Malaysia between 1962 and 1964 with the help of Master Kim, Bok Man and Master Woo, Jae Lim.

Po-Eun was the pseudonym of Jeong Mong-Ju, who was born in Yeongcheon, in the province of Gyeongsang, Korea in 1337 during the Goryeo Dynasty. His family was part of the Yeongil Jeong (Chong) clan. Po-Eun means *'Secret or Hidden Garden'* or more literally *'Hidden Treasure'*.[111]

In 1350, when Jeong Mong-Ju was 23 years old he became a civil servant after taking and passing three different civil service literary exams, passing each with the highest marks achievable.

---

[110] This should actually read '14th Century', not '1400' as he lived from 1337 to 1392.

[111] According to an online conversation with Master Doug Nowling (Kido Kwan) who translated the Hangul for Po-Eun. Another translation I came across said it meant *'Recluse of the vegetable plot'*.

From Creation To Unification
The Complete Histories Behind The Ch'ang Hon (ITF) Patterns

In 1367, at the age of 30 he taught Neo-Confucianism[112] at the Gukjagam[113], as well as holding his position in the government and was a servant of King U, who he served faithfully until his death in 1392. Jeong Mong-Ju was known as a scholar and also became a pioneer in the field of Physics.

Due to his wide knowledge and sound judgement in important matters, he was highly respected by King U. His scholarly work and involvement in national projects also gained him a lot of respect in the Goryeo Royal court.

As part of his services to King U, he participated in several diplomatic missions. In 1372 he visited China as a diplomatic envoy and in 1377 he was sent to Japan as a delegate to discuss invasions on the Korean peninsula from Japanese pirates, where he gained help from the Japanese in defeating the pirates following his negotiations with them. In 1384 he was sent to China for peace talks with the Ming Dynasty and a peace settlement was founded in 1385.

King U, had originally been placed on the throne as an 11 year old child by an anti-Ming (China) group led by a High Government official and war hero, Yi In-Im, who had assassinated the former King[114] - this led to suspicions by the

Portrait of Jeong-Mong Ju

---

[112] See page 71, footnote 64 for an in-depth explanation of Neo-Confucianism

[113] The Gukjagam was the highest educational institution (University) of the Goryeo Dynasty, training students in advanced Chinese classics. It was known as the Seonggyungwan in Jeong-Mong Ju's day, as it has undergone various name changes throughout it's history.

[114] Another story of King U's ascension to the throne is that the former King; Gongmin was murdered after he become aware of an affair between a man named Hong Ryun and one of his concubines. Hong Ryun and a friend Choe Man-Saeng heard of the kings anger and decided to murder him, before he had Hong Ryun executed, which they did whilst the king slept, in 1374, following which a high court official and war hero, Yi In-Im assumed control of the government and installed the 11 year old King U

포은
Po-Eun

Ming's regarding the previous kings sudden death as well as the legitimacy of King U himself.

Fourteen years into his reign as king, the Ming Dynasties suspicions were enough to make them want to establish a command post in the northeast of Korea to protect their interests - this was seen as a threat to Goryeo. With tensions mounting, General Choi-Yong (see Choi-Yong chapter), supported by General Yi Seong-Gye decided the best way to avoid conflict and lower the Ming threat to Goryeo was to rid the government of the anti-Ming faction, which they did, following which General Choi-Yong took control of the government, whilst the King retained the throne.

However, the Ming threat was not over and in the same year (1388) a Ming envoy came to Goryeo and demanded a large area of Goryeo territory be returned to the Ming empire. Before King U, the previous government had had a policy of never attacking its neighbours, but with the growing threat, General Choi-Yong convinced King U to send General Yi Seong-Gye and his army to attack the Ming's.

General Yi and many others opposed the invasion due to the previous policy and though he did march to meet them, when he saw the strength of the Ming armies, he knew he would be crushed and decided to turn his troops around. He knew he had support from those who were against the attack in the first place, so General Yi marched on the capital only to be met by the armies of General Choi. Despite a valiant defence by General Choi, he was defeated and Yi Seong-gye stormed the palace, dethroned the King and banished Choi-Yong, whom he later executed.

Though he was to take the throne later, at first Yi Seong-Gye placed King U's son (Prince Chang) on the throne, but one year later he poisoned them both and replaced the throne with a distant royal, Gong-Yang, as his puppet king. In 1392 he dethroned King Gong-Yang, exiled him (where he is said to have had murdered both the former King and his family a couple of years later) and installed himself as the 1st king of the Joseon Dynasty, bringing the Goryeo Dynasty to an end.

From Creation To Unification
The Complete Histories Behind The Ch'ang Hon (ITF) Patterns

Jeong Mong-Ju was fiercely loyal to the Goryeo Dynasty and its kings to the bitter end, but despite this, King Yi Seong-Gye still thought highly of him. Yi Seong-Gye's 5th son, Yi Bang-Won held a banquet for Jeong Mong-Ju in order to convince him to forget his loyalty to the former Goryeo Dynasty and cross over to the Yi (Joseon) Dynasty.

At the banquet, Yi Bang-Won recited a poem to discourage Jeong Mong-Ju from still remaining loyal to the Goryeo Dynasty. One English translation reads as follows:

> *What if one goes this way, or that way?*
> *What if arrowroots of Mt. Mansu be tangled together?*
> *Tangled likewise, let us prosper for hundred years.*

However, Jeong Mong-Ju replied with his own poem to affirm his unerring loyalty. Its English translation reads:

> *Though I die and die again a hundred times,*
> *That my bones turn to dust, whether my soul remains or not,*
> *Ever loyal to my Lord, how can this red heart ever fade away?*

Having failed to convince Jeong Mong-Ju, Yi Bang-Won ordered he be assassinated instead and on his way home from the banquet, on 4th April, 1392, Jeong Mong-Ju was murdered by five men on the Sonjukkyo bridge in Kaesong (which is now in North Korea).

As Jeong Mong-Ju was known as a great diplomat, with ties to both China and Japan, Yi Seong-Gye rebuked his son for the killing. The bridge is now a monument in North Korea and there is a brown stain on one of the stones that is said to be the actual place Jeong Mong-Ju died. The stain is said to turn red like blood whenever it rains!

Over the years, various other monuments to Jeong Mong-Ju have been erected near Sonjukkyo bridge, including the Songin monument, which was erected in 1641 to commemorate Jeong Mong-Ju's loyalty; the Kuksa monument was erected in memory of the coach driver that died alongside Jeong Mong-Ju on the bridge that night; and the Hama monument was erected in memory to Jeong Mong-Ju and meant that

포은
Po-Eun

Sonjukkyo Bridge

all those that passed should dismount their horses as a sign of respect.

The mark on the stone is said to be Jeong-Mong Ju's blood stain from the murder and is also said to turn red when it rains.

Opposite the Sonjukkyo bridge is the Pyonchung pavilion which houses two huge stone tablets (known as stele), laid on the backs of stone turtles. The first was erected by King Yeongjo in 1740 and the second by King Gojong in 1872 and both were laid to commemorate the execution of Jeong Mong-Ju as affirmation of his loyalty to the ruling Goryeo Dynasty of the time. Behind the pavilion is the lecture hall where Jeong Mong-Ju lived.

The pattern diagram, which forms a straight horizontal line is said to represent Jeong Mong-Ju's unerring loyalty to the Goryeo Dynasty.

"To many fame comes too late."

- Luis De Camoens

계백
Ge-Baek

Ge-Baek is named after Ge-Baek, a great general in the Baek Je Dynasty (660 A.D.). The diagram represents his severe and strict military discipline

Ge-Baek is the twelfth pattern of Ch'ang Hon Taekwon-Do, usually taught at 1st Degree Black belt. It has 44 moves and was developed in Korea in 1961 with the help of Master C. K. Choi. Though it is the twelfth pattern practiced by students, it was the fifth pattern developed for Ch'ang Hon Taekwon-Do.

Ge-Baek was a famous General from the Baekje Dynasty. Although there is little known about his early life, research has revealed that he was born in Buyeo County[115] in South Chungcheong Province in what is now, South Korea, though his date of birth remains a mystery![116]

Ge-Baek was a martial artist from a young age and several mythical stories have been passed down about him. One story tells how his mother fainted when she had given birth to Ge-Baek and that a tiger took Ge-Baek and suckled him! In another story, it is said that Ge-Baek climbed Cheondung mountain in Buyeo, where he lived and as

---

[115] In Kim Jeong-ho's book *'Daedong Jiji'*, written in 1865 he recorded that Ge-Baek's real (first) name was Seung and that his surname is the same as Baekji. This has led to inference that his last name is Buyeo, which was also the last name of the Baekje royal family. In 'Buyeoji', which was published in 1928, it stated that Palchoongmyeon (Chungcheong province) was named after 8 of the most loyal subjects of Baekje, including General Ge-Baek and it is from this that historians came to their conclusion that Ge-Baek was born in Buyeo County.

[116] According to the Korean Drama Series (2011) Gye-Baek was born 612 AD to father Mu-Jin, a faithful General to King Mu (Ul-Ja's father) and mother Myeong Mu, who died whilst Ge-Baek was still a child.

From Creation To Unification
The Complete Histories Behind The Ch'ang Hon (ITF) Patterns

he did so, the pine trees fell like reeds and the rocks he stepped upon were left marked from his feet.

From 18 BC the Baekje Dynasty had flourished for over 6 centuries until Silla defeated it in 660 AD. Though allied with the Kingdom of Goguryeo, Baekje had fallen into disarray as King Uija had neglected the running of the country. During his reign the government had been hampered by internal power struggles and corruption issues and King Uija was known to be overly decadent and ignored pressing issues of state.

In 660 AD Baekje was invaded by 50,000 Silla troops led by General Kim Yoo-Sin (the noted General that Yoo-Sin tul is named after). The Silla troops were also supported by 130,000 Tang Chinese troops led by Chinese General, Su Ding Fang. King Uija quickly promoted General Ge-Baek to Commander of the Baekje Armed forces and sent him to meet the joint Silla and Chinese forces. Unfortunately, with little time at hand and lack of support from the king, General Ge-Baek could only muster up 5,000 troops, so was vastly outnumbered.

Shortly before the battle, knowing he had little chance of victory,

An old portrait of Ge-Baek next to actor Lee Seo Jin, in his role as 'Gye-Baek' in the 2011 Korean drama series of the same name.

계백
Ge-Baek

General Ge-Baek is said to have killed his wife and children so they could not be captured and used against him during the battle, but also possibly because he knew it was a suicide battle, one which he wouldn't be coming back from and he didn't want them captured and tortured after he was gone or to live in shame as slaves of the enemy.

General Ge-Baek arrived at the battlefield first and it is said that the general made a heroic speech to his men, mustering their courage and fortitude as they prepared to face the massive army of the Silla and Tang forces. General Ge-Baek reminded them of stories of old, particularly one of a Chinese King; King Goujian of Yue, who reputedly defeated an army of 700,000 with only 5,000 – coincidently, the same amount of men General Ge-Baek had under his command! Ge-Baek was also reputed to have stated that he would *'Rather die than be a slave to the enemy'*, ensuring his men would fight to the bitter end if needed!

Despite the odds, initially the battle went in Ge-Baek's favour, where he won the first four clashes between the troops, causing severe casualties to the Silla forces. Yoo-Sin's troops were becoming demoralized and upon seeing this, General Kim Pum-Il sent his 16 year old son, Kwan Chan, a Hwa-Rang warrior, alone into the Baekje camp to kill General Ge-Baek. Kwan Chan rushed fearlessly into

A statue of Ge-Baek leading his warriors into battle

the camp and was easily captured. However, it is said that General Ge-Baek was so impressed by this young Hwa-Rang warrior, who reminded him of his own son, that he released him unharmed, back to the Silla forces.

The following day, Kwan Chan once again charged at the Baekje forces and once again he was captured. However, Kwan Chan almost

From Creation To Unification
The Complete Histories Behind The Ch'ang Hon (ITF) Patterns

escaped by killing his guards and it is said he also killed Ge-Baek's 2nd in command, kicking him off his horse with a flying kick to the head, breaking his neck! He was recaptured and executed, but as a sign of respect for this young Hwa-Rang warrior General Ge-Baek sent his body back to the Silla camp to be honoured and it was Kwan Chan's act of bravery that inspired the Silla troops and roused them again!

With renewed morale and inspired by the courage of their fellow soldier Kwan Chan, the Silla forces attacked again and with his troops thinning and exhausted, General Ge-Baek was surrounded and overwhelmed. General Ge-Baek and all his men were killed after Ge-Baek ordered them all to *'Hold or Die'* and shortly after that battle, the Baekje Dynasty fell altogether. The battle is known as *The Battle of Hwangsanbul* or *The Battle of Hwangsan Field*, which is where it took place.

History is written by the victors as they say and as the Baekje Dynasty fell, the name of one its greatest heroes was almost erased from history, but once Neo-Confucianism became popular in Korea, many years later, General Ge-Baek was recognized by Korean historians for his principles of Confucianism, his patriotism and his loyalty to his king and remains a hero to the Korean people some 1,300 years after his death.

Strangely enough, there is a Korean comedy war film depicting this battle. Made in 2003, it is called *'Hwangsanbul'* (or in English known as *'Once Upon a Time in a Battlefield'*) and stars Park Joong-Hoon, Jeong Jin-Yeong and Oh Ji-Myeong.

In 2011 there was a Korean drama series released, which detailed the life of Ge-Baek. Titled *'Gye-Baek'* and starring Lee Seo-Jin, it details his and his parents life and that of King Uija. It is a great series to watch, however, I`m not sure how much of it is historical fact and how much of it is fictional drama, as it spans over 30 plus episodes!

Although I can find no 'official' real reason why this pattern has 44 moves, having watched most of the 'Gye-Baek' episodes of the Korean drama series, it seems that it could be based on the number of battles Ge-Baek fought under King Uija's reign (which only lasted 19 years) where Ge-Baek came to prominence as a General. As the series progressed, there is a part where the royal court discuss Ge-Baek's amazing achievement of capturing 39 cities, which is noted as a record in the history of the kingdom. King Uija takes command of the 40th battle, so as not to be over shadowed by Ge-Baek's rise to fame, though it was Ge-Baek who did all the preparations etc. A couple of episodes later Ge-Baek is recalled from his 41st battle and an alliance to run the city (he was going to attack) is made instead, leaving the total still at 40. In the series, a little while later there is talk in the royal court of how General Kim, Yoo-Sin of Silla had captured 3 of Baekje's cities, and General Ge-Baek is tasked to recapture them, which makes 43 in total! Of course, the final battle is 'The Battle of Hwangsan Field', making it his 44th battle, but sadly not his 44th victory! Of course, this is pure speculation on my part, based on a series that is part fact and part fiction, but the maths do add up this way!

The pattern diagram is said to represent his severe and strict military discipline, which is portrayed in the drama series. In one scene, King Uija travels to a battle front in order to ensure the glory of the battle becomes his by taking command personally, as Ge-Baek is becoming too popular with the people, above the King, due to his numerous victories for Baekje. On his arrival, all the officers are waiting in his tent, standing up. The King comes in and instructs them all to sit down, but they all wait for General Ge-Baek to sit first before sitting down themselves. King Uija, partly in disdain, comments on their *'admirable discipline'*. The King then calls forward the officers who will be leading the main assault and pays them a compliment before offering one of them a cup of wine. In that era, to refuse an order by the king was punishable by death, but the officer asks to be forgiven for not taking the cup and asks for tea instead, saying that he has, like all the soldiers, made a pledge with General Ge-Baek that no-one is to drink wine until victory is completed. Ge-Baek intervenes and tells King Uija, that by forcing the officer to drink the wine it will affect the military discipline of his troops.

A statue of Ge-Baek in Buyeo County

의암
Eui-Am

Eui-Am is the pseudonym of Son Byong Hi, leader of the Korean independence movement on March 1, 1919. The 45 movements refer to his age when he changed the name of Dong Hak (Oriental Culture) to Chondo Kyo (Heavenly way religion) in 1905. The diagram represents his Indomitable Spirit, displayed while dedicating himself to the prosperity of his nation.

Eui-Am is the thirteenth pattern of Ch'ang Hon Taekwon-Do, usually taught at 2nd Degree Black belt. It has 45 moves and was finalised in Korea around 1968 with the help of Master Cho, Sang Min.[117]

Eui-Am (meaning Righteousness)[118] was born Son Byong-Hi on 8th April 1861, at Cheongju, in Chungcheong province of what is now South Korea.

Not much is known of his childhood, but at the age of around 23 (1884) he came across the Donghak[119] religion and became a member. Donghak stressed equality of all human beings.

As a new member, his training was very in-depth and included reading and reciting

Son Byong-Hi

---

[117] Master J. C. Kim, Master Park, Jong Soo, Master Lee, Byung Moo and others may also have helped in the formulation of this pattern.

[118] As translated by Master Doug Nowling.

[119] Donghak is a Korean religion founded in 1860 by Choe Je-u. Donghak venerated the god Haneullim ("Lord of Heaven") and believed that man is not created by a supernatural god but man is instead caused by an innate god. Koreans have believed in Haneullim from ancient times, so Donghak would be an Indigenous Korean religion, unlike Buddhism or Christianity. *Source:* Wikipedia

From Creation To Unification
The Complete Histories Behind The Ch'ang Hon (ITF) Patterns

the Donghak *"Incantation of Twenty-One Letters"* thirty thousand times a day! He did this for around three years whilst making straw sandals to sell at the local market. Eventually he became a student of Choe Si-Hyeong, the 2nd leader of Donghak and became his disciple, devoting his life to the religion and study.

By 1892, the small groups of Donghak members had formed a guerrilla army, by banding together. They armed themselves and attacked government offices, killed foreign traders and rich landlords and distributed their wealth to the poor. In the province of Cholla they organised a mass protest against abuses by local officials, where Choe Si-hyeong petitioned Emperor Gojong saying:

Choe Si-hyeong

"We the ordinary subjects of His Majesty's benevolent reign, after having read the Confucian writings, living on His Majesty's soil, are determined to follow this new doctrine only because we want people to reform themselves, to be loyal to their king, to show filial piety to their parents, to respect their teachers, and to show friendship to their fellow men".[120]

Emperor Gojong ignored the petition and by 1894 the Donghak Peasant Revolution had begun as more and more poor famers rose up against the ruling classes. The revolution was led by Choe Si-Hyeong and Son Byong-Hi became one of his commanders. The revolution started because at the time, incredibly high taxes were forcing the poor farmers to sell their homes to rich land owners, at rock bottom prices just to survive. The landowners also sold the rice they made to the Japanese and sent their (the

Emperor Gojong

---

[120] As quoted in *'Korea Since 1850'*, by Stewart Lone and Gavan McCormack.

의암
Eui-Am

landowners) children to Japan for an education and this resulted in much anti-Japanese sentiment.

Unable to suppress the revolution on their own, the government asked for help from China, who sent 3,000 troops into Korea, despite an agreement with Japan not to do so following the Tientsin Convention[121] which they both signed in 1885. Japan saw this as a threat to their own country and also sent troops into Korea.

With the additional Chinese troops, the Korean Government wanted to call a truce and end the revolution, but once the

Donghak rebels gather at the foot of Mt. Baektu, March, 1894

revolution ended, further tensions would rise between China and Japan as neither side wanted to vacate Korea before the other – this actually resulted in a Sino-Japanese war where they both fought over control of Korea (1st August 1894 – 17th April 1895), which the Japanese eventually won following a new treaty in which China declared Korea an independent nation, which in effect meant it renounced any claims to Korea, leaving it in the hands of the Japanese!

It was actually the Japanese that eventually suppressed the revolution as on the 16th October 1894 pro-Japanese forces and Japanese troops planned a trap and forced the peasant army into a decisive battle at Gongju, known as the Battle of Ugeumchi which started on 22nd October, 1894. The Donghak forces were ill-equipped with bows and

---

[121] The Tientsin Convention was an agreement by both Japan and China in Tientsin, China on 18th April 1885. It followed tensions between both Japan and China regarding influence over the Korean peninsula. It was negotiated by Hirobumi-Ito (see Joong-Gun) and Li Hongzhang and part of the convention involved both countries removing all troops from Korea and not sending any back in without notifying the other.

From Creation To Unification
The Complete Histories Behind The Ch'ang Hon (ITF) Patterns

arrows, spears, swords and some flintlock muskets, whilst the Japanese forces had modern rifles and cannons. Despite this, the battle raged for nearly 3 weeks (ending 10th November, 1984) but eventually the Donghak forces were overcome by the superior firepower of the Japanese.

A Japanese scroll depicting the Battle of Ugeumchi in 1894

Choe Si-Hyeong escaped and lived as a fugitive, but was eventually captured in 1898 and executed. However, Choe Si-Hyeong had the foresight to see this eventuality and prior to his capture he had ordained Son Byong-Hi to be the 3rd Leader of Donghak – this was on the 24th December, 1897.

After Choe Si-Hyeong's execution, Son Byong-Hi asked for political asylum in Japan and remained there whilst Japan and Russia fought over control of Korea (Russo-Japanese War)[122], returning to Korea in 1904.

Upon his return he established the Jimbohoe (Progressive Society), a new movement designed to reverse the current misfortunes of Korea by creating a new society. Using

Statue of Son Byong-Hi [123]

---

[122] A war fought between Russia and Japan for control of Manchuria and Korea. It started on the 8th February, 1904 and ended on the 5th September, 1905

[123] Photo by Gaël Chardon. Cc. License

의암
Eui-Am

Donghak, he reintroduced old customs and ways of living before recent events. Thousands of Donghak members followed him, cutting their hair short and wearing basic, modest clothes.

Throughout 1904 non-violent demonstrations took place, asking for social reforms to the country. These demonstrations were organized by Donghak and known as the Gapjin Reform Movement.

The Japanese occupiers didn't take kindly to the demonstrations and severely persecuted Donghak members, so Son Byong-Hi decided he needed to make Donghak more legitimate to the Japanese, so they would be seen as more open and thus persecuted less. Son Byong-Hi modernized Donghak on 1st December, 1905, officially changing its name to Chondo Kyo (Heavenly Way), establishing it as a modern religious organization by 1906, basing its headquarters in Seoul.

A Chondo Kyo temple

Japan was occupying Korea (annexing it altogether in 1910) and Son Byong-Hi yearned for freedom for his country and independence from Japanese rule, as all Koreans of that time did. Eventually he had had enough and set up a new anti-Japanese movement, although, unlike the previous efforts it became an underground movement, seeing Chondo Kyo, Buddhists and Christians unite under a common cause. Son Byong-Hi founded the movement, insisting that it must remain non-violent.

On 1st March 1919, as Korea mourned the death of Emperor Gojong, a public Declaration of Independence was announced at Pagoda Park in Seoul, known as the 1st March Movement or Sam-Il (see Sam-Il chapter). The Declaration of Independence was signed by 33 prominent leaders, 15 of which belonged to Chondo Kyo.

The declaration ignited the Korean population, with thousands upon

From Creation To Unification
The Complete Histories Behind The Ch'ang Hon (ITF) Patterns

thousands joining and peacefully demonstrating in the streets, all calling for Korean Independence. The movement became nationwide, with the whole country joining in, regardless of social status.

The Japanese did not take kindly to the calling and used their police to put down the non-violent demonstrations with brutality, killing over 7,500 Koreans, wounding almost 17,000 and arresting over 47,000, which included Son Byong-Hi .

Son Byong-Hi was released on bail after he became ill in prison. He returned home to recover, but his illness worsened and he eventually passed away on 19th May, 1922, aged 62. He died at his home in Sangchunwon which is just outside the Dongdaemun gate[124], Seoul.

Dongdaemun Gate

---

[124] The Dongdaemun gate (meaning Great East gate) was the major gate in the east wall that surrounded Seoul during the Chosen dynasty. It was built in 1398, renovated in 1453 and then rebuilt in 1869.

충장
Choong-Jang

Choong-Jang is the pseudonym given to General Kim Duk Ryang who lived during the Yi Dynasty, 14th century. This pattern ends with a left-hand attack to symbolize the tragedy of his death at 27 in prison before he was able to reach full maturity.

Choong-Jang is the fourteenth pattern of of Ch'ang Hon Taekwon-Do, usually taught at 2nd Degree Black belt. It has 52 moves and was developed in Malaysia between 1962 and 1964 with the help of Master Kim, Bok Man and Master Woo, Jae Lim.

Contrary to the written text in the Encyclopedia of Tae Kwon Do and copies on web sites, Choong-Jang was not born in the 14th century, but rather the 16th century, as he was born in 1567, during the Yi (Joseon)[125] dynasty of Korea. Nor was he 27 but 29 when he died.

Born into the peasant class in 1567 (in Seokjeo village, Chunghyo-Dong near Mudeung Mountain), Kim Duk-Ryang was the 2nd son of Kim Boong-Seob. He became a student of Seong-Hon (penname Woo-Gye), a Neo-Confucian scholar, politician, and soldier.

In 1592, when the Japanese invaded Korea led by Hideyoshi Toyotomi (known as the Imjin War)[126], Kim Duk-Ryang, along with his brother (Kim Duk-Hong) joined the militia

---

[125] The Joseon (or Chosŏn) Dynasty lasted from 1392 to 1897. Often referred to as the Yi Dynasty, after its founder Yi Song-Gye.

[126] The Imjin War also known as the 'Seven Year War'. See page 23, footnote 17 for more details.

From Creation To Unification
The Complete Histories Behind The Ch'ang Hon (ITF) Patterns

led by General Ko Kyung-Myeong. Sadly, at the battle of Guemsan his brother was killed. During his brother's funeral, Kim mustered local volunteers to form an army and rejoined the fight. With the Japanese attacks still going on, Kim led an army of 5,000 volunteers and met them at Damyang. He left a message before he departed that read *"Scholars, know this. The Japanese invaders are a great evil to us in these days. We must purge them from our country at once!"* Following this battle, Kim was appointed a senior official of the Ministry of Justice by King Seonjo after a recommendation by the Magistrate of Damyang and the District Magistrate of Jangseong.

In (January) 1594 he was appointed Seonjeonggwan (Royal Messenger), and given the name General Yikho by King Seonjo. Under the leader ship of Kwon Yul[127], he defeated Japanese troops at both Jinhae and Goseong. He also caused large defeats to the Japanese army as part of some joint amphibious operations with Admiral Yi, Sun-Sin (of Choong-Moo fame). Despite his small stature, Kim was known for his agility, bravery and outstanding ability in battle and the Japanese army named him General Seokjeo. In June, 1595, following a successful joint operation with another local leader, Gwak Jae-Woo, at the battle of Jeongam (which had taken place in March), King Seonjo awarded him the military title of Choongyonggun.[128]

In July, 1596 a rebellion was started by Yi Mong-Hak and General Kim Duk-Ryang marched to Jeolla Province to quell it, but he withdrew when he found out Yi Mong-Hak had died. However, Kim was falsely implicated as having joined the rebellion by subordinates of the king, who were growing jealous of Kim's ever increasing reputation and he was arrested. King Seonjo bound him to a tree with chains, but Kim laughed and said *"I bowed [to] you to defeat the Japanese invaders because you gave me many rewards. But how could I ever plot against this country? If I were such a person, what kind of a punishment is this helpless tree?"*. It is said he then tore off the chains with his own brute strength!

Many of the ministers tried to aid his release, but sadly he remained a

---

[127] Kwon Yul (1537–1599) was a Korean Army General and the Commander-in-chief of the Joseon Dynasty

[128] As far as I can ascertain, Choongyonggun means something along the lines of *'loyal and best man'*.

충장
Choong-Jang

prisoner. He was executed at the age of 29 (not 27) following some extreme torture, which is said to have left the skin peeled from his body and his shins broken.

Sixty five years after his death, General Kim was exonerated and his government position restored to him, after it was revealed that the previous charges were based on false testimonies.

Kim Duk-Ryang's loyalty and bravery did not go unrecognised by future generations and in 1681 he was awarded the posthumous title 'Minister of War' by King Suk-Jong. During his reign in the late 18th century, King Jeong-Jo also bestowed upon him another posthumous title; Chungjanggong[129], as well as changing the name of Kim's hometown from Seokjeo village into Chunghyo-ri, meaning the place of loyalty and filial piety. And then in 1788 he was posthumously declared 'Head of Parliament'.

Chigajeong Pavillion

In 1889, a shrine was built by Kim Duk-Ryang's ancestors, in honour of his patriotism and loyalty called the 'Chigajeong Pavillion'. At the pavilion is a tombstone carved with a poem (*Chisiga*) after a legend

---

[129] '*Chungjanggong*' is a military title equivalent to Lieutenant-General (it also relates to Vice-Admiral). 'Gong' is possibly an honorary title attached to his name, kind of like 'Sir'. Choong-Jang can also be translated as 'Loyalty /Great' meaning something like 'Great loyal One'.

From Creation To Unification
The Complete Histories Behind The Ch'ang Hon (ITF) Patterns

that spoke of Kim appearing in a dream of Kwon-Pil, where he sang a song about his fate. After the dream, Kwon-Pil wrote the poem down to appease the Generals soul. 'Chigajeong' refers to the Generals drunken requiem (below):

> *"The song which I sing when I'm drunk,*
> *Is the song to which nobody listens.*
> *I don't want to be drunk with the flowers and moon ,*
> *I don't want to boast of my deeds.*
> *Having done deeds is just a cloud of vanity,*
>
> *Being drunk with the flowers and the moon is just a cloud of vanity.*
> *The song which I sing when I'm drunk,*
> *Is the song which nobody knows.*
> *My heart from the blade of a long sharp sword*
> *Want to serve a wise and great ruler."*

The Chisiga

Kwon-Pil felt the poem was fuelled with anger and sadness, so wrote his own poem as well, to describe Chisiga:

> *"In the past General fought with the sword,*
> *But his intentions were frustrated before completed;*
> *To this he was doomed.*
> *Now burning with revenge in the pits of Hades,*
> *This is the song of Chisiga."*

충장
Choong-Jang

In 1975, another shrine called the Chungjangsa shrine was built at Kim's ancestral home. The shrine was built to face Mudang mountain. In this shrine are some of Kim Duk-Ryang's clothes which were excavated from his burial place at the foot of the mountains, which was the original Kim clan grave site. Samples of his handwriting can also be found in the shrine, as well as his coffin. Kim Duk-Ryang is buried in a tomb behind the shrine, where his gravestone can be found.

A picture of General Kim Duk-Ryang inside the Chungjangsa shrine

Kim Duk-Ryang's Burial Clothing

From Creation To Unification
The Complete Histories Behind The Ch'ang Hon (ITF) Patterns

There is a book called *'The Biography of Kim Deokryeong'* about his legendary battles, his bravery and his character, although the author is unknown, as is when it was written.

Kim Duk-Ryang's Grave Stone

고당
Ko-Dang

Ko-Dang is the pseudonym of the patriot Cho Man Sik, who dedicated his life to the Korean Independence Movement and to the education of his people. Ko-Dang has 39 movements which signify his times of imprisonment and his birthplace on the 39th parallel.

Ko-Dang is the fifteenth pattern of of Ch'ang Hon Taekwon-Do, usually taught at 2nd Degree Black belt.[130] It has 39 moves and was developed in Malaysia between 1962 and 1964 with the help of Master Kim, Bok Man and Master Woo, Jae Lim.

Ko-Dang was the penname of Cho Man-Sik, who was born on 1st February 1883, in Kangso-kun County, Pyongyang, which is now part of North Korea. Cho Man-Sik was a young Christian and an activist within Korea's Christian Movement. He also became an elder in the Presbyterian Church he attended in Pyongyang.

Like many Koreans during the occupation by Japan, Cho Man-Sik went to Japan to further his education and graduated in law at Meiji University. By the age of 27 Cho Man-Sik had returned to Korea and, having been

Cho Man Sik

influenced by the likes of Ahn Chang-Ho (Do-San) he became involved with the Korean Independence Movement, which had flourished after Japan annexed Korea in 1910. He became an activist and took part in the famous Sam-Il[131] protest marches in 1919, for

---

[130] Some organisations teach pattern Juche instead of Ko-Dang

[131] The 3rd Degree pattern, Sam-Il tul, is named after these marches. See also, Do-San and Eui-Am chapters.

From Creation To Unification
The Complete Histories Behind The Ch'ang Hon (ITF) Patterns

A rare photograph of Yo Un Hyung, Dosan and Cho Man Sik in Seoul, 1935

which he was arrested, along with tens of thousands of other Koreans.

When he was released, he decided to continue with non-violent resistance, for which he became known as *'The Ghandi of Korea'*, although the real truth is that it was the peaceful Sam-Il protest marches that actually inspired Mahatma Ghandi's own non-violent resistance movement, one year later, as well as many others that followed in Asia.

Cho Man-Sik formed the *Korean Products Promotion Society*, which encouraged Koreans to buy Korean goods and instil a sense of nationalism and through this, Cho Man-Sik advocated self-sufficiency for the nation.

In August 1945, the Japanese surrender of Korea was imminent and Cho Man-Sik (now 52) was asked by the Japanese Governor-General of Pyongyang province to organise a committee to take over control of the area, in order to provide stability for the people, once the Japanese left. Cho Man-Sik agreed and set up Governing Councils around North Korea, known as the *Provisional People's Committee for the Five Provinces*, of which he became chairman.

고당
Ko-Dang

Days after the Japanese surrender, the Soviet Union arrived in Pyongyang as per an agreement with the USA, who were to take control of the country in the South, whilst The Soviet Union took control of the North, meeting at the 38th parallel (which now permanently divides North and South Korea). Supported by the Soviet Union, Kim Il-Sung returned to Korea, having been training under the Russians for 10 years!

With their arrival, the Soviet Union put pressure on Cho Man-Sik to reorganise the councils so more communists were able to be part of the committees. Though Cho Man-Sik is seen as the 'real' first leader of North Korea, he was forced to share power with the communist supported Kim Il-Sung,

Cho, Man Sik (far left) at the first meeting with Kim, Il Sung (holding the chop sticks) at a restaurant in Pyongyang, September 1945.

which led to a lot of tension due to their differing ideologies, meaning clashes were often inevitable. Labelled by the Russians as a *'Bourgeois nationalist'*[132], Russian General Terenti Shtykov, Stalin's main General in Korea, reported back that he considered Cho Man-Sik to be anti-soviet and anti-Stalin and thus, Cho Man-Sik's days were already numbered!

Following a conference in Moscow in 1945, the victorious Allied powers had decided to run Korea for a period of 5 years under a *four power trusteeship*[133], after which Korea would become independent. Cho Man-Sik (along with many others) refused to co-operate with this plan, as it meant too much foreign interference and influence on Korea. In January 1946, Cho Man-Sik, along with other council

---

[132] A Bourgeois nationalist was a label given to those who didn't seem to understand that all important decisions were to be made back in Moscow by Stalin.

[133] Consisting of the USA, USSR, China and Great Britain

members, was ordered to sign an expression of support for the trusteeship, which he refused to do and a month later he was forced to resign as Chairman of the Council and placed under house arrest, being kept at a reasonably nice hotel where he still vocally opposed the communists!

Cho Man-Sik stood in a vice-presidency election in 1948, but the communist grip on North Korea was so strong, he only received a small portion of votes and thus was defeated. His resistance to all things involving the Russians allowed General Shtykov to gain Stalin's permission to get rid of Cho Man-Sik once and for all, some feel possibly at the request of Kim Il-Sung, and a short time later Cho Man-Sik was transferred to a prison in Pyongyang, which is where confirmed reports of him finish, though some believed he was executed on 15th October 1950, along with other political prisoners[134] of the time, just after United Nations troops marched northwards on the 7th October, 1950, on route to capture Pyongyang, during the Korean war, forcing Kim Il-Sung's regime to retreat to the northwest border of the country (the border with China) where, in order that there were no automatic political replacements should the South now occupy the North as well, Cho Man-Sik and others were executed. Cho Man-Sik was 67 at the time of his execution.

In 1970, the South Korean Government declared Cho Man-Sik a martyr and awarded him the *Order of the Republic of Korea*, a posthumous title in recognition of his contribution to his country.

Many Taekwon-Do organisations have reverted back to pattern Ko-Dang, dropping Juche tul and replacing it (either with the whole pattern or simply by name only)[135] with Ko-Dang once more. The reason for this is most often cited as being because of Juche's obvious

---

[134] Some feel he was executed, not only because of his opposition to Kim Il-Sung and the USSR, but also because he was a Christian, as at that time there was a steep rise in the persecutions of Christians in North Korea as they were seen to be in opposition to the new 'Juche ideals' Kim Il-Sung had brought in.

[135] See *Juche* chapter for full explanation.

고당
Ko-Dang

links with the North Korean 'Juche' ideology and its obvious links with communism.

However, according to a blog post[136] I read, the author notes that although Ko-Dang was opposed to Soviet-Communism (as he was opposed to the Soviets, or anyone else, having any influence over North Korea), he was in fact a (Christian) Communist[137] himself and his own philosophies were not too far removed from the 'Juche' ideology itself! Here is an excerpt from the blog:

A statue of Cho Man-Sik, found in South Korea. His pointing finger signifies a reunited Korea, as one nation.

"Juche is often translated as "spirit of independence" or "self-reliance." Cho Man-sik is well known for having advocated not only independence, but also "self-sufficiency"; in other words, that the state should be autonomous, not requiring any outside support for its survival. This is practically the same as the Juche-ideology which Kim Il-sung summarised as: (1) independence in political work, (2) self-sustenance in economic endeavours, and (3) self-defence in national defence. The idea of self-sufficiency / self-reliance is present in both the term Juche and, by association, in the name Kodang. Choosing the name Kodang over Juche because you think the latter is associated with communism while the former is

---

[136] http://sooshimkwan.blogspot.com/2010/12/kodang-juche-controversy.html

[137] Christian communism is a form of religious communism based on Christianity. It is a theological and political theory based upon the view that the teachings of Jesus Christ compel Christians to support communism as the ideal social system. Although there is no universal agreement on the exact date when Christian communism was founded, many Christian communists assert that evidence from the Bible suggests that the first Christians, including the Apostles, created their own small communist society in the years following Jesus' death and resurrection. As such, many advocates of Christian communism argue that it was taught by Jesus and practiced by the Apostles themselves. *Source:* http://en.wikipedia.org/wiki/Christian_Communists.

From Creation To Unification
The Complete Histories Behind The Ch'ang Hon (ITF) Patterns

not only reveals your ignorance of Cho Man-sik's life. No, both "Juche" and "Kodang" has communist overtones."

Hard to believe I know, more so as South Korea celebrate and recognises Ko-Dang's achievements, even having a museum in South Korea in his honour. However, in South Korea any mention of communism or association with it has always been taboo and is still a criminal offence (so I`m told). In the past, offenders faced severe penalties under the South's broad National Security laws, put in place by its military Generals, who ruled South Korea with iron fists, justified because of the constant threat from the communists in the North - so it's easier and better for most to not even go into it in the first place.

CHO MAN - SIK (pen - name "Kodang")

Cho Man-Sik (pen-name "Kodang") was born in Kangsuh-Gun (County), Pyungnam Province, on February 1st, 1883. He spent his whole life for his country and people. His firm faith, noble character, solid will power and ability to carry out his beliefs in reviving national independence as well as his efforts to conduct non-violent resistance activities against the Japanese colonialism is a living lesson for us.

He contributed much to society, education, culture and industry through his leadership in the Sanjunghyun Church in Pyungyang, the Young Men's Christian Association, and in schools such as Osan, Sungin, and Sungshil, and through work at the Kwansuh Athletic Association and the Chosun Daily Newspaper.

After the liberation from Japanese occupation, he dedicated himself to establi-shing a unified, democratic nation when he was recruited to be the premier of North Korean civil politics and head of the Chosun Democratic Party. He stood up to the strong-arm tactics of the Communist political forces. He chose to make his own the lot of his countrymen of the north and thereby sacrificed himself showing a martyr's love. Hence, he is our pride and an everlasting symbol of our nation's ebullient spirit.

In 1950, Cho Man-Sik was martyred by the communists in Pyungyang.

He was awarded Order of Merit for National Foundation, Republic of Korea Medal by the Korean Government in 1970.

Plaque, at the base of Cho Man-Sik statue, in South Korea

No matter his politics, Cho Man-Sik should be (and is) remembered as a great patriot who's main aim was bringing Korea back to stand tall, on its own two feet, once again.

주체
Juche

Juche is a philosophical idea that man is the master of everything and decides everything. In other words, the idea that man is the master of the world and his own destiny. It is said that this idea was rooted in Baekdu Mountain which symbolizes the spirit of the Korean people. The diagram represents Baekdu mountain.

Juche is the fifteenth pattern of of Ch'ang Hon Taekwon-Do, usually taught at 2nd Degree Black belt.[138] It has 45 moves and was developed in the early 1980's with the help of Master Park, Jung Tae[139], becoming an official ITF pattern sometime between 1983 and 1985.

Juche was a pattern instituted by General Choi in the 1980's. Contrary to what one ITF organisation (surprisingly[140]) tells its members, it was never originally called Ko-Dang, but instead replaced Ko-Dang tul, which was removed entirely from the 24 patterns of the ITF.

At the time, the official explanation for the replacement of Ko-Dang with Juche was that General Choi was still developing Taekwon-Do and that new techniques needed to be added after the completion of the 24 patterns. General Choi said that these new *advanced* techniques needed to be incorporated via a pattern and, because he (General Choi) considered them to be very difficult and also felt that most students achieved their physical peak around 2nd degree, before natural ageing diminishes physical capabilities, that is where they needed to be placed. Ko-Dang was the most junior patriot, plus a 2nd

---

[138] Some organisations teach pattern Ko-Dang instead of Juche

[139] With the possible assistance of Master Lim, Won Sup, Master Choi, Jung-Hwa, Michael McCormack (General Choi's son in law) and early North Korean instructors.

[140] I find this incorrect version of Juche's history surprising because the head of the organisation that issued this statement was thought to have possibly helped in its creation whilst in North Korea and would have undoubtedly learnt Ko-Dang prior to it as well, so would know that it was a new pattern created and never named Ko-Dang at all!

From Creation To Unification
The Complete Histories Behind The Ch'ang Hon (ITF) Patterns

degree pattern already, so was the pattern General Choi Chose to replace.

However, for those who have studied this episode of Taekwon-Do history, it is generally agreed that Juche tul was introduced to appease the North Korean dictator Kim Il-Sung in return for funding for the ITF[141], after such funding was refused by other entities. Ko-Dang (the pen-name of Cho Man-Sik), whom the pattern Ko-Dang was named after, was a former (and main) political rival of the North Korean dictator Kim Il-Sung; more than that however, there was a rumour that Kim Il-Sung had him executed.

Kim Il-Sung [142]

Obviously, there would be no funding for the ITF (and we are talking millions of dollars here[143]) as long as Ko-Dang remained an honoured hero portrayed in the ITF patterns. However, apparently just taking it out wasn't enough and the rumour goes that to gain the desired funding, Kim Il-Sung actually wanted Taekwon-Do to be renamed *Juche Taekwon-Do*, after his own regime, perhaps in recognition[144] of his place in Korean history, perhaps as a resistance fighter for Korea

---

[141] There are a myriad of reasons that led General Choi to North Korea. Apart from ITF funding, he wanted to introduce Taekwon-Do there anyway and hoped in some way, it would help foster relationships between the North and the South. Due to pressure from the KCIA, many of his Korean instructors had left the ITF, so he hoped going into North Korea would bolster his ranks again and help combat the continued attacks from the KCIA of South Korea. As an aside, he eventually got his 15 Volume Encyclopaedia's printed in North Korea after the KCIA put pressure on publishers around the world (who had expressed an interest in printing it) so they wouldn't print it!

[142] Picture courtesy of Yeo, Kok Leng. Used with permission and thanks.

[143] North Korea, through the Korean Taekwon-Do Federation, also loaned money for the ITF Headquarters in Vienna Austria and the DPRK Government constructed the Taekwon-Do Palace in North Korea, 1992.

[144] Recognition Kim Il-Sung either felt was deserved or felt would further enforce his history propaganda - see page 31, footnote 23.

주체
Juche

The Taekwon-Do Palace, built in North Korea in 1992 [145]

against the Japanese occupation or simply as the 'Supreme Leader', but General Choi's compromise was to name a pattern *Juche* instead.[146] This is a bigger deal than one might think, as Juche is forever connected with Kim Il-Sung and is listed, via the Taekwon-Do patterns, amongst the names of Korean heroes and patriots going right back through history, to the actual founding of Korea via Dan-Gun tul!

Also, what many do not know (or fail to realise) is that General Choi was a master strategist when it came to achieving what he wanted or felt was needed! Before the whole *Juche* saga, when General Choi supported Syngman Rhee, the first President of South Korea (the only man who had the authority to authorise the name 'Taekwon-Do' that General Choi wanted), the General actually named a pattern after Presidents Syngman Rhee's penname of *Unam!*[147] Whist this pattern never materialized, the name is strikingly similar to the 2nd degree pattern *Eui-Am*, which we now practice! What this goes to show, is that General Choi wasn't opposed to using Taekwon-Do's patterns, to help gain the advancement he wanted and perhaps he simply felt the

---

[145] The DPRK has since built another spectacular training facility in Pyongyang, North Korea, known as the Taekwon-Do Sanctuary or Taekwon-Do Holy Place - which opened in 2012.

[146] Another rumour was that Kim Il-Sung wanted the pattern named directly after himself but apparently General Choi knew that wouldn't go down too well, so the compromise was naming it Juche.

[147] Information courtesy of Grandmaster CK Choi, via research by Dr. George Vitale, VIII.

From Creation To Unification
The Complete Histories Behind The Ch'ang Hon (ITF) Patterns

same with *Juche* tul![148]

Interestingly enough, at the first demonstration that introduced Taekwon-Do to North Korea in 1980, the 7th ITF Taekwon-Do Demonstration team performed Ko-Dang tul, not Juche, as it wasn't created yet. Even the North Korean students of the first two Special Instructors Courses (in North Korea), which lasted 7 months each, trained with Ko-Dang tul until Juche was finalised and replaced it.

Apart from the name of the pattern itself, Juche, even upon mild inspection contains references to Kim Il-Sung within it – The ready posture itself is based on a well known posture of Kim Il-Sung, as is possibly the 1st movement in the pattern; the pattern diagram is said to be based on the Baekdu mountain[149] where Kim, Il Sung supposedly had his 'light-bulb' moment and the Juche idea was born - which is a disputed idea in itself, as many believe the idea was formed whilst at a military base in the former Soviet Union and not even by Kim himself!.

While some see the introduction of Taekwon-Do to the communist state of North Korea as a really bad move, to General Choi it seemed a necessary business move, as in the 1970's pressure from the South Korean Government had caused all but around 10 of the Korean masters to leave the ITF, so apart from the money side of things, he also gained many Korean instructors back into his art and the ITF and the Korean instructors would help General Choi to continue to spread his

A picture of Kim, Il Sung, showing a similar position to the ready posture of Juche tul!

---

[148] Further supported in *'A Modern History of Taekwondo'* by Kang Won-Sik & Lee Kyong-Myong.

[149] Baekdu mountain is a special place as it is where Dan-Gun, the legendary founder of Korea was born in 2333 BC, according to the legend of Dan-Gun. Due to this, it is a place of great significance to both North and South Korean people and a reason why it was fabricated that North Korean leader Kim Jong-Il was born there, when in fact he was born in Vyatskoye, in Russia (USSR at the time) in 1941 according to his birth records in Soviet archives.

주체
Juche

Taekwon-Do around the world, especially in the communist and socialist countries, however, it was always to be a double edged sword.

It must also be remembered that General Choi fought against communist North Korea during the Korean War, as part of the South Korean army, so was highly unlikely to favour their political ideals himself. His birthplace also now rested in an artificially created North Korea and this was where many of his family members, whom he had not seen for around 35 years, still resided! He also felt Taekwon-Do should be spread worldwide regardless of race, religion or political ideals, so therefore why should it exclude North Korea! Finally he had his own dream of reunifying both North and South Korea and felt Taekwon-Do could help to achieve that in some way.

So what is Juche really?
According to Wikipedia[150] *'The Juche Idea'* is a political thesis of Kim Il-Sung, the founder of the Democratic People's Republic of Korea, which says that the Korean masses are the masters of the country's development.

In Korea, the term *Juche* is originally thought to have come about during the Japanese occupation of Korea, where there was a hated term used by the Japanese to describe Koreans. This term was *sadae* and meant 'subservience', so Koreans started using the antithesis[151] of *sadae*, which was *Chuch'e*, which is now written as *Juche*.

Kim Il Sung encourages service personal - notice the posture again!

The *Juche Idea* is actually thought to have been the brainchild of a North Korean politician called Hwang Jang-Yop who, after reading a

---

[150] http://en.wikipedia.org/wiki/Juche

[151] Something in direct contrast or opposition

From Creation To Unification
The Complete Histories Behind The Ch'ang Hon (ITF) Patterns

1955 speech by Kim Il-Sung, noticed some of the words saying 'Juche means Chosŭn's revolution' and knowing Kim Il-Sung wanted to develop his own version of communism, helped to create and craft the *Juche Idea* and reinvent North Korean history to reflect this to the people! Interestingly enough, Hwang Jang-Yop defected to South Korea in 1997 and in 2010 two North Korean assassins were arrested in South Korea after being sent to kill Hwang Jang-Yop. When asked about this Hwang said *"Death is just death. There is no difference from dying of old age or being killed by Kim Jong-Il".*

From the 1950s to the 1970s, Kim elaborated the *Juche Idea* into a set of principles that the government used to justify its policy decisions. Among these are independence from great powers, a strong military posture, and reliance on Korean national resources.

Juche, when translated, means *"main body"* or *"mainstream"* and is sometimes translated by North Korean sources as *"independent stand"* or *"spirit of self-reliance."* It has also been interpreted as *"always putting Korean things first."* According to Kim Il-Sung, the Juche Idea is based on the belief that *"man is the master of everything and decides everything."*

1946 - A young Kim Il-Sung

주체 (主體)

Juche in hangul and hanja

Whilst the Juche Idea is usually accredited to Kim Il-Sung, some years ago, while I was researching an article related to Juche and Ko-Dang[152], Master Doug Nowling (7th Dan, Director of Kido Kwan International), who also supplied the Hangul/Hanja picture above, made an interesting observation in that he felt the original origins of Juche may actually be of Chinese origins, as opposed to Korean, as if you look at the way it's written in Hanja (Chinese) Juche simply means

---

[152] The full article: www.raynerslanetkd.com/Press/ARTICLES_juchekodang2.html

주체
Juche

"*Master of the Body*" or "*Master of Self.*" The Wikipedia article also alludes to this as well!^153

Juche Tower, built in Pyongyang in 1982 to celebrate Kim Il-Sung's 70th Birthday

The Juche *Idea* and the Juche *Reality*, in truth bear scant resemblance to each other. Human Rights Organisations (that monitor North Korea) agree and say that the real situation in North Korea bears no resemblance to the theory of Juche at all!

---

[153] According to a passage about Juche in Wikipedia "Political thinking from Maoist China has greatly influenced North Korea, such as the North's Chollima mass mobilization movements, which were based on China's Great Leap Forward. However, the ruling party in Pyongyang strongly denounces any Maoist influences on Juche in an attempt to appear independent. So even though the influence of Mao Zedong is also not formally acknowledged in North Korea, WPK ideologists and speech writers began to openly use Maoist ideas, such as the concept of self-regeneration, in the 1950s and 1960s. Maoist theories of art also began to influence North Korean musical theater during this time. These developments occurred as a result of the influence of the Chinese Army's involvement during the Korean War, as well as during the Sino-Soviet split when Kim Il-sung sided with Mao against Soviet de-Stalinization. Kim attended middle school in China, he was conversant in Chinese, and he had been a guerrilla partisan in the Communist Party of China from about 1931-1941. The postwar Kim Il-sung regime had also emulated Mao's Great Leap Forward, his theory of the Mass line (*qunzhong luxian*), and the guerrilla tradition. Juche, however, does not exactly share the Maoist faith in the peasantry over the working class and the village over the city. *Source:* http://en.wikipedia.org/wiki/Juche

From Creation To Unification
The Complete Histories Behind The Ch'ang Hon (ITF) Patterns

The 45 moves of this pattern may be in reference to the year 1945, when Korea was divided into North and South, with Kim Il-Sung taking power in the North, which eventually lead to the Juche Idea.

A statue of Kim Il Sung in Pyongyang subway - notice the posture![154]

---

[154] Photo courtesy of Master Doug Nowling VII, *Kido Kwan Martial Arts International.* Reproduced with permission and thanks.

삼일
Sam-Il

Sam-Il denotes the historical date of the independence movement of Korea which began throughout the country on March 1, 1919. The 33 movements in the pattern stand for the 33 patriots who planned the movement.

Sam-Il is the sixteenth pattern of of Ch'ang Hon Taekwon-Do, usually taught at 3rd Degree Black belt. It has 33 moves and was developed in Korea by General Choi, with the assistance of Sgt. Park Won Ha sometime prior to or around 1958/1959.

Sam-Il is named after the *'Sam-Il Movement'* which, when translated means literally the *'Three One Movement'*[155] due to the date it occurred: 1st, March, 1919, sometimes it is also called the 'March 1st Movement'.

---

[155] Sam is Korean for 3rd and Il is Korean for 1st i.e. The first day or the third month.

175

From Creation To Unification
The Complete Histories Behind The Ch'ang Hon (ITF) Patterns

As you will have read in previous chapters, Korea was declared a Japanese protectorate in 1905 with the signing of the Japan–Korea Protectorate Treaty (Eulsa Treaty) and officially annexed in 1910. The oppressive and harsh rule by the Japanese gave many Koreans cause to form resistance movements against the Japanese overlords.

Korean organizations in America had been putting pressure on the President, Woodrow Wilson, to speak on Korea's behalf at the Paris Peace Conference[156] which took place in January, 1919. Japan was also in attendance, wanting to control Germany's possessions in the Pacific and needed to show its best face. Were news of Japan's brutal and harsh rule in Korea to get out and be accepted worldwide, it would not bode well at the peace talks and as such, a propaganda war[157] ensued between Japan and Korean activists.

President Woodrow Wilson, 1919

Though both Japan and the USA blocked any Korean delegates from directly addressing the conference themselves, Woodrow Wilson made a speech known as *'The Fourteen Points'*; though not officially directed at Korea, he spoke of *'the right of nations to self-determination'*, which, gave those at the conference (such as Do-San) confidence to demand freedom from the Japanese occupation and is thought to have led directly to the Sam-Il movement.

Paris Peace Conference - 1919

---

[156] The Paris Peace Conference was a meeting of the victorious allies following the end of World War I.. 32 countries took part to discuss their post-war future, sign treaties between them and put sanctions on Germany. The borders of countries throughout the world were reshaped and changed forever because of this conference.

[157] A fascinating account of the propaganda war can be read at
http://populargusts.blogspot.co.uk/2008/03/battle-for-american-perceptions-of.html

삼일
Sam-Il

Fed up with the oppressive Japanese occupying their country and treating Koreans as 3rd class citizens in their own homeland, Koreans had had enough, and the speech by President Wilson, along with the suspicious death of Emperor Gojong[158] on the 21st January, 1919 became the catalyst for Koreans demanding their freedom more vocally.

It was planned that on 1st March, 1919, during a mourning period for Emperor Gojong leading up to his funeral scheduled for 3rd March, that 33 Korean patriots would present the *Korean Declaration of Independence* in Pagoda Park to the people of Korea and the Japanese authorities.

On the run up to this day, the Korean media had run a series of articles based on President Wilson's *Declaration of the Principle of Self Determination*. The articles pointed out:

⇒ That no Koreans held influential government positions, and of those that did hold them, both Japanese and Korean, they were too arrogant.
⇒ That administrative processes were too complicated for the general population to follow, whilst laws were made too frequently for the general public to keep up!
⇒ That there was a big difference between the education of Korean and Japanese children and also that Korean village teachers were being forced out of their jobs due to the Japanese attempts to suppress their heritage.
⇒ That the government discriminates when employing Koreans and Japanese workers, in the Japanese's favour and that Koreans scholars, and those of the upper classes were afforded no special treatment!
⇒ That taxes were too high and didn't equate to the services received and land was still being confiscated from Koreans for no reason except for Japanese financial gain.
⇒ That there was too much forced labour put upon Koreans and while Koreans worked towards developing their country, they were not reaping the rewards of benefits of their own work!
⇒ And that the Japanese despised Koreans generally, which led to their mistreatment by the Japanese!

---

[158] It was wide spread suspicion that Emperor Gojong was poisoned by the Japanese.

From Creation To Unification
The Complete Histories Behind The Ch'ang Hon (ITF) Patterns

A painting showing the signing of the Korean Declaration of Independence by the patriots

On 1st March, 1919 the meeting took place against the backdrop of Korean dissent. Large crowds had gathered at Pagoda Park to mourn Emperor Gojong and, fearing it could create a riot, the 33 patriots decided to meet in a more secluded location, instead meeting at the Taehwagwan Restaurant in Seoul.

At the meeting, the *Korean Declaration of Independence*, which had been written by Korean historian Choe Nam-Seon was read out and then signed by the 33 patriots. A copy was then sent to Yoshimichi Hasegawa (the 2nd Governor-General of Korea), following which they called the police and informed them of what they had done... a short while later, all 33 were arrested.

Yoshimichi Hasegawa

Despite the concerns over causing a riot by declaring Independence publically to such large crowds, a student called Chung Jae-Yong read the declaration to the public that had gathered in Pagoda Park. The crowds formed a procession which the Japanese police tried to break up. However, at the same time, on the same day (2pm) when the 33 patriots were reading the Korean Declaration of Independence, other

삼일
Sam-Il

The crowds gather outside the City Hall to hear the reading

appointed delegates around the country were also reading it to crowds of Koreans.

The Declaration of Independence
Written by Choe Nam-Seon
Translated by Yer-Ae K. Choi

We herewith proclaim the independence of Korea and the liberty of the Korean people. This we proclaim to all the nations of the world in witness of human equality. This we proclaim to our descendents so that they may enjoy in perpetuity their inherent right to nationhood.

Inasmuch as this proclamation originates from our five-thousand-year history, inasmuch as it springs from the loyalty of twenty million people, inasmuch as it affirms our yearning for the advancement of everlasting liberty, inasmuch as it expresses our desire to take part in the global reform rooted in human conscience, it is the solemn will of heaven, the great tide of our age, and a just act necessary for the co-existence of all humankind. Therefore, no power in this world can obstruct or suppress it!

Victims of the outdated notions of aggression and brute force, we have now suffered for a decade, for the first time in our long history, under foreign tyranny; our right to existence deprived, our spiritual growth stunted, our national pride and honor damaged, and our opportunity to make our own creative contribution to the progress of world civilization lost.

From Creation To Unification
The Complete Histories Behind The Ch'ang Hon (ITF) Patterns

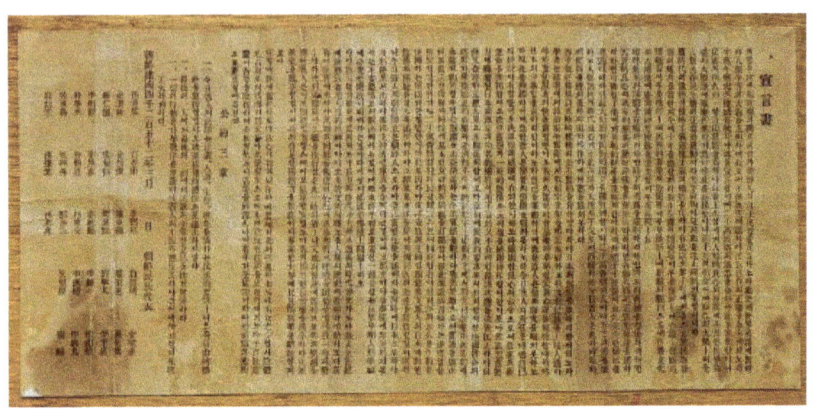

The original Declaration of Independence, written by Choe Nam-Seon

Surely, if we are to eradicate our longstanding sense of injustice, if we are to extricate ourselves from today's pain, if we are to forestall tomorrow's threat, if we are to resuscitate our trampled national pride, if we as individuals are to reach our full potential, if we are to deliver our children from the legacy of shame, if we are to bequeath to our future generations blessing and prosperity, our first and foremost duty is to secure the independence of our people. If each and every twenty million of us carry a sword in our hearts and if we are supported by today's shared human conscience ready to stand by us equipped with arms of justice and morality, what can stop us from pressing forward to defeat the strongest? If we regroup and build up our strength, what aim can we not accomplish?

Though Japan has repeatedly violated its promises since the Treaty of 1876, we do not here condemn its perfidy. Though its scholars and government officials dismiss our great dynastic achievements in order to prop up its claim that our history began as a foreign colony with a primitive civilization, though it merely seeks a conqueror's gratification willfully ignoring the ancient foundation and the outstanding characteristics of our people, we do not here take it to task. We are pressed to reprimand ourselves, and thus have little time to reproach others. Busy with today's work, we have little time to chastise yesterday's actions.

Today, our only duty is to rebuild ourselves, not to demolish others. It is to explore our new destiny according to the solemn dictates of our conscience, not to squabble with others over fleeting grudges and old animosities. It is to restore our natural, rational foundation by rectifying the unnatural, irrational ambition of the Japanese politicians in the grip of obsolete ideas. The annexation made without national consensus has inevitably led to intimidation used as a temporary measure, inequality caused by discrimination, and statistics falsified to justify it. Just look at the result today! The chasm of rancor has grown so wide that bridging the two peoples with differing interests seems all but impossible.

To boldly right old wrongs, opening a new relationship based on true mutual understating, is certainly the best way for both countries to avert disaster and foster amity. To forcibly bind twenty million people filled with bitterness and enmity will

삼일
Sam-Il

not secure lasting peace. Moreover, it will exacerbate the apprehension and distrust of four hundred million Chinese people who hold the key to East Asian stability, which will undoubtedly lead to the unrest and eventual downfall of the entire region. Therefore, establishing Korean independence today will permit Koreans to return to their rightful lives, will enable the Japanese to break away from their wrongful path and concentrate on their responsibility as a major player in East Asia, and will free the Chinese from their nightmare of uncertainty and anxiety about Japan. Korean independence will indeed be an indispensable step toward the stability of East Asia, which will in turn contribute to the attainment of world peace. With the well-being of all humanity at stake, the establishment of Korean independence is a grave issue that transcends mere animosity between two nations.

Behold! A new world is approaching before our very eyes! The age of might has receded, and the age of morality has arrived. The spirit of humanism cultivated throughout the past century now begins to throw its light on a new chapter in world history. Just as a new spring has come, hastening the rebirth of every living thing, our pulse, once frozen in the bitter cold and snow, now quickens in the warm breeze and sunshine. The good fortune of heaven and earth has returned to us, and we ride the changing tide of the world. Do not hesitate or flinch! By protecting our inalienable individual right to freedom, we will enjoy our lives to the full. By realizing our bountiful creativity, our national civilization will flower in the warmth of spring that pervades the world.

We hereby rise up! Conscience is on our side, and truth marches with us. Men and women, young and old, leave your darkened corners and partake in the joyful resurrection along with all creation! The spirit of our many ancestors protects us from within, and the tide of the new world from without. To begin is to succeed! Let us march straight into the light!

We hereby pledge the following:

Today's undertaking reflects the demands of our people for justice, morality, survival, and prosperity. Therefore, we will act solely in the spirit of liberty, never in the spirit of enmity.

1. To the last person and to the last moment, we will forthrightly express the will of the Korean people.
2. We will respect order in all our actions and ensure that our demeanor and claims are always honorable and upright.

The first day of the third month of the 4252nd year of the founding of Korea,

The Representatives of the Korean people:

(the names of 33 signatories)

From Creation To Unification
The Complete Histories Behind The Ch'ang Hon (ITF) Patterns

One of the Sam-Il protest marches

Protests, marches and demonstrations formed throughout the country, with as many as 2 million Koreans taking part, which the Japanese local, and even military police, could not suppress. The army (and even the navy) was called in to assist and though the demonstrations were non-violent in nature, the police and army brutally put them down, firing into unarmed crowds. Brutal beatings, stabbings, beheadings and even crucifixions were reported by American missionaries in Korea.

"Crucifixion in 1919: This photograph was taken by the International Film Company a few minutes after the execution by the Japanese soldiers."
- Taken from a pamphlet

The brutal put down ended up killing over 7,500 Koreans, wounding almost 17,000 and arresting over 47,000. Amongst the many atrocities reported, one tells of how Japanese police herded the population of an entire village into a locked church, and then burnt it to the ground, shooting through the windows as it burnt so no one escaped. Many of

삼일
Sam-Il

those arrested were taken to the infamous Seodaemun Prison where they were tortured and held without trial. Hundreds were put to death at the back of the prison, again without trial, at a place known as the 'death house'!

The notorious Seodaemun Prison

Though Korea was not to gain its independence from the Japanese until 1945, the Sam-Il movement did result in some big changes in Korea. The Governor-General was replaced due to his lack of control and handling of the 'riots', the military police force was replaced with a civilian police force, some of the most objectionable rules imposed by the Japanese were removed and surprisingly women were allowed to express their views on female liberation more freely!

Outside of mainland Korea, the *Provisional Government of the Republic of Korea* was formed in Shanghai on 13th April, 1919, which included such notables as Ahn Chang-Ho (Do-San) and Syngman Rhee, who became its first President and remained in office for 6 years before being impeached, though the provisional government itself, lasted in exile, until 1945. When Korea was finally liberated from the Japanese in 1945, Syngman Rhee would return from his exile in America and become South Korea's 1st President, as well as the man who authorized Taekwon-Do to be named and thus become the national martial art of Korea.

During the 1930's and 1940's the provisional government coordinated armed resistance against the Japanese occupier. In 1920, at the Battle of Qingshanli, Korean resistance fighters fought and beat Japanese

From Creation To Unification
The Complete Histories Behind The Ch'ang Hon (ITF) Patterns

troops in Manchuria and in 1932 they assaulted the Japanese military leadership that was based in Shanghai. By 1940, the provisional government had managed to bring together all the separate armed resistance groups and formed the Korean Independence Army.

The Korean Independence Army formerly declared war against the Axis powers (Germany, Italy and Japan) on 9th December, 1941 and fought in the Second World War and by this action; Korea was finally liberated from Japanese rule on 2nd September, 1945

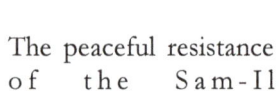

Provisional Government of the Republic of Korea. Taken 11th October, 1919

An early Korean Independence Army unit in Manchuria

The peaceful resistance of the Sam-Il movement went on to inspire Mahatma Ghandi's own non-violent resistance movement in India one year later and in 1949, the 1st March was designated a public holiday in South Korea.

유신
Yoo-Sin

Yoo-Sin is named after General Kim Yoo Sin, a commanding general during the Silla Dynasty. The 68 movements refer to the last two figures of 668 A.D., the year Korea was united. The ready posture signifies a sword drawn on the right rather than left side, symbolizing Yoo Sin's mistake of following his King's orders to fight with foreign forces against his own nation.

Yoo-Sin is the seventeenth pattern of of Ch'ang Hon Taekwon-Do, usually taught at 3rd Degree Black belt. It has 68 moves and was developed in Malaysia between 1962 and 1964 with the help of Master Kim, Bok Man and Master Woo, Jae Lim.

Kim Yoo-Sin was born in Gyeyang, Jincheon county in 595 AD to the daughter of King Jin-Heung of the Silla Dynasty. His father was Kim Seoh-Yeon, a General in the Silla army. At aged 15, with Silla under the rule of King Jin-Pyeong, Yoo-Sin became a Hwa-Rang warrior. He became an accomplished swordsman and soon rose through the ranks, gaining the rank of Kuk-son (Unit commander) in an unprecedented 3 years! His unit was the Yonghwa-Hyangdo (Band of the Dragon Flower Tree). His quick rise through the ranks may have been due to his already heightened position within the bone rank system (see Hwa-Rang chapter, Page 94, footnote 79) due to his royal bloodlines, but his position was further elevated as it was thought that he was a great grandchild of

A drawing of Kim Yoo-Sin [159]

---

[159] Picture by artist widyarahayu. *www.widyarahayu.deviantart.com*

another former King, Guh-Yeong of Gaya[160] and by the age of 34, in 629 AD Kim Yoo Sin had become the Commander in Chief of Silla's armed forces after proving himself in many battles against Silla's neighbour Baekje.

Legends of Kim Yoo-Sin are plentiful. In the Samguk Sagi there is a passage that tells how a young Kim Yoo Sin was forever planning attacks on Baekje and Goguryo and a spy, who was well placed as he had been mingling with the Hwa-Rang for many years, tried to lure Yoo-Sin into a trap. The spy convinced Yoo-Sin that they should set out secretly to spy on the enemy forces, but as they travelled across a mountain, Yoo-Sin paused for a rest and saw visions of three beautiful girls (Goddesses of the sacred mountains) who warned him about the trap. Yoo-Sin turned around, saying that in his haste he had forgotten his purse and needed to return to get it, leaving the spy none the wiser. On his return to the camp, he had the spy arrested, interrogated and upon his admission of guilt – executed!

Another story tells of a battle where Yoo-Sin's father was trying to take a Goguryo castle and Kim Yoo-Sin was fighting under him. The battle was not going well as each attempt to attack it was repulsed, with many soldiers losing their lives. The spirit of the Silla forces from the constant defeats and deaths of their fellow soldiers was so low, that they refused to fight any more. Dismayed, Kim Yoo-Sin sought out his father and said, bowing down on one knee, *"They've defeated us. But throughout my life I have been guided by loyalty and filial piety. In the face of battle one must be courageous. Now, I have heard that if you shake a coat by its collar, the fur will hang straight. And that, if you lift up the headrope, the whole fishing net will open and it can be thrown far and wide. Let me become the collar and the border ropes."*. He then mounted his horse, drew his double edged sword and charged at the enemy castle solo. He jumped a trench and fought his way in and beheaded the general defending the castle. On seeing this, the rest of the Silla troops regained their spirit and charged at the castle, following Yoo-Sin's lead, it is said they cut

---

[160] Guh-Yeong of Gaya was the final ruler of the Gaya Confederacy (see page 132, footnote 106). With Gaya under constant attack from Silla's King Beop-Heung, King Guh-Yeong chose to surrender Gaya which became absorbed into Silla. Due to his actions, King Guh-Yeong not only saved many lives but was welcomed into the Silla aristocracy at the 2nd highest level of the bone rank system (just one tier lower than the King of Silla himself) and was also allowed to keep and govern his former territory.

유신
Yoo-Sin

off 5000 enemy heads and captured the castle, as those left were to afraid to fight back!

In 632 AD King Jin-Pyeong died and was succeeded by Silla's (and Korea's) first queen; Queen Sun-Duk (see Sun-Duk chapter). Queen Sun-Duk was so impressed with General Kim Yoo-Sin's abilities that she kept him on as Commander in Chief after her ascension to the throne, which was unusual in those days.

In 645 AD General Kim had just won a big victory over a Baekje army and was travelling home. As he neared his home news arrived that another Baekje army was readying for an attack. Without even visiting his wife and family, General Kim turned his troops around and set off to meet the second army who, upon seeing the Silla forces, turned around and fled. Again he returned home, firstly visiting the palace to file a report. As he did so, again news arrived that Baekje were advancing on Silla and once again, without visiting his wife, General Kim went to meet the enemy.

Kim Yoo-Sin as played by actor Uhm Tae-Woong in the Korean television drama, Queen Seon Deok

On this occasion however, General Kim and his troops actually passed his own house and as they approached the household servants were lined up outside waiting for him. It is said he was so resolute, that he passed his house without even looking back at it! Suddenly however, he stopped and ordered one of his soldiers to fetch a drink of water from the household well. He drank it and exclaimed that it still tasted the same! The tired and hungry soldiers, who had seen the General return towards battle over and over without even visiting his family, were inspired saying *"When our leader is like this, how can we be sad to be parted from our meat and bread"* and with that they marched on with a new vigour. Upon arriving, once again the Baekje army did not dare engage Yoo-Sin's troops and fled! Queen Sun-Duk was so impressed that she rewarded General Kim with money and another title!

A statue of General Kim Yoo-Sin. Hwangseong Park, South Korea

Many stories relate how Kim Yoo-Sin was not only courageous himself, but also a wise leader of his troops. On one occasion the troops were travelling across a snowy mountain and, tired, weary and freezing cold, they kept stumbling and falling down. Yoo-Sin saw this and instead of issuing any orders, simply threw off his jacket, whipped his horse and sped forwards. His men tried to keep up and in doing so, started to warm up and even sweat!

In 642 AD future Silla King, Kim Chun-Chu (later to become King Muyeol) who was a high minister at the time, travelled to Goguryo to ask for assistance to counter continuous Baekje attacks, which had seen Baekje take a number of Silla territories. Before he left Kim Chun-Chu made a pact with his childhood friend, Kim Yoo-Sin, asking if something would happen, would Yoo-Sin be distressed. Yoo-Sin said if he did not return, he would climb on his horse and ride at Goguryo (meaning he would come and rescue him). Kim Chun-Chu and Kim Yoo-Sin became blood brothers that day and as he left, Kim Chun-Chu said that if he did not return in sixty days, then they would not meet again! Goguryo had plans of their own however and when Kim Chun-Chu arrived, the Goguryo King imprisoned him and sentenced him to execution.

As the sixty days drew near, Yoo-Sin choose 3000 of his bravest Hwa-Rang and started his preparations. He told the troops that a hero of Silla had been imprisoned and he intended to rescue him. Kim Yoo-Sin said to his men *"If a man is ready to give himself up to death, then he is worth one hundred men; if one hundred men are ready to give themselves up to*

유신
Yoo-Sin

death, then they are worth one thousand men; if one thousand men are ready to give themselves up to death, then they are worth ten thousand men. In this case, it is possible, through faith, to march straight through the world.". And with this, the troops swore their allegiance to General Kim, saying even if the mission only had a small chance of success, they would follow his orders to the death! A Goguryo spy informed the Goguryo King that the great General Kim, Yoo-Sin was coming to rescue Kim Chun-Chu, with his 3,000 specially trained Hwa-Rang and before Yoo-Sin and his troops had even left, the King of Goguryo released Kim Chun-Chu!

Though Silla and Baekje had fought for many years, they eventually formed an alliance in order to counter attempts from the powerful Kingdom of Goguryo, as it tried to expand southwards into Silla and Baekje territory. The alliance pre-empted Goguryo and successfully attacked it, taking two major Goguryo territories. However, Silla betrayed Baekje and tried to take both territories for itself and due to this betrayal, Baekje formed an alliance with Goguryo against its betrayer!

In 647 AD Queen Sun-Duk was succeeded by Queen Jin-Duk (her cousin) who was herself succeeded by King Muyeol in 654 AD King Muyeol was Kim Chun-Chu the childhood friend and now blood brother of Kim Yoo-Sin who had married Kim Yoo-Sin's sister. Kim Yoo-Sin had retained his position throughout, despite the change of kings and Queens. Years later, following the death of his wife, Kim, Yoo-Sin would remarry, and his new wife was King Muyeol's sister, Lady Jiso.

King Muyeol of Silla

King Muyeol was also on good terms with the Tang (Chinese) Emperor, whom he had been friends with for many years, before he had even assumed the role of the Tang Emperor. In 655 AD Baekje and Goguryo attacked Silla and with the odds against them, Silla called for aid from the Tang Dynasty of China. The Tang sent 13,000 Tang troops to assist and in 660 AD the most famous battle of Kim Yoo-

From Creation To Unification
The Complete Histories Behind The Ch'ang Hon (ITF) Patterns

Sin's career took place, when he led 50,000 Silla troops, backed up by the 13,000 Tang troops and attacked the capital of Baekje; Sabi!

The capital was well defend by Baekje General, Ge-Baek (see Ge-Baek chapter), who held off the attack with just 5,000 men for days, before he was defeated by Kim Yoo-Sin, which saw the fall of Baekje once and for all. This famous battle became known as *The Battle of Hwangsanbul* or *The Battle of Hwangsan Field*, which is where it took place.

Just prior to the battle, the Tang General had seen a buzzard (or similar bird) circling his camp and took it as an omen that he was to die in battle. According to the story, the Tang General was so fearful that he was about to order his men to turn back, but Kim Yoo-Sin saw the General trembling in fear, pulled his sword and struck the bird down. Laying the dead bird at the Tang Generals feet, Yoo-Sin said *"A small grotesque bird cannot interfere with our great expedition against a bad king".*

After the final battle, the Tang Emperor had heard the great stories of General Kim Yoo-Sin and was so impressed that he sent an emissary with his personal praise. The Tang General spoke to Kim Yoo-Sin, Kim Inmun (King Muyeol's son) and another general and offered the three of them all of the conquered lands of Baekje, as a reward. However, they thanked the Tang General for his troop's assistance,

유신
Yoo-Sin

but refused the offer saying that it is the whole of Silla that celebrates the downfall of Baekje so how could just the three of them enrich themselves by accepting such an offer!

In 661 AD a new King; Moon-Moo (see Moon-Moo chapter) took the throne following the death of his father, King Muyeol - King Moon-Moo was not only Kim Yoo-Sin's new King but also his nephew by family line!

With Baekje now annexed, the combined Silla and Tang forces headed towards Goguryo, which up until now had been considered an impregnable kingdom. In 661 AD they attacked Goguryo from two directions and although they were unsuccessful, they weakened Goguryo considerably. In 667 AD the Silla and Tang forces started another offensive against Goguryo, who had not recovered fully from its attack 6 years earlier and in 668 AD Goguryo was finally beaten and a unified Silla was formed!

Kim Yoo-Sin was well rewarded for his efforts in the campaigns against Baekje and Goguryo. The King was reputed to have bestowed upon him the title of *Taedaegakgan* (meaning something similar to Grand Sub-Chief), which elevated him even higher than his current position. He was also given a village of 500 households, his own officers all received titles and he was allowed to enter the royal palace whenever he wanted too. A year later King Moon-Moo also gave him 142 horse farms that were spread throughout the kingdom.

Stories of Kim Yoo Sin existed during his day and led to his legendary status. One was told of a time when one of General Kim's commanders was involved in a heated argument with a Tang General, that was about to erupt into violence. It was said that General Kim's sword leapt from its scabbard into his hand and as a warriors sword was believed to contain his soul, it scared the Tang General so much that he immediately apologised to Kim's commander. Years later, when the Tang General was ordered to attack Silla (during the Silla-Tang war), the Tang General refused, saying Silla and their Hwa-rang could not be defeated!

Another story recites how his (General Kim's) troops refused to attack

From Creation To Unification
The Complete Histories Behind The Ch'ang Hon (ITF) Patterns

a rebel army after seeing a falling star in the sky and taking it as a bad omen! General Kim constructed a large kite, big enough to carry a ball of fire into the night sky. He flew it away from his troops and when they saw it, they thought the star had returned to heaven, took up their arms and defeated the rebel army. Though this legend may seem simply that[161], it may also have much truth in it as General Kim was known to use kites as a way of communicating with his forces when they were split!

Despite their previous alliance that defeated the other two Kingdoms of Korea, the Tang tried to place the whole of Korea under its control, even placing a Protectorate General's office in Silla territory. King Moon-Moo resisted these attempts and eventually drove the Tang out of Korea for good.

In June, 673 AD it is said that people saw visions of warriors, with shields and weapons walking out of Yoo-Sin's house crying, then disappearing into thin air! Upon hearing of this, Yoo-Sin said that they must have been his *'guardian soldiers'* who had protected him all these years and now, understanding that his time has come, they have left! Ten days later he was struck down with a sickness! King Moon-Moo wept at his bedside at the thought of losing Silla's greatest warrior, wondering how the kingdom would carry on without him!

On the 1st July, 673 AD, aged 79, Kim Yoo-Sin passed away, having served three Silla Kings and two Silla Queens. Though he was a

---

[161] There is another story of Kim Yoo Sin and a flaming kite, where he advised Queen Sun-Duk to send a flaming kite into the sky after a falling star was seen during a revolt against a 'female on the throne' and used by the opposition to signify that her reign had come to an end. Once again, the flaming kite was to make it seem as if the star had returned to its rightful place in the sky!

유신
Yoo-Sin

Kim Yoo-Sin's tomb in South Korea [162]

soldier of Silla, he always held a strong belief throughout his life, that the Kingdoms of Korea should be united as one and he is remembered as the driving force for the unification of Korea. He is considered a foremost master of the Korean sword and was posthumously awarded the honorary title of *'King Heung-Mu'* (Great King of War) by King Heung-Deok (the 42nd ruler of Silla). Kim Yoo-Sin was buried at the foot of Songhwa mountain, in a tomb said to be as splendid and magnificent of that of a king!

Kim Yoo-Sin had 10 children, one of which (his 2nd son) Kim Won-Sul became a general himself and served King Moon-Moo. Though a (low level) general himself Kim Won-Sul never achieved the heights of his father. In fact, at one battle, which went on whilst his father was still alive in 672 AD, Kim Won-Sul was fighting and winning in a battle against Tang troops. However, as the Tang retreated he chased them but fell into a trap that killed seven of his own generals and countless others. Realising the tide of battle had changed and that defeat was now inevitable, he tried to do the honourable thing and drive his horse into the enemy ranks, saying *"a man does not live a humiliating life"* – but his soldiers stopped him.

---

[162] Picture by Alain Seguin. Cc-by-sa-3.0

From Creation To Unification
The Complete Histories Behind The Ch'ang Hon (ITF) Patterns

His father however was outraged as he wrongly thought his son was a coward, so angry was he that he asked King Moon-Moo to execute his son for his shame of not dying on the battlefield, when he had lost so many men under his command, but, though Kim Yoo-Sin was deadly serious with this request, the King decided that he had lost too many generals already and decided not to punish Kim Won-Sul at all. Kim Won-Sul still felt shamed and retreated from sight, but upon his father's death returned to his household home to attend the funeral. His mother, Lady Jiso also wrongly believed he was a coward and would have nothing to do with him except for saying *"How can I be the mother of a son who was not a son to his father"*. After the traditional 3 years of mourning, which Kim Won-Sul spent alone, he returned to the battlefields to fight the Tang once more. It was said that when he fought, it was as if he was anxious to die and because he had no fear, he won many great victories which helped end the war.

For his victories and actions in the war, Kim Won-Sul was meant to return to the capital of Silla and be rewarded, but he never returned home and instead headed into the mountains to live out the remainder of his short life, with the regrets he had regarding his impiety towards his parents. History however, recognizes him for his efforts for the role he played in gaining independence for Korea from the Tang.

A statue of Kim Yoo-Sin in Namsan, Seoul, South Korea [163]

---

[163] Picture by Integral. Cc-by-sa-2.0-kr

최영
Choi-Yong

Choi-Yong is named after General Choi Yong, premier and commander in chief of the armed forces during the 14th century Koryo Dynasty. Choi Yong was greatly respected for his loyalty, patriotism, and humility. He was executed by his subordinate commanders headed by general Yi Sung Gae, who later became the first King of the Yi Dynasty.

Choi-Yong is the eighteenth pattern of of Ch'ang Hon Taekwon-Do, usually taught at 3rd Degree Black belt. It has 46 moves and was developed in Malaysia between 1962 and 1964 with the help of Master Kim, Bok Man and Master Woo, Jae Lim.

Choi-Yong was born in 1316 in Cheorwon, Gangwon Province, Korea. Although he was born into reasonable wealth as the son of a government official, it didn't seem to matter to him. He didn't wear elaborate clothes or dine on the finest food, but instead chose to live a simple lifestyle, something which continued throughout his life, even when he became a famous general of the Goryeo Dynasty, this was all due to his own motto that his father gave to him, which simply said *"look at gold as if it were stone"*.[164] As a youth he was said to have been born strong and possessed extraordinary strength. He studied military strategy books and practiced martial arts to master his fighting skills.

A bust of Choi-Yong

---

[164] Another translation said his Fathers motto was simply *"Do not be covetous of gold"*

From Creation To Unification
The Complete Histories Behind The Ch'ang Hon (ITF) Patterns

As a young man, Choi-Yong joined the military and quickly progressed up the ranks. His many battles fighting Japanese pirates who were raiding the Korean coastline around 1350, gave his men much confidence in his abilities and gained him the attention of King Gong-Min. Choi-Yong became committed to fulfilling King Gong-Min's wish of restoring the sovereignty of Goryeo Dynasty from the Chinese Yuan Dynasty[165], of which they had been a tributary state, since the 13th century.

King Gong-Min

He rose to prominence in 1352, aged 36, when he helped crush a rebellion by Jo Il-Shin whose insurgents had surrounded the palace, killed many of the officials and pronounced a new king! This made Choi-Yong a national hero in the eyes of the people and only 3 years later, he was to crush a second rebellion, this time by a group called the Red Turbans.[166]

The Yuan Dynasty of China was of Mongol ancestry and a faction, known as the White Lotus Society[167] had always resisted and opposed Mongol rule. This resistance had grown into a rebellion which at first was just small sporadic outbursts, where White Lotus members would attack Yuan Dynasty officials, but as it grew, it spilled onto Goryeo territory and General Choi-Yong along with General Yi Seong-Gye (who was also considered a great general by the nation) were sent to help the Yuan forces crush the rebellion, as well as reclaim the areas of Goryeo that had been overrun by rebels, this they did with Choi-Yong fighting in over 30 battles, which increased his fame and gained him even more grace with the king back home.

---

[165] The Yuan Dynasty was the successor to the Mongol Empire established by Kublai Khan, a Grandson of Ghengis Khan. The Dynasty was officially founded in 1271 and ruled China until 1368, when it was succeeded by the Ming Dynasty.

[166] Known as 'Red Turbans' due to the red headwear they wore and red banners they flew to distinguish themselves.

[167] It is believed that the White Lotus Society was one of the original founding members of the Chinese Triads!

최영
Choi-Yong

Following his victories, General Choi-Yong returned to Goryeo and reported back about the problems within the Yuan Dynasty and how it was weakening. King Gong-Min decided that with the Yuan Dynasty in a weakened state, it was a good time for Goryeo to reclaim some of its northern territories previously lost to the Mongols. General Choi-Yong was dispatched and much to the Kings delight, recovered many of the territories on the Korean side of the Yalu river.[168]

The Yalu river, dividing North Korea and China [169]

Lee Min Ho plays Choi-Yong in the Korean drama 'Faith'

As he grew older he became Mayor of Pyongyang, which had been suffering a famine. Choi-Yong increased crop production in the area and ended the famine, which gained him even more favour and fame. However, he didn't stay as Mayor long, as in 1363 he returned to the military in order to combat another rebellion after a powerful court official, Kim Yon-An tried to overthrow the Goryeo Government with the help of the Mongols (Yuan Dynasty). General Choi-Yong and his troops defeated a Mongol force of 10,000 men and protected the Kingdom once again.

---

[168] The Yalu river (Amrok river to Koreans) is a dividing river that runs on the border between China and North Korea.

[169] Picture by Kmusser. Cc-by-sa-3.0

From Creation To Unification
The Complete Histories Behind The Ch'ang Hon (ITF) Patterns

Choi-Yong had a dream one day and in it, it showed a Buddhist monk would save his life! A short while later, King Gong-Min promoted a monk named Shin-Don to a high position within the Goryeo court and it seemed Choi-Yong's dream had come true! Shin-Don became a teacher to King Gomg-Min and worked to help the lives of the Goryeo peasant class. He also became the Kings advisor and tried to reform the government, driving out some of the ministers and putting in place his own group of officials! Even though other ministers in the court opposed him, he had the full support of the King and Shin-Don's power grew considerably. Power corrupts however, and as Shin-Don became powerful he also became corrupt and Choi-Yong joined the officials and vocally opposed him. Knowing that his fame might affect his standing with the King, Shin-Don engineered false allegations against Choi-Yong and accused him of misconduct. King Gong-Min believed the allegations and almost executed Choi-Yong, but instead, due to his previous glorious past in serving the kingdom, he exiled him.

Choi-Yong remained in exile for 6 years, but was allowed to return following Shin-Don's death. King Gong-Min had finally realised that Shin-Don had become corrupt and had him executed in 1371. Upon his return, Choi-Yong's position was restored and he was asked to prepare a fleet to combat the problem of Japanese pirates, who were once again raiding the coast of Korea, but most of all to drive the remaining Mongol forces, from the Goryeo owned, Jeju Island (the place where many years later, General Choi Hong Hi would locate his 29th Infantry Division).

An old drawing of Choi-Yong

Choi-Yong went straight to Jeju Island and engaged the Mongol forces, who doggedly held fast and fought well, but were eventually beaten by Choi-Yong's forces. During this time however, the Japanese pirates had grown in strength and in 1376 they had attacked and taken the Goryeo city of Gongju. Two years prior to

최영
Choi-Yong

this, King Gong-Min had died[170] and been succeeded by King U.[171] King U had sent an emissary Jeong-Mong Ju (Po-Eun) to Japan to secure the help of Japanese forces in defeating the pirates, but they were unsuccessful. However, a Korean scientist, Choe Mu-Seon[172], had recently introduced General Choi-Yong to gun powder weapons, which Choi-Yong used to easily beat the pirates. It is said that between Jeju Island and the battles with the Japanese pirates, Choi-Yong fought in over eighty battles!

A portrait of scientist Choe Mu-Seon and the Singijeon Rocket Launcher he invented

While all this was going on, the Yuan Dynasty of China had been replaced by the Ming Dynasty which was growing more powerful as each day went by and in 1388; a Ming envoy visited Goryeo and

---

[170] King Gong-Min was actually murdered after becomig aware of an affair between a man named Hong Ryun and one of his concubines. Hong Ryun and a friend Choe Man-Saeng heard of the Kings anger and decided to murder him, before he had Hong Ryun executed, which they did whilst the King slept, in 1374.

[171] There are two stories regarding King U's ascension to the throne. The first is that following the murder by Hong Ryun and Choe Man-Saeng, a high court official and war hero, Yi In-Im assumed control of the government and installed the 11 year old King U. Another is that Yi In-Im had led a coup and had the King killed so he could seize control of Goryeo due to his dismay at the growing influence of the Ming dynasty over the King. He did this by killing the King and then placing the young King U on the throne, which he could control. King U's mother is, according to record, said to be the maid of the monk, Shin Don!

[172] Choe Mu-Seon is noted for having introduced gun powder to Korea after obtaining the formula after bribing a Chinese merchant for the recipe – an illegal act under Chinese and Mongol law at the time. This allowed Korea to produce its own gun power and Choe Mu-Seon gained much support from king U which enabled him to establish his own gun powder factory where he created many gun powder based weapons, including one that is similar to modern day rocket launchers.

From Creation To Unification
The Complete Histories Behind The Ch'ang Hon (ITF) Patterns

demanded the territories taken earlier were returned to the Ming Empire. During this time, General Choi-Yong, supported by General Yi Seong-Gye (who was against actually attacking the Ming) decided that the best way to lower the Ming threat was to rid the government of the anti-Ming factions and thus ease tensions between both governments, which they did, leaving King U to remain on the throne, but with General Choi-Yong (being the senior General) taking control of the government himself.

However, Choi-Yong convinced King U to send an army to attack the Ming, in fact he convinced the King to send General Yi Seong-gye and his forces, whom he now saw as a rival. General Yi supported the governments previous policy of never attacking its neighbours which is why he supported the previous action of ridding the Goryeo government of the anti-Ming factions, instead of direct action against the Ming Empire, and though he did follow orders and march to meet the Ming armies at the Yalu river, he decided to turn around when he saw how large the Ming forces were as he knew he would be crushed. After considering the alternatives and the fact that he had much support from ministers back at the palace who also agreed with the previous policy, he turned his forces around and marched back to Goryeo in what is known as the Wihwa[173] Retreat.

General Yi's return to the capital was seen as (or actively was) a revolt against the King. General Choi-Yong's army went to meet General Yi Seong-Gye's forces and defend the palace, but General Yi Seong-Gye was superior and won, despite a valiant effort from Choi-Yong. Yi Seong-Gye then took control of the palace, dethroned King U and replaced him with King U's own son, Prince Chang whilst he himself took full control of the military. General Yi Seong-Gye banished Choi-Yong to a small town outside the capital (Goyang) and a little while later, in 1388, Choi-Yong was sentenced to execution by beheading when he is famously known to have said that *'Grass would never grow on his grave due to the unjust end'* and in over 600 years since his death it never did.[174] The grave of Choi-Yong is known as jeokbun (red grave).

---

[173] Wihwa Island was an island on the Yalu river, where General Choi-Yong was to engage the Ming forces.

[174] Not until 1979 did the first blade of grass sprout from the Choi-Yong's grave.

최영
Choi-Yong

The tomb of General Choi-Yong

A year or so later, General Yi Seong-Gye also executed the former Kings; U and Chang (who was just 9 years old), placing on the throne a distant relative, King Gong-Yang as his puppet king. A couple of years later General Yi once again deposed and exiled the current king before taking the throne himself in 1392, ending the Goryeo Dynasty forever as he became the 1st King of the Joseon Dynasty (often referred to as the Yi Dynasty).

Opinions of General Choi-Yong are as plentiful as they are of General Yi Seong-Gye, whilst many see them both as great general's; devoted to the Goryeo Dynasty (especially Choi-Yong) others see them as usurpers to the throne/government. Either way, General Choi-Yong fought many times for the Goryeo Dynasty, risking his life in many battles. Whatever his politics or thoughts on the kings of the time, his loyalty to Goryeo never wavered and ended up costing him his own life!

There is no information as to why this pattern has 46 moves, however it is very close to the age he would have been when he resumed his military career in order to counter yet another rebellion, in which he

From Creation To Unification
The Complete Histories Behind The Ch'ang Hon (ITF) Patterns

defeated a force of 10,000 Mongols.

ROKS Choi-Yong
- a Yi Sunshin Class destroyer

In modern times, there is a Korean Navy Destroyer named after Choi-Yong, which successfully rescued the crew of the cargo ship Samho Jewelry, in what was described as *a 'perfect military operation'*, after it was hijacked by Somali pirates in the Arabian sea in 2011.

연개
Yong-Gae

Yong-Gae is named after a famous general during the Koguryo Dynasty, Yon Gae Somoon. The 49 movements refer to the last two figures of 649 A.D., the year he forced the Tang Dynasty to quit Korea after destroying nearly 300,000 of their troops at Ansi Sung.

Yong-Gae is the nineteenth pattern of Ch'ang Hon Taekwon-Do, usually taught at 4th Degree Black belt. It has 49 moves and was developed in Korea around 1968 with the help of Master Cho, Sang Min.[175]

Yong-Gae Somoon[176] was born the first son of the Prime Minster of the Goguryo Dynasty, Yeon Tae-Jo. Born in 603 AD under the reign of King Yeong-Yang, his family line held much status in the dynasty – apart from the current King, his father had also been prime minister to the previous King; Pyeong-Won and his grandfather, Yeon Ja-Yu was the prime minister before that.

Not much is known about Yong-Gae's younger years except that his father died when he was around 13 after much infighting within the Goguryo Royal Court. The court was split into two factions; one side, which included Yong-Gae's father, along with Ul-Ji Moon Dok (see Ul-Ji chapter) and other military commanders, wanting to take

---

[175] Master J. C. Kim, Master Park, Jong Soo, Master Lee, Byung Moo and others may also have helped in the formulation of this pattern.

[176] General Choi had his name as 'Yon-Gae' and later 'Yong-Gae'. This may be because some Korean and Chinese text say his first name was Somum (or Somoon), with his surname as Yeongae (or Yon/Yong-Gae), however the majority of sources list his family name as Yeon with Gaesomun as his first name. For the purpose of this chapter, I have kept Yong-Gae's name as General Choi used it, but use the more common historical names for his family members.

From Creation To Unification
The Complete Histories Behind The Ch'ang Hon (ITF) Patterns

advantage of the Chinese Sui Dynasty's internal problems to expand the Goguryo Empire and the other side; consisting of Grand Prince Go Geon-Mu (later to become King Yeong-Nyu) and other scholars wanting a peaceful existence for the kingdom. Yeon Tae-Jo ended up being on the losing side meaning he was unable to pass on his position of Prime Minister to his son, however Yong-Gae did gain a governor's title and became Governor of the Western province of Goguryo.

In 618 AD King Yeong-Yang was succeeded by King Yeong-Nyu and the Tang Dynasty had succeeded the Sui Dynasty in China. A relative peace ensued, as the Goguryo Dynasty was still recovering from the Goguryo-Sui wars and the Tang Dynasty was still building itself. The two dynasties sent emissaries and even conducted a prisoner exchange in 622 AD, at the Tangs request. By 624 AD the Tang Dynasty had introduced Taoism to Goguryo and scholars went to China to study. However, the Tang Dynasty grew quickly and in 631 AD they sent a small number of troops into Goguryo to destroy a monument that was built to celebrate the victories over the previous Sui Dynasty.

In response to the incursion, in 631 AD, Governor Yong-Gae began a project named *'Cheolli Jangseong'* (Thousand Unit Wall), which saw a great wall built along the border with China, to defend against future incursions from the Tang Empire. This wasn't just a wall however, but much like the Great Wall of China, it housed military garrisons every 500 yards or so. The *Cheolli Jangseong* took 16 years to complete, being finalised in 647 AD. At the same time, Goguryo forces were battling the Silla Dynasty in the South, to recover territories that they had previously lost, including one battle with Silla's famous General Kim Yoo-Sin (see Yoo-Sin chapter), who had taken one of their cities. This would not be the only time Yong-Gae would encounter Kim Yoo-Sin!

With so many forces along the wall, the now General Yong-Gae was considered too powerful, which made King Yeong-Nyu nervous. King Yeong-Nyu along with some court officials wanted to get rid of Yong-Gae and planned to have him killed, however news of the plan was leaked to Yong-Gae and he put in place a plan of his own. In 642 AD having recently become Governor of the Eastern Province of Goguryo as well, Yong-Gae invited 100 opposing court officials to a banquet he had prepared in celebration of his new position. As the

연개
Yong-Gae

officials travelled to the banquet, Yong-Gae's troops ambushed and killed all of them. Yong-Gae then took his troops and attacked the palace itself, defeating the guards and beheading King Yeong-Nyu.

Yong-Gae placed a nephew of the former king on the throne; King Bo-Jang and assumed the role of supreme head of all of Goguryo military forces and with such power, Yong-Gae basically took control of the entire kingdom. Whilst some historians see Yong-Gae's decision to dethrone the king as a simple lust for power, others feel, that due to the fact that he was a hard-liner against the Tang Dynasty and wanted to strengthen Goguryo which was, at the time, basically submitting to the Tang in the interests of peace that Yong-Gae, as his father did before him, saw that as weakness.

Also in 642 AD a high minister from Silla had travelled to Goguryo to request help due to continuous Baekje attacks on Silla. The minister's name was Kim Chun-Chu, who was destined to later become a Silla King (King Muyeol). However, it is said that upon his arrival, King Bo-Jang recognised him as a great man and thus dangerous to Goguryo's ambitions and instead imprisoned him and sentenced him to death. In reality, as Yong-Gae was now in charge of Goguryo, it was probably Yong-Gae who recognised Kim Chun-Chu's traits and forced the Kings actions. Unbeknown to either of them however, was that Kim Chun-Chu was a blood brother of the great Silla General, Kim Yoo-Sin and upon hearing of his imprisonment, Kim Yoo-Sin trained a special Hwa-Rang army to rescue Kim Chun-Chu. A spy reported that Kim Yoo-Sin and his troops were coming to Goguryo and Kim Chun-Chu was released before any blood was shed.

Yong-Gae's hard-line approach to the Tang empire had far reaching consequences, as Silla allied with the Tang to attack Goguryo, who they both saw as a common enemy, which eventually saw the fall of Goguryo altogether in 668 AD by a Silla-Tang alliance. However, at first, Yong-Gae attempted to pacify the Tang somewhat, possibly as he expected an invasion very soon, due to his ambitions towards Silla. To this end, he supported the rise of Taoism above the countries current religion of Buddhism and sent emissaries to China to request Taoist sages to study under, which was well received as China sent 8 sages back to Goguryo. Just 3 years later however, Goguryo and the

From Creation To Unification
The Complete Histories Behind The Ch'ang Hon (ITF) Patterns

Tang would be at war, as General Yong-Gae attacked Silla!

Silla was already at war with Baekje who had formed an alliance with Goguryo. With Silla weakening, Queen Sun-Duk (see Sun-Duk chapter) formed the Silla-Tang alliance and moved to conquer Baekje, which it finally did at *The Battle of Hwangsan Field* (see Ge-Baek and Yoo-Sin chapters) in 660 AD

Prior to that however, attacks on Goguryo had already begun and in 645 AD the Tang Emperor; Taizong (a great military tactician himself who had never been beaten) sent 170,000 troops towards the Goguryo fortresses of Lyodong and Ansi, which were located close to the border. Goguryo prepared for the attack with 100,000 men of its own. The Tang forces won many battles that were fought outside the castles and using some clever tactics, took the Lyodong fortress.

Emperor Taizong of the Tang Dynasty

The fortress at Ansi Sung was a different matter however and it was well defended by troops under the command of Yang Man-Chun[177]; Commander of the Fortress. With the weather worsening in late September Emperor Taizong ordered a 'earthen siege ramp' to be built, but Commander Yang Man-Chun captured it and used it to his own troops advantage. Meanwhile, General Yong-Gae's own troops had defeated Elite Tang Marine's, sent by Emperor Taizong to capture Pyong-Yang and immediately following

Commander Yang Man-Chun

---

[177] When Yong-Gae took control of Goguryo, Yang Man-Chun had refused to give up the Ansi Sung fortress to General Yong-Gae. General Yong-Gae attacked it, laid siege to it, but could never take it, so left control of it to its commander, Yang Man-Chun.

연개
Yong-Gae

General Yong-Gae in battle

the victory, Yong-Gae led his troops towards Ansi.

Eventually, Emperor Taizong's troops retreated, due to the worsening weather conditions, low food supplies and the threat of being caught between two large Goguryo forces. General Yong-Gae's troops pursued the retreating Tang forces, killing many Tang soldiers - this was Emperor Taizong's first and only defeat!

Despite the defeat at Ansi the main Tang force survived and they had also inflicted heavy casualties on the Goguryo troops. More so, it led to Emperor Taizong becoming obsessed with defeating Goguryo, an obsession that was carried on by his son; Emperor Gaozong, following Taizong's death in 649 AD.

In 661 AD Emperor Gaozong of the Tang Dynasty led another massive attack on Goguryo, sending 350,000 troops to attack, but the invasion failed. In 662 AD the Tang army once again attacked Goguryo and once again failed in an even worse defeat than the previous year, as one of the great Tang Generals and his sons were killed during one battle. Despite the loses, both the Tang and Silla Dynasties kept up assaults on Goguryo for another 8 years, slowly grinding it down.

From Creation To Unification
The Complete Histories Behind The Ch'ang Hon (ITF) Patterns

In 666 AD General Yong-Gae passed away; in his time as the real leader of the Goguryo, neither Silla nor Tang or even their combined forces had managed to capture Goguryo. Following his death, a power struggle ensued between Yong-Gae's three sons; Yeon Nam-Saeng, Yeon Nam-Geon, and Yeon Nam-San for control of the kingdom and with Goguryo in turmoil, the way was finally paved for a successful Silla-Tang victory over the kingdom and Goguryo fell in 668 AD, just 2 years after Yong-Gae's death. The fall of Goguryo, along with the earlier fall of Baekje united the county under what is known as Unified Silla.

Historian's opinions on Yong-Gae are divided; ancient Silla and Tang records portray him as a brutal dictator and disloyal subject, hell bent on power, saying that he carried no less than 5 swords and forced subjects to become his 'steps', by bending over so he could stand on their backs and mount his horse! They say that Yong-Gae unnecessarily provoked the Tang into war and that led to the dynasty's downfall.

On the other side, defenders of Yong-Gae claim that the Tang would have invaded regardless as that was their ambition anyway and the rest (of the Silla/Tang writings) are simply history written by a jealous and bitter enemy and in fact Yong-Gae should be seen as a patriot as he did what was necessary for the sake of the Goguryo Dynasty, which he defended so resolutely.

In 2006 a Korean television series aired over 100 episodes about the life of Yong-Gae; titled '*Yeon Gaesomu*'

을지
Ul-Ji

Ul-Ji is named after General Ul-Ji Moon Dok who successfully defended Korea against a Tang[178] invasion force of nearly one million soldiers led by Yang Je in 612 A.D., Ul-Ji employing hit and run guerrilla tactics, was able to decimate a large percentage of the force. The diagram represents his surname. The 42 movements represent the author's age when he designed the pattern.

Ul-Ji is the twentieth pattern of Ch'ang Hon Taekwon-Do, usually taught at 4th Degree Black belt. It has 42 moves and was developed in Korea around 1957 with the help of Master Han, Cha Kyo. Though it is the twentieth pattern practiced by students, it was the third pattern for Ch'ang Hon Taekwon-Do ever developed.

Ul-Ji Moon Dok was born in the middle of the 6th Century[179] and came from an area known as Mt. Seokda, Pyongyang. He was born into the Kingdom of Goguryo, which had grown large and powerful and often warred with its neighbours; Silla and Baekje (to the South) as well as the Chinese Sui Dynasty to the North and West.

Not much is known about Ul-Ji's early years, but he grew into an educated man, skilled both in politics as well as military tactics and became Prime Minister of Goguryo.

In 589 AD the Sui Dynasty of China defeated the former Chen Dynasty and united China for the first time in over 300 years. The Sui

---

[178] It was actually the Sui Dynasty invasion force, the Tang Dynasty succeeded them.

[179] His exact birth date is unknown.

From Creation To Unification
The Complete Histories Behind The Ch'ang Hon (ITF) Patterns

Dynasty now saw themselves as a mighty power throughout all of Asia and started to assert their dominance all over the Far East. While most countries submitted, the Korean Kingdoms did not and Goguryo, being the closest to the border simply felt they were the equals of the Sui Dynasty and tried to maintain a balanced relationship with them – much to the Sui's displeasure, which was further heightened as despite the uneasy peace, Goguryo often sent small raiding parties over the border to some of the Sui villages.

The Sui Dynasty was already involved in several conflicts; on their home soil they were at war with Turkish nomads, whilst further afield they were fighting in Vietnam, trying to regain former territories which were originally parts of earlier Chinese dynasties. Then in 596 AD Chinese spies spotted Goguryo diplomats in the hut of a Turkish leader and the Sui Emperor had had enough. The Sui sent an envoy to Goguryo, demanding they break all ties with the Turks, as well as to stop the raiding of the Sui villages across the border and finally to acknowledge the Sui Dynasty as their lords! At first it seemed to the Sui that King Yeong-Yang (of Goguryo) was going to comply with their demands, but it was simply a delaying tactic, as a year later, in 597 AD, a joint force of Goguryo and Mohe[180] soldiers attacked Sui outposts along the borders of China.

The Sui Emperor (Wen) retaliated by ordering one of his sons (Yang Liang), along with an Admiral Zhou, to destroy and conquer Goguryo. General Yang Liang took 300,000 troops into Goguryo but a heavy rainy season bogged the troops down and hampered their supply efforts leaving them at the mercy of many attacks by Goguryo troops, which eventually led General Yang to retreat and create a combined attack force with the navy led by Admiral Zhou. However, this course of action didn't fare any better, as when the Chinese forces landed, they were immediately attacked by Goguryo troops. At the end of this first expedition, the Sui Dynasty had lost 90% of its total forces!

In 604 AD Emperor Wen died and was succeeded by Emperor Yang. Emperor Yang rebuilt the Sui Empire, most notably building a canal

---

[180] The Mohe were a race from ancient Manchuria, often considered the ancestors of the Jurchen's (which we first heard about in the Choong-Moo chapter - see page 110).

을지
Ul-Ji

(known as the Grand Canal) to connect the north and south of China and in 611 AD he ordered all his soldiers to what is now Beijing, with the canal allowing the movement of so many troops much more easily than marching across thousands of miles of land! According to the *Book of Sui*[181] the army was *"one of the greatest in civilization"*.

The following year (612 AD) over a million troops started to march towards Manchuria, en route to Pyongyang in Goguryo. It is said that the army took 40 days to depart due to its massive size and that the line of soldiers stretched back for over 250 miles!

Emperor Yang of the Sui Dynasty

Faced with such a massive force, King Yeong-Yang gave up the Sui territories he had taken and ordered all Goguryo troops back beyond the Liao River. The river was frozen, so the Goguryo forces crossed it quickly, but by the time the Sui troops had arrived, the river had melted and the Sui troops were forced to build three bridges to cross it, all the while under constant attacks from Goguryo troops.

Ul-Ji Moon Dok was commissioned as a Field Marshal and ordered to defend the nation. Faced with the superior size of the Sui force, Ul-Ji decided on a tactic of deception, where his troops would attack and then feign retreat. Another tactic he employed was *Chongya*, which was similar to a 'scorched earth' policy and Ul-Ji ordered the land be cleared of all food supplies or anything else that may help

A bronze statue of Ul-Ji Moon Dok

---

[181] A book that compiled the history of the Sui Dynasty

the enemy. He sent all non-military people South, deeper into Goguryo, carrying their belongings, so nothing was left for the approaching enemy.

Prior to the campaign, Sui Emperor Yang had ordered his own Generals not to make individual decisions regarding troop movements and that all orders must go through him first – this was a strategy that would hamper the Sui for the whole war. Once the Sui had crossed the Liao River, Emperor Yang ordered a contingent of soldiers to take the Goguryo city of Yodong. The besieged city was close to surrender but by the time the Sui General in charge had sent a messenger back to Emperor Yang to approve the surrender, an Admiral sent by Ul-Ji (Admiral Gang I-Sik) had arrived and reinforced the fortress's defences and the Sui siege was defeated. Similar situations happened elsewhere and five months into the campaign, neither Yodong or any other Goguryo castle had been captured!

The rainy season had held the Sui troops back from any major offensives, but as it closed Emperor Yang moved all his troops to the banks of the Yalu river[182] in order for a decisive battle. However, the major battle never came as Ul-Ji was too smart to take on such a big force head on and instead chose to attack small contingents of Sui troops when and where he wanted, before retreating, forcing Emperor Yang to decide on a new strategy.

As supplies and provisions were easily carried through China, but the lands of Goguryo were basically void of anything that the troops could use, Emperor Yang set up a main base in Manchuria and ordered 305,000 Sui soldiers, with the support of 200,000 sailors of the Sui Navy, to take the fortress at Pyongyang.

The Sui navy reached Pyongyang before the ground troops and a small force of Goguryo ships were sent to engage them; after a short battle the Goguryo ships retreated – which was all part of a bigger plan. Upon seeing the retreat, the Sui Navy commander felt he had a chance to defeat the fortress on his own and by doing so he would

---

[182] A dividing river that runs on the border between China and North Korea, known as the Amrok river to Koreans. See map on page 197.

을지
Ul-Ji

gain higher position (within the Sui Dynasty). Admiral Lai Huni led 100,000 of his men to assault the fortress, but as they approached they noticed the main gates were open and the walls were unguarded – it looked as if the troops guarding the fortress had fled! As they entered the fortress, the Sui troops saw weapons and valuables just sitting there in the open – however, Admiral Lai was cautious and didn't allow his troops to loot the weapons or valuables and instead ordered them forward into the fortress. As Admiral Lai's troops passed a huge Buddhist temple, Goguryo soldiers flooded out and ambushed them, but the Sui troops held them off, forcing the Goguryo troops to flee further back in to the fortress. Admiral Lai saw the small victory as a good omen and allowed his men to loot the valuables and weapons they had passed by earlier. However, Admiral Lai was mistaken in thinking that the soldiers that had tried to ambushed them earlier on were the only soldiers in the fortress and as his men looted around the fortress, special contingents consisting of thousands of Goguryo troops were dispatched and with their guard down, the Sui sailors were defeated, forcing Admiral Lai to run for his life and return to his ships. With his forces now down to just a few thousand from the previous 200,000, the Admiral decided to wait and combine his troops with the Sui army approaching by land.

However, as the attack on the fortress was being repulsed, the Sui land troops continued towards Pyongyang. To combat the problem of the distance between the Sui troops and their main supplies, the soldiers had been ordered to carry their own personal food supplies, however, this increased what they had to carry considerably, tiring the soldiers out, so many simply discarded much of the provisions and by the time they drew close to Pyongyang, many were tired and hungry and provisions all round were running out.

King Yeong-Yang wanted to know the strength of the approaching Sui forces and ordered Ul-Ji to visit the Sui forces to assess them, under the pretence of establishing a peace agreement. Ul-Ji did this, but what he didn't know was that the Sui Generals had secret orders to capture either King Yeong-Yang or Field Marshal Ul-Ji should the chance arise, however, the Sui Generals advisors convinced them it would not be a wise move to capture a peace negotiator and Ul-Ji was free to leave with the Sui's terms of surrender and was able to report

From Creation To Unification
The Complete Histories Behind The Ch'ang Hon (ITF) Patterns

back to the King that his plan was working and the Sui troops were tired and low on supplies.[183] General Yu (one of the two Commanding Sui Officers) later regretted the decision to let Ul-Ji go and tried to redress his error by inviting Ul-Ji back for further talks – a plan that failed as Ul-Ji was aware of the plan and knew it was a trap!

The two Sui Generals were undecided as to whether to pursue Ul-Ji or continue with their original plan and carry on towards Pyongyang as they recognised their men were exhausted and that the taking of the fortress seemed less and less likely. Ul-Ji wanted them to continue and taunted them by sending a poem[184] that read:

Ul-Ji Moon Dok

> **Your divine plans have plumbed the heavens;**
> **Your subtle reckoning has spanned the earth.**
> **You win every battle, your military merit is great.**
> **Why then not be content and stop the war?**

Despite the setback of allowing Ul-Ji to remain free or the fact that the Sui troops were tired, cold and hungry, they continued their advance to Pyongyang. Knowing the weakening state of the enemy, Ul-Ji decided to make their advance take longer than needed and thus tire the troops out even more than they were already. As they continued towards Pyongyang, Ul-Ji's troops attacked them up to seven times a day, each time feigning defeat and withdrawing back towards Pyongyang. The idea was that they would further weaken and

---

[183] Some stories say that Ul-Ji surrendered to fulfil his goals, where as another story says that as the Navy was attacking the Pyongyang fortress, Ul-Ji raced into the enemy camp alone, riding his horse through the camp to assess their strength, before finally coming face to face with one of the Sui Generals. Ul-Ji shouted at the General *"Don't you understand that it's always the people who suffer the most from the warfare? There is no need to continue this crazy war which brings nothing but evils and pains. Why not bury the hatchet and kiss good bye to your losing battle?"* and with that, whilst the stunned General looked on, Ul-Ji sped away before the Sui troops could capture him!

[184] The poem is called the *Ul-Ji Moon Dok Hansi* and is the oldest surviving example of poetry in Korean literature.

을지
Ul-Ji

Ul-Ji's troops using 'hit and run' tactics against the Sui forces

dwindle the number of Sui troops, whilst making it seem like the Sui were still going to be victorious.

The Sui troops continued onwards and reached the Cheongcheon River in South Pyongyang province. Prior to their arrival, Ul-Ji had built a dam on the river[185] and when the Sui troops arrived, the water level of the river was very low so the Sui troops began to cross. As they did so, Ul-Ji ordered his troops to open the dam which sent cascades of water down the river, flooding it and drowning many thousands of Sui soldiers. Ul-Ji then ordered his cavalry units to

A picture showing the river flooding and Ul-Ji's Calvary at Salsu

charge the remaining Sui troops, who were already running around in confusion. As Ul-Ji's Calvary charged, the Sui troops fled in full retreat, but Ul-Ji's cavalry troops pursued and killed as many as they could. Known as the *'Battle of Salsu'* it is said of the original 305,000 soldiers sent to Pyongyang only 2,700 returned alive. It is listed as one of the most lethal classical formation battles in history, due to the

---

[185] Another version says he also destroyed a bridge to force the troops to cross the river bed.

From Creation To Unification
The Complete Histories Behind The Ch'ang Hon (ITF) Patterns

Confusion reigned at the Battle of Salsu

number of Sui casualties, compared to the minimal loses of Goguryo troops!

Following the defeat at Salsu winter set in and low on men and provisions, the remnants of the Sui army were forced to return to China. Though the Sui army was to attack Goguryo again in 613 AD, once more the invasion would fail, partly due to the tactics of Ul-Ji, which were employed so successfully before, but also due to internal conflicts within the Sui Dynasty itself. In 614 AD Emperor Yang tried one more unsuccessful campaign against Goguryo and once again, the hit and run tactics Goguryo employed worked well, and with the Sui forces dwindling once again, sensing a chance to end the wars once and for all, King Yeong-Yang pressed for peace, which Emperor Yang accepted as he felt further battles against Goguryo forces would yield the same results and instead, withdrew his troops and returned to China in order to deal with the Sui's own internal conflicts. The wars with Goguryo had left the Sui Dynasty in a very weakened state and its people started to rebel. A few years after returning to China, Emperor Yang was assassinated and the Sui Dynasty came to an end in 618 AD,

을지
Ul-Ji

paving the way for the Tang Dynasty to rise.

Ul-Ji passed away[186] shortly after the fall of the Sui Dynasty, having defined the strategies that defended the empire from Chinese domination, however the wars were also costly to Goguryo and though peace with China remained for a while, as Goguryo recovered and the new Tang Dynasty concentrated on building itself within, Goguryo would eventually fall to a Silla-Tang alliance some 50 years later.[187]

300 years later, during his reign, King Hyeon-Jong of Goryeo had a shrine built near Pyongyang to honour Ul-Ji and in 1680, King Suk-Jong of the Joseon Dynasty built another shrine in Ul-Ji's honour. During the Japanese occupation of Korea in the 20th Century, Korean historian, Sin Chae-Ho wrote a biography of Ul-Ji's life which was used to promote Korean nationalism, showing the achievements of Ul-Ji as a shining example of Korea's tradition of resisting oppression. Ul-Ji remains a hero of Korea and is recognized as one of its greatest Commanders with the 2nd Highest Military medal of South Korea[188] named in his honour and a South Korean Naval Destroyer is also named after him. Every couple of years, South Korea and the USA run simulated computer exercises named the '*Ul-Ji Freedom Guardian*', which are designed to simulate how South Korea would defend itself against a North Korean attack!

A Korean stamp commemorating Ul-Ji's victory at Salsu

Though the pattern definition now states that the number of moves in the pattern represent the authors (General Choi's) age when he designed it, the math's do not exactly add up, as General Choi would

---

[186] The actual date or even year he passed away is unknown.

[187] See Yong-Gae chapter for details of Goguryo's eventual demise.

[188] 'Field Marshal Lord Ul-Ji's Order of Military Merit'

From Creation To Unification
The Complete Histories Behind The Ch'ang Hon (ITF) Patterns

had been 38 or 39 when it was made, it does however, coincide with the dates he first published it in print, which was in his first book on Taekwon-Do, released in 1959. Originally however, his first English book didn't include this part of the definition, which was added later.[189]

ROK Destroyer Ulchi Mundok

A statue of the Great Commander Ul-Ji Moon Dok in North Korea [190]

---

[189] Choi's first English book was released in 1965, so I presume he didn't include it in his 1959 book, which was in Korean, otherwise it would have been transferred over to the English book.

[190] Picture courtesy of Dr. George Vitale, VIII

문무
Moon-Moo

Moon-Moo honours the 30th King of the Silla Dynasty. His body was buried near Dae Wang Am (Great King's Rock). According to his will, the body was placed in the sea "where my soul shall forever defend my land against the Japanese." It is said that the Sok Gul Am (Stone cave) was built to guard his tomb. The Sok Gul Am is a fine example of the culture of the Silla Dynasty. The 61 movements in this pattern symbolize the last two figures of 661 A.D. when Moon Moo came to the throne.

Moon-Moo is the twenty first pattern of Ch'ang Hon Taekwon-Do, usually taught at 4th Degree Black belt. It has 61 moves and was developed in Korea around 1968 with the help of Master Cho, Sang Min.[191]

Moon-Moo was born in 626 AD as Prince Kim Beom-Min and was the son of King Muyeol, the 29th King of the Silla Dynasty (see Yoo-Sin and Yong-Gae chapters). His mother, Queen Mun-Myeong was the younger sister of Kim, Yoo-Sin.

During his father's reign he held a governmental position that was responsible for all of Silla's maritime affairs. His father was a friend of the Chinese Tang Emperor, Gaozong, whom he had known even before he had assumed the role of Emperor and

King Moon-Moo

---

[191] Master J. C. Kim, Master Park, Jong Soo, Master Lee, Byung Moo and others may also have helped in the formulation of this pattern.

From Creation To Unification
The Complete Histories Behind The Ch'ang Hon (ITF) Patterns

when Goguryo and Baekje combined their forces and attacked Silla, in 655 AD King Muyeol called on his old friend, Emperor Gaozong, for aid.

In 660 AD a combined Silla and Tang army defeated Baekje (see Ge-Baek chapter) and turned their sights on Goguryo, however a year later (in 661 AD) King Muyeol passed away and his son, Prince Beom-Min took the throne, taking the name King Moon-Moo, becoming the 30th King of the Silla Dynasty. King Moon-Moo continued with his fathers plans to defeat Goguryo and attacked it in the same year, but they (the Silla and Tang forces) were unsuccessful.

Despite the initial defeat, Moon-Moo did not give up and in 667 AD he attacked again. Goguryo had not fully recovered from the earlier attack and in 668 AD Goguryo finally fell, making Moon-Moo the 1st King of 'Unified Korea' – the first time in Korea's history that it was fully united under one King.

Though it was a combined Silla and Tang army that brought about a Unified Silla, the Tang were eager to expand and dominate the Far East and wanted the whole of Korea under their control, even their ally, the Silla Dynasty. As they asserted their authority, the Tang placed a protectorate general's office[192] in Silla territory but Moon-Moo resisted their attempts and their previous alliance fell apart. Tang General Xue Li was in charge of the protectorate general's office and former Goguryo King; Bo-Jang became a governor for a period, before eventually being banished for helping form rebellions against the Tang, as he tried to revive his old kingdom.

By 674 AD the Silla and Tang were engaging in frequent battles, as Moon-Moo attempted to defend not only the original territory that Silla held, but the new Unified Silla territories that were formerly Baekje and Goguryo. In order to bolster his forces, Moon-Moo sought help from a resistance group that had emerged in Goguryo following its fall. The resistance was led by Geom Mojam and An-Seung, with Geom thought to have been the illegitimate son of Goguryo's last King; Bo-Jang and An-Seung also a great nephew. An-

---

[192] Its full name was 'the office of Protectorate General to Pacify the East'

문무
Moon-Moo

Seung was proclaimed the new leader of Goguryo which was attempting to establish a new state within the Unified Silla territories and, in order to gain their help and support, King Moon-Moo proclaimed An-Seung as 'King of Bodeok' and commissioned some territory for him to rule, telling him to gather his former people, keep their old traditions but also give them new lives, to be as a neighbour to Silla and to conduct affairs as brothers. However, this territory wasn't in Goguryo, but rather in the former state of Baekje and former Goguryo people flocked there, unbeknown to them that the state was set up as a buffer between a Tang invasion and the main capital and lands of the old Silla!

Emperor Gaozong grew angry at Moon-Moo's resistance to Tang rule and proclaimed his younger brother, Kim In-Mum as the true King of Silla. Kim In-Mum had been working in the service of Emperor Gaozong at the request of his father, King Muyeol, for 23 years. Kim In-Mum was ordered to return to Silla with a Tang army and take the throne from Moon-Moo. However, as he traveled towards Silla, Moon-Moo apologised and offered tributes to Emperor Gaozong, which, possibly due to his previous good

Emperor Gaozong

relationship with Moon-Moo's father, Gaozong accepted and recalled Kim In-Mum back to China and rescinded the previous claim.

The peace didn't last long as in 675 AD Mohe[193] forces attempted to occupy land owned by Silla after crossing into Silla from Manchuria. Even though the Silla forces defeated the Mohe, as they had previously submitted to the Tang Empire, it was considered a Tang incursion. A year later, the Tang sent one of its greatest Generals, Xue Li along with a naval fleet across the Yellow Sea, to invade Silla. However, his fleet was met by Silla's own navy and defeated and when Xue Li returned home, he was stripped of his rank and exiled by the

---

[193] The Mohe were a race from ancient Manchuria, often considered the ancestors of the Jurchen's (which we first heard about in the Choong-Moo chapter - see page 110).

From Creation To Unification
The Complete Histories Behind The Ch'ang Hon (ITF) Patterns

Tang Emperor.

Following the defeat of General Xue Li, Emperor Gaozong ordered all Tang forces to withdraw from Silla and moved the protectorate general's office to China. By 679 AD any future plans to invade Silla were put to rest as a revolt against the Tang Empire by Eastern Turks made Emperor Gaozong realise he could not expend his forces or resources overseas, whilst also trying to combat problems at home. Eventually he renounced all claim to Unified Silla (Korea) and King Moon-Moo was left to rule the whole of Korea. This would also be the last time China would ever invade Korea, though Chinese troops would return to Korean soil a thousand years later, to aid the Joseon Dynasty against the Japanese invasion in the 16th Century; known as the Imjin war (see Choong-Moo and Choong-Jang chapters) and again during the Korean war in 1950.

In 681 AD, five years after the last major battle with China, King Moon-Moo fell ill and on his deathbed abdicated the throne to his son saying *"A country should not be without a king at any time. Let the Prince have my crown before he has my coffin. Cremate my remains and scatter the ashes in the sea where the whales live. I will become a dragon and thwart foreign invasion"*

As requested, Moon-Moo's ashes were scattered into the sea at Dae Wang Am (the Rock of the Great King), which is just 100 metres off the coast of Korea. His son, King Sin-Moo also built a temple in memory of his father – Gomun-sa Temple (the Temple of Appreciated Blessing) - the temple was connected to the sea by a

Dae Wang Am (the Rock of the Great King)
Picture courtesy of Dr. George Vitale, VIII

문무
Moon-Moo

Gomun-sa Temple
Picture courtesy of Jordan VanHartingsveld

waterway, so that his father; the sea dragon could travel between the sea and the land, it was also built with empty space below its floor, where the 'dragon' could sleep. Finally, he built a pavilion that over looked Dae Wang Am, where future kings could look out over Moon-Moo's tomb and pay their respects.

It is said that King Sin-Moo had a dream and in it, his father Moon-Moo and Kim Yoo-Sin appeared and told him that *"Blowing on a bamboo flute will calm the heavens and the earth"*. When he awoke, he rode to the sea and found a bamboo flute and, upon blowing it, invoked the spirits

Dae Wang Am viewed from above

From Creation To Unification
The Complete Histories Behind The Ch'ang Hon (ITF) Patterns

of Moon-Moo and Yoo-Sin so that they would push back enemy troops, cure illnesses and control the rains during floods or droughts!

King Sin-Moo ruled Unified Silla for 11 years until he died in 692 AD. In that time he reorganized the Kingdom into 9 provinces, expanded the government, fought off revolts and established the Gukhak (National Academy), a place where government officials could study the Confucian classics.

In 1796 a stele dedicated to Moon-Moo was discovered in Gyeongju, a coastal city in South Korea, but somehow it went missing. Part of it turned up again in 1961 and in 2012 another part (the top) was found in a traditional Korean house (a hanok), where it had been used as a platform for a water basin. It has yet to be fully translated.

Moon-Moo Steele

Sok Gul Am (Stone Cave)

서산
So-San

So-San is the pseudonym of the great monk Choi Hyong Ung (1520-1604) during the Yi Dynasty. The 72 movements refer to his age when he organized a corps of monk soldiers with the assistance of his pupil Sa Myunh Dang. The monk soldiers helped repulse the Japanese pirates who overran most of the Korean peninsula in 1592.

So-San is the twenty second pattern of Ch'ang Hon Taekwon-Do, usually taught at 5th Degree Black belt. It has 72 moves and was developed in Korea around 1968 with the help of Master Cho, Sang Min.[194]

Choi Hyong-Ung was born in 1520 during the reign of King Jung-Jong of the Joseon (Yi) Dynasty. His childhood remains a mystery and all that is known is that he was educated in Neo-Confucianism before he became a Buddhist monk. At that time in Korea, in fact since the start of the Yi Dynasty over 100 years before[195], Buddhism was frowned upon in favour of Taoism, but Choi Hyong-Ung felt that even though the state opposed Buddhism the Dharma[196] didn't allow him to turn his back on those that needed its teachings, so he travelled the land teaching Buddhism, staying at various monasteries as he did so.

---

[194] Master Kim, Jong Chan (J.C.), Master Park, Jong Soo, Master Lee, Byung Moo and Master Kim, Young Soo and others may also have helped in the formulation of this pattern.

[195] Yi Seong-Gye, founder of the Joseon Dynasty, had brought Taoist monks from China to pacify the ruling Ming Dynasty and rebuild relationships with them, as the former government had pushed for war against the Ming.

[196] Dharma; Law of the Universe or Natural Law, as well as referring to the doctrines of the founders of Buddhism

From Creation To Unification
The Complete Histories Behind The Ch'ang Hon (ITF) Patterns

Following the death of King Jung-Jong in 1544, his first son (In-Jong) took the throne, but only ruled for a year and died[197] himself in 1545 and was succeeded by Jung-Jong's second son, Myeong-Jong. However, King Myeong-Jong was only 12 years old when he took the throne, so his mother, Queen Mun-Jong (the 3rd wife of King Jung-Jong) became Queen Regent and ruled the country in his name.

Queen Mun-Jong's influence was far reaching and she did much good for the people of Korea. Even after her son reached twenty years of age, the age considered mature enough for him to rule without a regent, his mother still remained in control. She gave land formerly owned by nobility to the common people but most importantly for So-San, she lifted the previous ban on Buddhism and supported its resurgence into the kingdom.

A picture of Choi Hyong-Ung

So-San had grown to become a Zen master, known as a 'Seon' or 'Meditation' Master, he taught and guided hundreds of pupils, many of whom also became Seon Masters. He authored many religious texts; the most important of which is called the 'Seonga Gwigam' (Mirror for Seon), which is a guide to religious practice and is still studied by monks today. So-San believed in meditation as well as the reading of Buddhist doctrines, seeing them as the two wings on the bird to enlightenment. He saw the doctrines as the information to practice Buddhism, whilst meditation was the most effective path to 'truth'. Initially schooled in Neo-Confucianism before converting to Buddhism, So-San believed that, along with Confucianism as well, the essence of each taught the same thing – the truth of the mind – which

---

[197] Though always a sickly child, some historians believed that In-Jong was poisoned by one of the government factions at the time, so his half-brother could take the throne which would give them more power.

서산
So-San

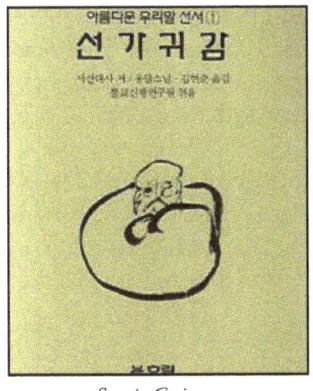

Seonja Gwigarn

was the foundation of all humanity, heaven and earth and thus, the mother of the universe and it is within the mind that good, evil, assumptions and ideologies are born.

King Myeong-Jong was impressed enough to give him an important position at the Seon School, however, So-San did not enjoy the role and soon resigned, returning to his travelling ways, teaching at the monasteries.

In 1567 a new king came to the throne, following the death of King Myeong-Jong (whose mother had died a couple of years earlier). King Seonjo continued with various governmental reforms, but a serious divide in the government started to form (see Yul-Gok chapter – East/West divide); this weakened the kingdom and caused much political bickering. By the late 1580's, a united Japan was trying to expand its empire and was viewed as a possible threat to the Joseon Dynasty.

In 1583 the noted scholar Yul-Gok (see Yul-Gok chapter) had proposed that the government train a 100,000 man Army Reserve, to reinforce the regular army should the Japanese attack Korea, but due to the political bickering he was ignored. With the threat still present, the king was urged to send delegates to Japan to find out their intentions towards Korea, however, the divide within the government was so bad, the two sides couldn't even decide who the best delegate to go was, so in the end they sent one from each side! The delegates returned with a letter from Hideyoshi Toyotomi inviting the king to submit

An older Choi Hyong-Ung

From Creation To Unification
The Complete Histories Behind The Ch'ang Hon (ITF) Patterns

to Japan and fight with them in their intended invasion of China. The delegates also reported that Toyotomi had raised a huge army, but one of the delegates told the king that he thought the army was to quell internal problems in Japan and was not a threat to Korea. After many discussions within the court, it was decided that the letter was not a real threat and Japan was simply trying to sort out its own problems and raise its army to fight China, not Korea. The court debated whether to inform the Ming Dynasty about Japans ambitions, in case they were seen as aligning themselves with the Japanese, but in the end, simply decided to remain quiet.

In 1591 a letter arrived for King Seonjo, requesting that Japanese troops be allowed to pass through Korea, so that they may invade China. The King refused the request, as he felt it was simply a ruse so that Japan could invade Korea and he finally made preparations for an attack. He built forts along the coast and sent an emissary to China to tell them of the Japanese intentions. In 1592 the Japanese invaded Korea and though King Seonjo had started preparations, it was really too little, too late and the Imjin War began![198]

The invasion began with 7000 Japanese troops arriving and taking the port of Busan. The poorly trained Joseon soldiers were continually defeated in land battles, even though at sea, the Joseon Navy were faring much better (See Choong-Moo chapter). King Seonjo fled the capital and in desperation called on So-San[199], asking him to form his monks into guerilla units and help defend the country – So-San was 72 years old at the time!

Despite his age, So-San did as the King had asked and established a secret base in a monastery high in Yeong-Chwisan Mountain, which he operated from. At this base he formed the 'Righteous Army'; a guerilla army which eventually consisted of over 5000 warrior monks, with So-San at the head. The monks were split into divisions, with So-San and his senior students leading them; So-San's own division had an estimated 1,500 warrior monks itself. The monks fought against the

---

[198] The Imjin War also known as the 'Seven Year War'. See page 23, footnote 17 for more details.

[199] Some accounts say that So-San formed the army on his own accord, with no prompting needed.

서산
So-San

Japanese troops firing arquebuses[200] with only sickles and spears and won many victories.

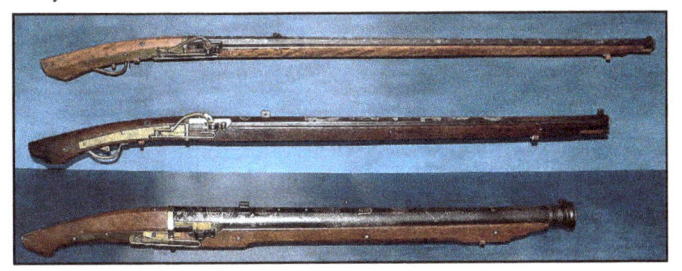

Japanese arquebus's [201]

Of his leading students, one of the most notable was Yu Jeong (Sa Myunh Dang in General Choi's original description[202]), who fought in many battles. Yu Jeong seemed fearless and would lead secret intelligence gathering operations himself, that saw his troops sneak directly into the enemy bases. Yu Jeong would sometimes use the information he gained in peace talks with the Japanese troops and on one occasion, he met with General Kiyomasa Kato and shocked him when he said that Korea's greatest prize was Kato's head, as peace would only come to Korea once Kato's head had been removed!

Yu Jeong

Inspired by the monks and incensed by the Japanese, other guerilla armies formed around the country. It is said that So-San, along with allied Ming soldiers, recaptured the capital Pyongyang.

In January, 1604 So-San gave his last lesson to his students and when

---

[200] An arquebus was an early flintlock rifle, the forerunner of the modern day rifle.

[201] Rama & World Imaging, Cc-by-sa-2.0-fr

[202] Yu Jeong is the Buddhist name of Sam Yeong-Dang aka Sa Myunh Dang

From Creation To Unification
The Complete Histories Behind The Ch'ang Hon (ITF) Patterns

he had finished he took out a portrait of himself and wrote one final teaching for his students, which numbered over a thousand by this time, it said:

"80 years ago, that image was me. 80 years later, I am that image now."

Following his final teaching, it is said that So-San went into the lotus position and entered Nirvana, passing away, aged 84.

His full title was Seosan Daesa which meant 'Great Master of the Western Mountain'. Apart from being revered as a great teacher of Buddhism and leading the fighting monks against the Japanese invaders, he was also thought to have

So-San

A statue of So-San at Daeheung Temple

230

서산
So-San

revived the Buddhist tea ceremony in Korea, after it died out following Yi Seong-Gye's persecution against Buddhists. In 1972 a film called 'The Great Monk Seo San' was released in Korea which, with some artistic license, notes So-San's famous role building the warrior monk army.

As a final note, when the Imjin war was over, King Seonja sent Yu-Jeong (So-San's pupil) to Japan for peace talks with Ieyasu Tokugawa (Toyotomi's successor), where he was met with respect and reverence for his actions during the war. When he returned to Korea, Yu-Jeong brought with him 3,500 Korean prisoners of war and returned to Japan many more times to lay a foundation for the future between Korea and Japan.

As with his teacher So-San, Yu-Jeong was also highly regarded for his Buddhist writings as well as his efforts during the war. A statue of Yu-Jeong was built at a temple in Kyoto (Japans former capital city of Imperial Japan), which shows just how much respect they had for him.

Yu-Jeong's statue in Kyoto

"It is from numberless diverse acts of courage and belief that human history is shaped. Each time a man stands up for an ideal, or acts to improve the lot of others, or strikes out against injustice, he sends forth a tiny ripple of hope."

- Robert Kennedy

세종
Se-Jong

Se-Jong is named after the greatest Korean King, Se-Jong, who invented the Korean alphabet in 1443, and was also a noted meteorologist. The diagram represents the king, while the 24 movements refer to the 24 letters of the Korean alphabet

Se-Jong is the twenty third pattern of of Ch'ang Hon Taekwon-Do, usually taught at 5th Degree Black belt. It has 24 moves and was developed in Malaysia between 1962 and 1964 with the help of Master Kim, Bok Man and Master Woo, Jae Lim.

Se-Jong (whose birth name was Yi-Do) was born the 3rd son of King Tae-Jong (the 3rd king of the Joseon Dynasty) on 7th May, 1397[203] and proclaimed a Grand Prince at the age of 12. He took the name Grand Prince Choong-Nyung and despite being the 3rd son, his father favoured him over his brothers as he excelled at his studies and even Se-Jong's older brother, the 1st born Yi-Je (later to become Grand Prince Yang-Nyeong) recognised Se-Jong's 'kingly' qualities, feeling that he himself lacked the skills required to make a great king and so believed it was his duty to ensure Se-Jong became king.[204] In order to achieve his 'duty' Grand Prince Yang-Nyeong manoeuvred his own banishment from the royal court and even the capital Seoul itself, by behaving rudely to court officials and

---

[203] Some sources give his birth date as 6th or 7th May 1397, whilst others state it as 15th May 1397. Consequently, his death dates also conflict, as some sources list it as 8th April 1450, while others list it as 18th May 1450.

[204] See next page for a different version of these events

From Creation To Unification
The Complete Histories Behind The Ch'ang Hon (ITF) Patterns

marrying a peasant girl[205]. Se-Jong's 2nd brother; Grand Prince Hyo-Ryeong felt the same about Se-Jong as his older brother and helped clear the way to the throne by becoming a Buddhist monk and living in a Buddhist temple.

Yi-Je recognising Se-Jong's 'kingly' qualities and stepping aside after feeling he lacked the 'kingly' skills himself and thus making it his 'duty' to ensure Se-Jong became king, may be the more romantic version of the story. However, history has shown us how rare it would have been for two older brothers to simply give up the throne so easily and it may have more to do with the kingdoms history than most stories would say; King Taejo (Yi Seong-Gye) was Se-Jong's grandfather and founded the Joseon Dynasty in 1392, when he overthrew the Goryeo dynasty (see Choi-Yong chapter). Yi Bang-Won (King Taejo's 5th son) was seen as King Taejo's most likely successor, as he had assisted his father when he took the throne. However, a number of court officials, led by Prime Minister Jeong Do-Jeon detested Yi Bang-Won and convinced King Taejo to name his 8th son Yi Bang-Seok as his successor and so Yi Bang-Seok was named the crown prince.

Whilst King Taejo was in mourning due to the loss of his wife, Jeong Do-Jeon hatched a plan to kill off Yi Bang-Won and his brothers to ensure Yi Bang-Seok took the throne, thus securing his own position as Prime Minister in the process. Yi Bang-Won came to hear of the plan and stormed the palace with his army and killed Jeong Do-Jeon, as well as two of his own brothers, including Yi Bang-Seok.

Shocked and horrified that his own sons were killing each other in order to gain power King Taejo immediately crowned his 2nd son, Yi Bang-Gwa as king (known as King Jeong-Jong) and abdicated the throne in 1398. Just two years later, Yi Bang-Won was fighting again, this time with another brother, Yi Bang-Gan. Yi Bang-Won's forces won and he banished his brother (Yi Bang-Gan) into exile. Upon hearing this, King Jeong-Jong was afraid of his brother and felt weak so abdicated the throne and named Yi Bang-Won as the 3rd king of

---

[205] Grand Prince Yang-Nyeong was stripped of his title of Grand Prince when he was banished. Though, once Se-Jong became King, all three brothers had a good relationship. Yi-Je would often visit him at the palace. Though Yi-Je felt he didn't have the same kingly qualities Se-Jong had, he was in fact known for his great calligraphy and literary skills. Yi-Je lived his later years travelling the land and passed away aged 67.

세종
Se-Jong

the Joseon Dynasty. Yi Bang-Won became King Tae-Jong, father of Se-Jong.

As King, Tae-Jong ruthlessly executed anyone who became too powerful, including members of his own court and even family! He executed his own wife's (Queen Wong-Gyeong) brothers, Se-Jong's father-in-law and brothers-in-law. The romantic story tells us that his 1st son (Yi-Je) stepped aside after seeing the 'kingly' qualities of Se-Jong, but it might be more likely that Yi-Je, as well as his younger brother either feared they themselves may be executed or stepped aside in disgust at their fathers actions, which paved the way for Se-Jong to become king.

Either way, in June 1418 King Tae-Jong abdicated the throne and two months later Se-Jong was crowned King of Joseon, aged just 21. Se-Jong began to revise the government in what was seen as a revolutionary act. He appointed government positions to people from all the various social classes instead of the usual upper classes that would of gained favour in the past, his selection process was based on merit, rather than status and he brought in people whom he felt would contribute to the kingdom, irrespective of their class. Se-Jong conducted official events along the guidelines of Confucianism and encouraged the people to follow suit in their own daily lives. He wrote books on Confucianism and as such, it became the norm in every day society.

Se-Jong always put his people first. He said *"If I have to choose two, amongst army, finances, and people's minds, I would discard the army. If I had to choose one between the rest, I would discard finance. The thing that should not be*

From Creation To Unification
The Complete Histories Behind The Ch'ang Hon (ITF) Patterns

discarded until the last, is the people's trusts and their minds"[206]

Se-Jong was able to maintain good relationships with those that may be considered threats to the kingdom or have even attacked Korea in the past; including the Ming Dynasty of China and even Japan, though in 1419 he invaded a Japanese island (Tsushima) which was a known base for Japanese pirates that kept raiding Korean coastal towns.

Prior to the invasion of Tsushima, the Joseon Dynasty had an agreement with the Ashikaga Shogunate of Japan to control the pirates in exchange for trading rights with Korea. This task was given to the islands ruler, Sadashige Sō but when he died, his son, who would have succeeded him, was only an infant and control of the island was taken by a known pirate leader, Saemontaro Soda. The island was suffering a famine and the pirates started to raid China and their route to China passed by Korea, of whom they requested food, but were turned away. In response to this denial they raided the towns for food instead and when Se-Jong, and the court heard of the raids, Se-Jong (under the advice of his father) approved what is known as the *'Gihae Eastern Expedition'* which was a full scale military invasion of the island and on 9th June 1419, Se-Jong officially declared war against the island of Tsushima, saying it belonged to the Joseon Dynasty.[207]

He ordered one of his Generals (Yi Jong-Mu) to take a fleet of 227 ships and over 17,000 soldiers and invade the island. General Yi at first tried diplomacy and sent pirates that he had previously captured to request surrender, but this fell on deaf ears, so he sent an expeditionary force onto the island. The force raided the pirate villages they came across and managed to free 131 Chinese captives, 21 island slaves (local islanders forced to work for the pirates), as well as 8 kidnapped Koreans. Almost 4 weeks into the expedition, a Japanese force ambushed the Korean forces[208] resulting in 150 Korean casualties and soon after a truce was negotiated between the Joseon Dynasty and the Sō clan, whereby Tsushima was granted trading

---

[206] From the book 'Leadership of *King Sejong, CEO of the Nation'* by Choi Gi-eok

[207] At one time, Tsushima Island, known as Daema Island in Korea, was under the rule of the Silla Dynasty.

[208] Known as the Battle of Nukadake

세종
Se-Jong

privileges with Korea in exchange for maintaining control of the island and its pirates. In the years that followed, Tsushima would eventually come under the control of the Joseon Dynasty and serve as a trading hub between Korean and Japan.

Originally, like his father before him, Se-Jong frowned upon Buddhism but soon changed his mind. In recompense he actually built Buddhist temples and even took the test required to become a Buddhist monk, though he didn't actually become one.

For the first 4 years of his reign, his father (Tae-Jong) had maintained control of the military, however, when his father passed away in 1422, Se-Jong showed his acumen in this area as well. He pushed for military technology to be developed, such as cannons, mortars and other gun powder based weapons and created various military regulations that helped strengthen his forces. In 1433, he sent forces against the Manchu's where they regained territory and captured several castles; he also built forts and outposts in the north to protect the people against the Jurchen nomads.

Se-Jong is known for the many technological advances that occurred during his reign as King. He created a book; the Nongsa Jikseol, which detailed various farming techniques and aided farmers in the different agricultural areas of Korea. Se-Jong's policy of selecting officials based on merit rather than status allowed a young man with an incredible thirst for invention to come to his attention. The man was called Jang Yeong-Sil, but was born at the very bottom of the social classes of Korea, so King Se-Jong promoted him to a government position and sent him to the 'Hall of Worthies'[209] and began to fund his inventions.

Se-Jong first instructed Jang Yeong-Sil to build a celestial globe, so they would know the position of the sun, moon and stars at any time of day. Jang Yeong-Sil is also credited with improving the iron printing press, which was originally invented in 1234 by Korean minister Choe Yun-Ui, but Jang Yeong-Sil's improvements made it

---

[209] The 'Hall of Worthies' was set up by King Se-Jong in 1420 and was a royal Institute for scholarly endeavours by those personally selected by the King.

From Creation To Unification
The Complete Histories Behind The Ch'ang Hon (ITF) Patterns

The Celestial Globe

Jang Yeong-Sil

twice as fast and gave works printed on it astounding clarity. Jang Yeong-Sil is further credited with improving or inventing water clocks, weaponry, sun dials and his most noted invention – the first Korean rain gauge in 1441. However, Jang Yeong-Sil fell out of favour in 1442 after building King Se-Jong a sedan chair to travel in. Unfortunately, the chair broke whilst the King was travelling in it and it allowed those who were jealous of Jang to get a decree issued, making Jang responsible and thus he was expelled from the court and actually jailed![210]

Se-Jong is also credited for reforming the Korean calendar, which originally was based around the primary meridian running through the Chinese capital and Se-Jong had it changed so it ran through the Korean capital of Seoul, making it much more accurate for the Korean people.

Along with inventions and some medicines, Se-Jong is most well known for inventing the Korean alphabet or Hangul as it is known today. King Se-Jong felt that Hanja (Chinese text) was too complicated for the common man and was something only the highly educated could read or write and he wanted something simpler for his country. By 1444 Se-Jong has devised 28 distinctly Korean letters[211]

---

[210] Nothing is recorded of his life, following Jang Yeong-Sil being jailed.

[211] Modern Hangul only uses 24 letters today

세종
Se-Jong

and this was to become the first phonetic alphabet of Korea. His purpose was that each letter should be easily understandable by all Koreans after just a few days of study, no matter which class they were from.

Many Korean scholars opposed the new alphabet but Se-Jong pushed forward and on 9th October 1446 (celebrated as 'Hangul day' in South Korea) he published a document explaining why his country needed a new alphabet. The document was actually written in hanja and was designed to describe the new system of lettering. In the first paragraph it reads:

> *"The sounds of our language differ from those of Chinese and are not easily communicated by using Chinese graphs. Many among the ignorant, therefore, though they wish to express their sentiments in writing, have been unable to communicate. Considering this situation with compassion, I have newly devised twenty-eight letters. I wish only that the people will learn them easily and use them conveniently in their daily life."*[212]

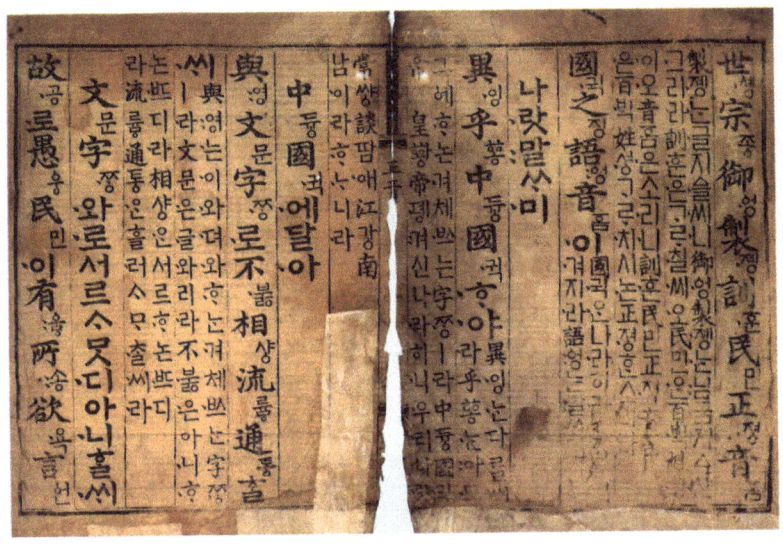

Pages from the Hunmin Jeong-Eum

---

[212] As quoted in *Sources of Korean Tradition: From Early Times through the Sixteenth Century (Hunmin Chongum, 1446)* by Peter Lee and William De Bary.

From Creation To Unification
The Complete Histories Behind The Ch'ang Hon (ITF) Patterns

The alphabet was originally called *Hunmin Jeong-Eum* after the document and it later became known as Hangul.[213] *Hunmin Jeong-Eum* means 'The Proper Sounds for the Instruction of the People'. Around one year later, King Se-Jong published the *Dongguk Jeong-un* or 'Dictionary of Proper Sino-Korean Pronunciation' (September 1447) and Hangul became the national written language of the Korean people.

As he grew older Se-Jong developed diabetes, which blinded him and eventually took his life and he passed away on 14th May 1450, aged 53. Se-Jong's reign is known as the *'Golden Age of Korean Culture'* and he is one of only two Korean kings to have been been bestowed with the additional title 'the Great', the other being King Kwang-Gae the Great.

The Korean 10,000 won note features Se-Jong on one side and the celestial globe, invented by Jang Yeong-Sil on the other.

Like many great figures in Korea's history, a South Korean Destroyer is named after Se-Jong and in 2008, a 134 episode Korean drama series aired about his life, titled *'King Sejong the Great'*.

Se-Jong's legacy lives on to this very day, as language experts recognise his invention of Hangul as scientifically sound and very beautiful, but above all a decent and honourable thing to do for the good of his people. In 1994, Hangul was described as 'the most logical language writing system in the world' by Discovery magazine and in 2009, the United Nations Development Programme reported that both North

---

[213] It was named Hangul (meaning 'Great Script') in 1912 by Korean linguist Ju Si-Gyeong. 'han' can also be translated as 'Korean', so it can also mean 'Korean Script'

세종
Se-Jong

and South Korea have a literacy rate of 99% thanks to the invention of Hangul and the ease it takes to learn it.

King Se-Jong remains revered throughout Korea, so much so, that every year his original inauguration in 1418, is re-enacted in a massive colourful ceremony, attended by both civil and military dignitaries from throughout South Korea. It takes place at the restored Gyeongbokgung Palace (meaning *Palace Greatly Blessed by Heaven*)[214] in Seoul, which was originally built by King Taejo (Founder of the Joseon Dynasty) and later expanded by King-Se-Jong.

Gyeongbokgung Palace, with the massive Gwanghwamun (Arch of Enlightenment} right at the front. - only the King was allowed to walk through the centre arch. [215]

---

[214] The palace was raised to the ground by the Japanese in 1592, rebuilt in 1867, then mostly demolished (90% of it) in 1915, by the Japanese during their occupation of Korea, where they built their own building on the site to show their dominance of Korea. Once freed from Japanese occupation, reconstruction work started on the palace again in 1990 and was finally completed in 2010, with the building of the 'Arch of Enlightenment', the palace gateway.

[215] Picture by 螺钉, Cc-by-sa-3.0

From Creation To Unification
The Complete Histories Behind The Ch'ang Hon (ITF) Patterns

A statue of Se-Jong, in Seoul, South Korea

ROKS Sejong the Great

통일
Tong-Il

Tong-Il denotes the resolution of the unification of Korea which has been divided since 1945. The diagram symbolizes the homogenous race.

Tong-Il is the twenty fourth pattern of Ch'ang Hon Taekwon-Do, usually taught at 6th Degree Black belt. It has 56 moves and was developed in Malaysia between 1962 and 1964 with the help of Master Kim, Bok Man and Master Woo, Jae Lim.

Tong-Il is, and always has been the final pattern of Ch'ang Hon Taekwon-Do. Even when there were only 20 patterns developed, Tong-Il was the last pattern to be taught. When the final four patterns were developed (Eui-Am, Moon-Moo, Yon-Gae and So-San), they were placed prior to Tong-Il, due to its significance to General Choi.

As the description says, Tong-Il represents the unification of North and South Korea into one nation, with the diagram representing *'the homogenous race'* or *'people of the same kind'* i.e. all Korean people.

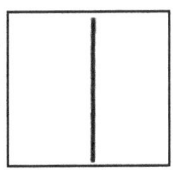

The pattern diagram of Tong-Il

When General Choi was born in 1918, Korea had been oppressed under the Japanese occupation following the annexation of Korea in 1910, by way of the Japan-Korea Annexation Treaty[216], but was still a single Korea. When Japan withdrew from Korea in 1945, following their surrender at the end of the 2nd World War, the victorious Allied powers decided to run Korea for a period of 5 years under a *four power trusteeship*[217], after which Korea would become independent again.

The country was divided into two halves along the 38th Parallel, with

---

[216] See Joong-Gun Chapter (page 87) for more information on the Japan-Korea Annexation Treaty

[217] USA, USSR, China and Great Britain

From Creation To Unification
The Complete Histories Behind The Ch'ang Hon (ITF) Patterns

the USSR[218] occupying the North and the USA occupying the South. Whilst the USSR had backed Kim Il-Sung to run the North, the USA had backed Syngman Rhee to run the South and he was appointed as head of South Korea in 1945 even though it was under US control. In 1948 the USSR withdrew most of its forces from North Korea and in the same year Syngman Rhee officially became South Korea's President. Unification talks followed, but due to Syngman Rhee being a hard-line anti-communist he clamped down on dissent within the South which hindered the talks.

However, talks of unifying the North and South continued, but now the view was that each side (both the South and the North) would take over the other with their own government, which were totally different from each other, with one being communist and the other (supposedly) democratic - obviously both sides opposed such a move!

When the USSR had left North Korea in 1948, much of its tanks, aircraft and heavy weapons remained, whereby in contrast, the USA refused to supply any heavy weaponry to South Korea, afraid that they would use them for more than internal peace keeping. This severely weakened South Korea and led to the start of the Korean War, when Kim Il-Sung's forces invaded South Korea on 25th June, 1950, knowing that the South's lack of heavy weaponry made them much weaker then the North.

It was in 1946 that General Choi had been commissioned as a 2nd Lieutenant in the newly formed South Korean Army, following the surrender of Japan at the end of the 2nd World War. General Choi was opposed to communism which is why he chose to join the South Korean Army, even though his actual birthplace now resided in North Korea. Since that time, he rose through the ranks of 1st Lieutenant, Captain, Major, Lieutenant Colonel, Colonel, and by 1951 was at the rank of Brigadier General.

General Choi, aged 33 - a 1 Star Brigadier General

---

[218] *'Union of Soviet Socialist Republics'* known as the USSR or Soviet Union – a collective of 15 republics with a centralized communist government based in Moscow, Russia, which existed between 1922 and 1991

통일
Tong-Il

The Korean War lasted for just over 3 years, finally ending on 27th July, 1953, during which time the United Nations had intervened; this in turn allowed the US Navy and US Air Force to support South Korea. The intervention by the US forces shifted or equalised the balance of forces, meaning little gain was made by either side for a number of years. Eventually an armistice was suggested by India at a United Nations meeting and put forward by new US President Dwight Eisenhower and thus, a ceasefire ensued.

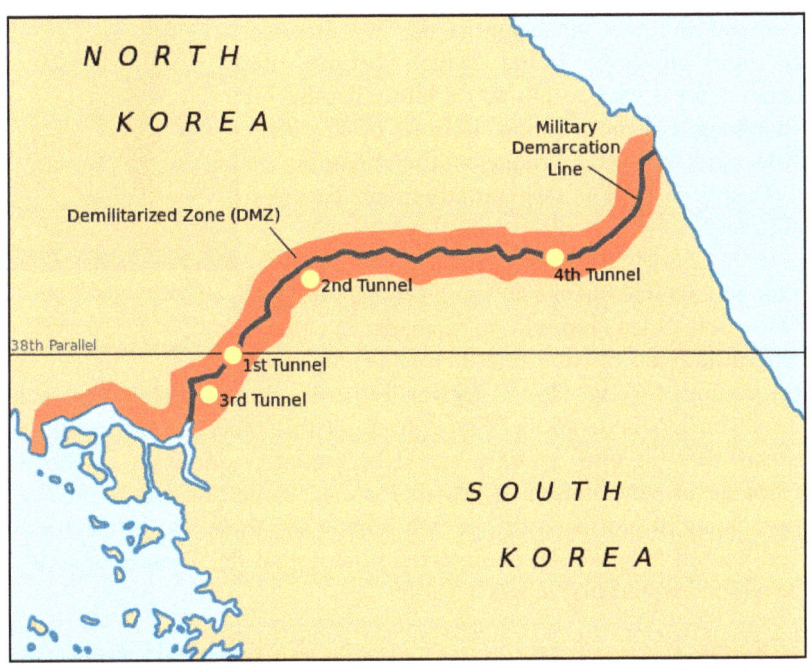

A map showing Korea divided into North and South, along with the 38th Parallel and the DMZ (Demilitarized Zone). The tunnels are thought to have been dug by North Korea over the years, ready for another incursion into the South, though this has always been denied by the North Korean leadership. [219]

Even though the fighting had taken land on both sides, moving backwards and forwards between the North and the South, when the fighting stopped following the armistice, the battle lines were

---

[219] Picture by Rishabh Tatiraju, Cc-by-sa-3.0

From Creation To Unification
The Complete Histories Behind The Ch'ang Hon (ITF) Patterns

approximately at the 38th Parallel, where it had all begun and it was around this that the DMZ (Demilitarized Zone) was established. The DMZ was set up to serve as a buffer zone between North and South Korea, it moved both forces back from its centre, which was the original front line, by 2,000 meters each, leaving a two and a half mile wide zone where neither country is allowed to install or take weapons, though each still continues to guard its border of the DMZ.

In 1954, General Choi was promoted to Major General and was in charge of the 29th Infantry division on Je-Ju Island, which became the catalyst for Taekwon-Do as we know it today[220]; following a demonstration in front of President Rhee and the arts subsequent official naming on 11th April 1955. The rest is pretty much Taekwon-Do history.[221]

Due to a regime change in South Korea, General Choi self-exiled himself to Canada in 1972, where he lived out the rest of his life, tirelessly promoting Ch'ang Hon Taekwon-Do and the ITF (International Taekwon-Do Federation). Throughout all this time, he continued to dream that his birth country would be united as one again. General Choi never saw himself as North Korean, as despite his birthplace now being in North Korea, he was born when there was just 'Korea' and wished it to be one again, often hoping that the Taekwon-Do he developed would play a part in this!

A rare photo of Major-General Choi in 2 Star Dress Uniform. [222]

Sadly, when General Choi passed away on 15th June, 2002, his dream remained a dream, but the pattern Tong-Il reminds all of us of General Choi's wish to see his country reunited. His patterns represent this, not just with Tong-Il, its final pattern, but with Chon-Ji, the first pattern representing the formation of Korea and the patterns in

---

[220] See Hwa-Rang Chapter for more information on this

[221] A full and detailed historical account of how Taekwon-Do really came to fruition, titled 'The True And More Complete History Of Taekwon-Do', written by Taekwon-Do Master and historian Dr. George Vitale VIII, can be found in my book "The Encyclopedia Of Taekwon-Do Patterns: The Complete Resource For Ch'ang Hon, ITF & GTF Students Of Taekwon-Do: Vol.1

[222] Picture courtesy of Dr. George Vitale, VIII

통일
Tong-Il

between its history, with the final, most important pattern to General Choi representing a unified Korea once more – General Choi's dream.

Tong-Il; movements 1 to 3 - demonstrated by Mr Gordon Slater VI

Some of the movements in Tong-Il are representative of General Choi's thoughts on unification and the divided Korea as well. The first movement for example is a *Twin Fist Middle Punch* executed in slow motion while moving backwards, this is said to represent the 2 Korea's, this is followed by the opening of the arms horizontally to the side, again in slow motion whilst moving backwards, to form *two knifehands* which is said to represent Korea being divided for too long.

The 3rd movement, where the student suddenly changes to the opposite direction and moves forward again, executing a *middle inward block*, with the left arm, at full speed, is said to represent the sudden attack of North Korea i.e. The start of the Korean war. The various *stamping motions* within the pattern are said to represent General Choi's anger and frustration at Korea's division, with the 38th movement; a *high twin fist vertical punch*, also with a *stamp*, said to represent the breaking of the 38th Parallel.

Movement 38, with the stamping motion

An interesting fact is that pattern Tong-Il has had the most changes, since it was first devised, out of all the patterns, numbering over 20 or more changes. For example, although the first two moves remain the

From Creation To Unification
The Complete Histories Behind The Ch'ang Hon (ITF) Patterns

same with the hand techniques, originally they were both executed from the first walking stance (meaning there was no second step backwards). The 3rd movement did originally step forwards, but it was executed in a left L-Stance using a middle inner forearm block with the right arm, as opposed to the right rear foot stance and middle inward block with the left arm, as is used now. The 38th movement however, has always remained the same. Many other moves have also changed, for example movement 16 was originally a front snap kick executed with the left leg; now it is downward kick executed with the right leg. Perhaps the changes were simply due to technical advances in Taekwon-Do or perhaps General Choi wanted even more movements to represent the dream of Tong-Il! Sadly, we will never know.

General Choi Hong Hi
1918 - 2002

Appendix i
The GTF Patterns

Grandmaster Park, Jung Tae was originally the ITF Secretary-General, as well as Chairman of the ITF Instruction Committee; the man responsible for teaching virtually all Taekwon-Do techniques and how they were executed and performed to the ITF before he left in 1990 and formed the GTF (Global Taekwon-Do Federation).

Shortly after the formation of the GTF (sometime after 1990) Grandmaster Park devised a number of patterns himself and incorporated them into the syllabus of the GTF, alongside the original Ch'ang Hon patterns. It is unclear as to whether he intended to eventually replace all the original Ch'ang Hon patterns with his new *Jee-Goo Hyung*' or simply to add to them[223], as Grandmaster Park, Jung Tae sadly passed away on 11th April, 2002 leaving six patterns finalised. As it stands, a student of the GTF will learn a total of 30 patterns between 10th Kup and Taekwon-Do Master (7th Dan) – all 24 of the current Ch'ang Hon patterns, with the exception that he reinstated the original Ko-Dang instead of Juche, plus the 6 *'Jee-Goo'* patterns that he devised.

Grandmaster Park, Jung Tae with General Choi [224]

---

[223] Although the fact he made a pattern named Dhan-Goon, after the mythical, legendary founder of Korea when pattern Dan-Gun already existed may be a sign that in the long term, he intend to replace the Ch'ang Hon pattern set in its entirety.

[224] Picture courtesy of Mr Stephen Gell, IV

From Creation To Unification
The Complete Histories Behind The Ch'ang Hon (ITF) Patterns

Of the six patterns taught exclusively within the GTF; three have very literal meanings or definitions and thus little in the way of historical context above and beyond what is already written for them and of course any unwritten meaning that Grandmaster Park may also of had in mind, these are patterns *Jee-Sang*, *Jee-Goo* and *Jook-Am*. Of the remaining three; *Dhan-Goon* tul is based on the legendary founder of Korea and thus has the same historical context as found in the Dan-Gun chapter, *Pyong-Hwa* is based on a historic event, that is only partially related to Korean history, but the last one; *Sun-Duk*, is based on a famous Korean historical figure who's history intertwines with some of the Ch'ang Hon patterns history, so deserves the same attention and research.

In this section I will list the patterns in order they are taught in the GTF syllabus, along with their definitions and any extra information on them, just as I have done in the previous chapters for the Ch'ang Hon patterns. I list the patterns in the order they appear in the GTF syllabus, noting their numerical order (one to six[225]) as they relate to the GTF.

지상
Jee-Sang

Jee-Sang means 'On Earth'. This pattern has 24 movements, which symbolize the hours of the day. The diagram represents the four directions: North, South, East and West.

Jee-Sang is the first of the GTF patterns, usually taught at 8th Kup and has 24 moves. Jee-Sang represents the spirit of the Global Taekwon-Do Federation. 'Jee' (지) means 'Earth' and represents the founding of the world. 'Sang' (상) means 'Top' possibly[226] representing 'Heaven'

---

[225] By 'first' 'second' etc. I mean the first one in that is taught to students of the GTF that isn't derived from General Choi's original syllabus of patterns. Not the actual first pattern taught (which would be Chon-Ji).

[226] I say 'possibly' as direct translations are not always possible and as there isn't much written information on this patterns meaning, so it could actually mean a number of things.

Appendix i
The GTF Patterns

and when combined Jee-Sang (지상) means 'On Top of Earth'[227], 'Heaven and Earth combined', or as Master Park wanted 'On Earth', which possibly represents the irrepressible strength and spirit he wanted to underpin the Global Taekwon-Do Federation, as well as the founding of the GTF itself, which is perhaps why it's the first of the GTF patterns!

The 24 moves are said to represent the 24 hours of each day, which is the time that all students have to learn and connect with others to gain knowledge and wisdom.

The pattern diagram represents the four points of a compass; North, South, East and West which stands for the students 'Inner' compass, with which they will never lose their way.

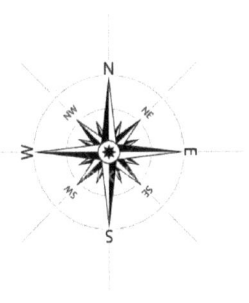

Personally, I feel this pattern definition is try to instil the true spirit of Taekwon-Do that Master Park hoped to instil in all students within his federation – that of training hard in the system, sharing knowledge to help fellow students and showing indomitable spirit and never quitting or giving up should things seem to hard.

단군
Dhan-Goon

Dhan-Goon was created after the holy Dan-Gun, the legendary founder of Korea in the year 2333 B.C. Dhan-Goon has 23 movements which stand for the first two digits of the year 2333 B.C.

---

[227] Another version of 'Sang' (상) that I have read is that it means 'Above' and represents the spirit of the GTF and when connected with 'Jee' (지) it symbolizes the spirit of the GTF on earth.

From Creation To Unification
The Complete Histories Behind The Ch'ang Hon (ITF) Patterns

Dhan-Goon is the second of the GTF patterns, usually taught at 5th Kup and has 23 moves.

Dhan-Goon is just a variation of the spelling of Dan-Gun, the legendary founder of Korea. Dhan-Goon is obviously a very important mythical figure for all Koreans, which is why Grandmaster Park may have felt the need to make a pattern of his own, named in his honour. For a full historical back ground on Dhan-Goon, please refer to the Dan-Gun chapter.

A painting of Dan-Goon

지구
Jee-Goo

Jee-Goo means *'The Globe'* or *'Global'*. Jee-Goo has 30 movements which consist of the numbers 24, 4 and 2. The number 24 represents the 24 hours of the day. The number 4 represents the four directions of North, South, East and West and covers all nations and people. The number 2 is demonstrated by student performing twice in each direction in order to underline the will to attain world peace and harmony.

Jee-Goo is the third of the GTF patterns, usually taught at 1st Degree and has 30 moves.

The ready posture of Jee-Goo is a parallel stance with the students forearms crossed in front of his chest. This is said to represent crossing out all the years of strife in Taekwon-Do. The first movement sees the student uncross his arms, chamber as he pivots to his left and execute a low block while moving into walking stance and

Appendix i
The GTF Patterns

The Ready Posture and first move of Jee-Goo tul

this is said to represent a breaking away from the past, the beginning of a new global Taekwon-Do movement and Master Parks desire for world peace and harmony.

The total 30 movements of the pattern are made up from the sum 24+4+2; with 24 representing the hours in a day, reminding the student of Master Parks desire for world peace and harmony all the time, in every second of every day. The number four represents a compass, which goes in all directions and thus represents all people, of all nations around the world and finally the 2 is representative of the student as he performs the pattern, moving twice in each of the four compass points and is meant to show his commitment to helping bring peace and harmony to the world.

죽암
Jook-Am

Jook-Am is the pseudonym of Grandmaster Park, Jung Tae. *'Jook'* means a bamboo which shoots up straight without any curvature, its roots intertwining to form an inseparable force. *'Am'* is an immovable rock, on which the bamboo strikes its roots to form an unshakable foundation. This pattern represents the life of Grandmaster Park, Jung Tae and his striving for perfection. The diagram

From Creation To Unification
The Complete Histories Behind The Ch'ang Hon (ITF) Patterns

symbolizes the bamboo, which grows high from the rock. Jook-Am has 95 movements which symbolize the year 1995, in which Jook-Am was created.

Jook-Am is the fourth of the GTF patterns, usually taught at 2nd Degree and has 95 moves.

To me, this pattern definition represents Grandmaster Park's mindset and focus, coupled with the belief, that to be strong and move forward unwavering, a strong foundation is needed.

평화
Pyong-Hwa

Pyong-Hwa means *'Peace'*. Grandmaster Park, Jung Tae dedicated this pattern to the United Nations Organisation (UNO). This pattern has 50 movements to symbolize the 50 countries which founded the United Nations Organisation in San Francisco, USA in 1950, after the 2nd World War. The diagram represents peace.

Pyong-Hwa is the fifth of the GTF patterns, usually taught at 3rd Degree and has 50 moves.

Pyong-Hwa is dedicated to the United Nations Organisation that was actually founded in 1945[228], at the end of World War II. The ending of World War II by the Allied powers freed Korea from its occupation by the Japanese and following the war's end, the United Nation's was

---

[228] The United Nations was founded on 25th April, 1945

Appendix i
The GTF Patterns

formed with the aim of preventing future world wars. It was the 2nd attempt at such a group, with the first one called *'The League of Nations'* which was founded after the Paris Peace conference in 1919 (which you will have read about in previous chapters), after the end of World War I, however despite having some impact on the world at large, it was disbanded when World War II broke out, as it had ultimately failed in what it was set up to do, which was also to prevent future World Wars.

The United Nations oversaw the elections in South Korea following the split into North and South and whilst its primary role is peace keeping and human rights, it did intervene during the Korean War on behalf of South Korea. Today, the highest position of the United Nations, that of Secretary-General, is held by South Korean diplomat Ban Ki-Moon and has been since 2007.

The emblem of the United Nations [229]

선덕
Sun-Duk

Sun-Duk is named after Queen Sun-Duk of the Silla dynasty in the year 668 A.D. Queen Sun Duk was known for bringing martial arts from China to Korea. Sun-Duk has 68 movements which refer to the year 668 A.D. and the diagram represents 'Lady'.

Sun-Duk is the sixth of the GTF patterns, usually taught at 4th Degree and has 68 moves.

---

[229] I have heard that General Choi was also inspired by the United Nations which is why the ITF logo (which was designed by Master J C Kim) has a blue back ground and the arm positions in Narani Junbi Sogi (Parallel Ready Stance) are said to reprsents the Wreath of Peace from the U.N. emblem.

From Creation To Unification
The Complete Histories Behind The Ch'ang Hon (ITF) Patterns

Sun-Duk was born in 606 AD a princess to King Jin-Pyeong (who ruled the Silla Dynasty around the time that Yoo-Sin became a Hwa-Rang warrior) and was the first of three daughters to the King. King Jin-Pyeong ruled Silla for 63 years but had no male heirs so he proclaimed Princess Duk-Man (as she was known before she became a Queen) as his successor, not just because she was his first daughter, but also because he felt she was highly intelligent. In Silla society at that time, women had influence and also held high positions, but none had ever become a Queen. Princess Duk-Man was to become the first Queen of Silla.

In 632 AD King Jin-Pyeong passed away (he was around 67 years old). Towards the end of his reign as King, the Silla dynasty was involved in many conflicts with its neighbour Baekje, and it was during these violent times that Sun-Duk ascended to the throne. In her early years as Queen, Sun-Duk not only had to continually deal with the minor wars with Baekje, but also rebellions within her own Kingdom.

A drawing of Sun-Duk [230]

However, in 646 AD, she cleverly tried to ally Silla with Goguryo following an invasion by Baekje, but Goguryo, sensing a weakness in the Silla Dynasty, decided to turn on them as well but instead of crumbling, Queen Sun-Duk strengthened her ties with the Tang Dynasty of China, meaning the Silla Dynasty had support from the large Tang forces, which all helped her keep the kingdom intact.

With her strengthened ties to China, Queen Sun-Duk took the advantage of learning from them, sending scholars and emissaries to China to be further educated. She also sent young Korean men to China to train in martial arts and is credited with an early formation of a Korean chivalric code.

---

[230] Picture by artist widyarahayu. *www.widyarahayu.deviantart.com*

Appendix i
The GTF Patterns

Queen Sun-Duk worked towards relieving poverty in her kingdom and, like her father before her, she also leaned towards Buddhism as her chosen religion. Queen Sun-Duk built (or completed) many Buddhist temples during her reign, one of which was the Hwangnyong[231] Temple, which was started in 553 AD during the reign of King Jin-Heung but not completed until 644 AD (During Queen Sun-Duk's reign). Along with completion of the temple itself, Queen Sun-Duk built a pagoda which was 9 stories high (around 70 to 80 meters tall) and was the largest pagoda ever built. Each storey

Miniature reconstruction of the pagoda at Hwangnyong temple. [232]

of the pagoda was inscribed with the names of the 9 nations that made up East Asia at that time, which was said to represent Silla's future conquests! The pagoda was burned to the ground during the Mongol invasions in 1238 AD and all that remains today is its massive foundations, made up of 60 stones that totaled an area of nearly 600 square meters.

A temple built under Queen Sun-Duk's reign that survives today is the Bunhwang[233] temple. Built in 634 AD, it is close to the Hwangnyong Temple and originally covered many acres. It was originally one of the four temples used by the state to ask for Buddha's blessing. It also has a pagoda, of which only the lower three levels remain today as it was built with andesite (a type of volcanic rock) as opposed to Hwangnyongsa's wooden structure. Though the upper levels of the pagoda (also thought to originally be 9 stories high) caved in, it was

---

[231] Meaning *'Emperor Dragon'*

[232] Picture by Renee Parker. Cc-by-sa-2.0

[233] Meaning *"Fragrant Emperor"*

257

From Creation To Unification
The Complete Histories Behind The Ch'ang Hon (ITF) Patterns

excavated in 1913 by the Japanese and they found the cremated remains of a priest hidden between the 2nd and 3rd floor, gold, coins, scissor and a needle, all indicating that the objects belonged to a woman of royal blood, perhaps Queen Sun-Duk herself! Queen Sun-Duk is thought to have built the first observatory in the Far East, known as Cheomseongdae or *'star-gazing tower'*.

Remains of the Bunhwang temple. [234]

In 647 AD there was a revolt against the Queens reign which was started by Lord Bidam, the highest ranking government minister under Queen Sun-Duk. Lord Bidam used a slogan to further his cause, which was *"Women rulers cannot rule the country"*. Legend has it that during the revolt a star fell from the sky, which Lord Bidam used to further enforce his claim, stating it was a sign that the Queen's reign was at an end. General Kim Yoo-Sin advised the Queen to send a burning kite into the sky, so the people thought the star had returned, she did so and the revolt ended!

Korean's 31st National Treasure, the Cheomseongdae Observatory. [235]

---

[234] Picture by Bifyu. Cc-by-sa-2.0

[235] Picture by Zsinj. GFDL, cc-by-sa

Appendix i
The GTF Patterns

Shortly after the revolt, on 17th February, 647 AD, Queen Sun-Duk passed away and was succeeded by Queen Jin-Duk (her younger cousin) who had Lord Bidam and his followers executed.

Apart from her cousin (her father's younger brothers daughter) becoming the next Queen of Silla, her sisters son eventually became King Muyeol of Silla, whilst her younger sister married King Mu of Baekje and became the mother of Baekje King; Ul-Ja.[236]

As with many historical figures, many legends follow. One legend tells of Queen Sun-Duk having an usual ability to perceive events before they happened! The legend goes that during one winter, Queen Sun-Duk heard a horde of white frogs croaking loudly by the Jade Gate pond at the palace. She is said to have interpreted this as an attack by Baekje, seeing the croaking frogs as soldiers of Baekje, who were in the northwest of Silla territory (as in astronomy white symbolised west) at the woman's valley (as the Jade Gate was a place where woman congregated) and with this thought, she sent some of her troops to the valley whereby they were able to capture two thousand Baekje soldiers!

Queen Sun-Duk

In 2009, South Korean television aired a 62 episode historical drama titled *"Queen Seondeok"*. It stared Lee Yo-Won as the older (non-child)

---

[236] This is disputed by some Korean historians as although historical records state Princess Sun-Hwa (Sun-Duk's youngest sister) married King Mu and was mother to King Ui-Ja, some evidence found in 2009 at Mireuksa Temple (the largest Buddhist temple in Baekje during that era) built by King Mu, seems to contradicts this and points to a Queen Sataek as King Ui-Ja's mother!

259

From Creation To Unification
The Complete Histories Behind The Ch'ang Hon (ITF) Patterns

Queen Sun-Duk, Uhm Tae-Woong as General Kim Yoo-Sin and Kim Nam-Gil as Lord Bidam and topped the TV charts nearly every week it was aired. The series won many awards even though it veered away from the history somewhat, preferring a more 'artistic license' instead.

As the 68 moves of this pattern are derived from the year 668 AD, yet it is not the death date of Queen Sun-Duk, the only connection to it that I can make is that it represents the unification of the three Kingdoms of Korea, following the conquering of Baekje, then Goguryo by the Silla Dynasty and formed what became known as 'Unified Silla' – however, this happened under the reign of King Moon-Moo, not Queen Sun-Duk!

Master Park Jung Tae [237]
1943 - 2002

---

[237] Picture courtesy of Mr Stephen Gell, IV

Appendix ii
Revising The Definitions

As you will have read in the previous chapters of this book, whilst many of the pattern definitions are fine, a few have some facts that should be corrected, so in this section I have revised the original definitions that General Choi left us, trying to keep as close as possible to the originals as General Choi first wrote them. These revised definitions include both corrections, as well as additional information gained from my own research, which I feel elevate and add to the definitions for the future. Any corrections or additions are in italics.

This section of the book is *copyright free*[238] and you are welcome (and encouraged) to use these definitions in your own syllabus's or web site.

Chon-Ji and **Dan-Gun** are fine and don't need revising.

Do-San is the pseudonym of the patriot Ahn Chang-Ho (*1878*-1938) who devoted his entire life to furthering the education of Korea and its independent movement. The 24 movements represent *the age he rose to prominence as a leader of his countrymen.*[239]

Won-Hyo was the noted monk who introduced Buddhism to the *common people* of the Silla Dynasty in the year *662 A.D.*

Yul-Gok is fine and doesn't need revising.

Joong-Gun is named after the patriot Ahn Joong-Gun who assassinated *Hiro-Bumi Ito*, the first Japanese *Resident-General* of Korea, known as the man who played the leading part in the Korea-Japan merger. Ahn Joong-Gun was executed at Lui-Shung prison in 1910

---

[238] For non-commercial work only. Commercial works may use them but must acknowledge this book and its author.

[239] The reasoning for the 24 for movements *(the age he rose to prominence as a leader of his countrymen)* is from my own research, as although a reason for the 24 moves wasn't originally part of the definition, but added later (see Do-San chapter), my reason is more exact to the life of Do-San than the same reference used as a reason for having 24 patterns in Taekwon-Do.

From Creation To Unification
The Complete Histories Behind The Ch'ang Hon (ITF) Patterns

aged only 30 years old.[240]

Toi-Gye is the pen name of the noted scholar Yi Hwang (16th century), an authority on Neo-Confucianism. The 37 movements *represent the years that he was one of the most influential government figures of the Joseon Dynasty*[241], the diagram represents "scholar".

Hwa-Rang is fine and doesn't need revising.

Choong-Moo was the name given to the great Admiral Yi Soon-Sin of the *Joseon* Dynasty. *He is credited with improving what is* reputed to have been the first armoured battleship (Kobukson) in 1592, which is said to be the precursor of the present day submarine. *The 30 movements of this pattern represent the number of ships Choong-Moo destroyed (out of a fleet of 333), with only 13 of his own ships, at the battle of Myeongnyang.*[242] The reason why this pattern ends with a left hand attack is to symbolize his regrettable death, having no chance to show his unrestrained potentiality, checked by the forced reservation of his loyalty to the king.

Kwang-Gae is named after the famous Kwang-Gae-Toh-Wang, the 19th King of the Koguryo Dynasty, who regained all the lost territories including the greater part of Manchuria. The diagram represents the expansion and recovery of lost territory. The 39 movements refer to the first two figures of 391 A.D. the year he came to the throne, *as well as the age he was when he passed away.*[243]

Po-Eun is the pseudonym of a loyal subject Chong-Mong-Chu *(14th Century)* who was a famous poet and whose poem "I would not serve a

---

[240] I have removed the section that states *'There are 32 movements in this pattern to represent Mr. Ahn's age when he was executed at...'*, as it is incorrect. I also changed the wording *'Mr. Ahn'* as it seemed more fitting to use his full name, as General Choi did at the start of the definition and in all other definitions. Finally, I removed his year of death from the original brackets and added his correct age at the time of his death.

[241] The reasoning for the 37 for movements (*..represent the years that he was one of the most influential Government figures of the Joseon Dynasty)* is from my own research, as I feel it fits better and makes more sense. The original definition is *'The 37 movements of the pattern refer to his birthplace on 37° latitude"*.

[242] This is from my own research, as there is no reason given for the 30 movements in the original pattern definition.

[243] This is from my own research as I feel it adds to the definition, representing Kwang-Gae's 39 movements even better than the original reasoning (which has been left in the definition anyway).

Appendix ii
Revising The Definitions

second master though I might be crucified a hundred times" is known to every Korean. He was also a pioneer in the field of physics. The diagram represents his unerring loyalty to the king and country towards the end of the Koryo Dynasty.

Ge-Baek is named after Ge-Baek, a great general in the Baek Je Dynasty *who was killed in battle in* 660 AD *following a final stand to protect the Dynasty against overwhelming Silla forces.*[244] The diagram represents his severe and strict military discipline.

Eui-Am is fine and doesn't need revising.

Choong-Jang is the pseudonym given to General Kim Duk Ryang who lived during the *Joseon* Dynasty, *16th* century. This pattern ends with a left-hand attack to symbolize the tragedy of his death at 27 in prison before he was able to reach full maturity.

Ko-Dang (the original version) is fine and doesn't need revising.

Juche doesn't need changing depending how you wish to interpret the meaning![245]

Ko-Dang (Juche performed but called Ko-Dang).
Formerly known as Juche, this pattern was devised in order to bolster the ITF's development. The name represents the first leader of North Korea. The 45 movements represent 45 degrees; the change in direction required at the time to fulfil the requirements needed and the diagram represents the forked path taken.[246]

Sam-Il, Yoo-Sin and **Choi-Yong** are fine and don't need revising.

Yong-Gae is named after a famous general during the Koguryo Dynasty, Yon Gae Somoon. The 49 movements refer to the last two figures of 649 A.D. the year he forced the Tang Dynasty to quit Korea

---

[244] This is my own addition, as I feel it shows the great sacrifice Ge-Baek made just prior to his passing in 660 AD.

[245] For those that have to perform this pattern, but don't like having to say the name 'Juche', you could simply say 'Jung Tae' - after Master Park, Jung Tae who helped design it, as it sounds like Juche but isn't!

[246] This is all my own work as when one of the ITF's changed the name from Juche to Ko-dang, but not the actual pattern movements, they never gave it a new definition, so none exists! Of course one may remove the first part (*Formerly known as Juche*) if the aim is to remove all reference to the word *'Juche'* totally.

From Creation To Unification
The Complete Histories Behind The Ch'ang Hon (ITF) Patterns

after *defeating* nearly *170,000* of their troops at Ansi Sung.

Ul-Ji is named after General Ul-Ji Moon Dok who successfully defended Korea against a *Sui* invasion force of *over a* million soldiers led by Yang Je in 612 AD, Ul-Ji employing hit and run guerrilla tactics, was able to decimate a large percentage of the force. The diagram represents his surname. The 42 movements represent the author's age when he *released* the pattern.

Moon-Moo is fine and needs no revisions.

So-San is the pseudonym of the great monk Choi Hyong Ung (1520-1604) during the *Joseon* Dynasty. The 72 movements refer to his age when he organized a corps of monk soldiers with the assistance of his pupil *Yu Jeong*. The monk soldiers helped repulse the Japanese *invaders* who overran most of the Korean peninsula in 1592.

Se-Jong is named after the greatest Korean King, Se-Jong, who invented the Korean alphabet in *1444*, and was also a noted meteorologist. The diagram represents the king, while the 24 movements refer to the 24 letters of the Korean alphabet *as it is now used today*.

Tong-Il is fine.

Of the GTF patterns, **Jee-Sang, Dhan-Goon, Jee-Goo** and **Jook-Am** are fine.

Pyong-Hwa means 'Peace'. Grandmaster Park, Jung Tae dedicated this pattern to the United Nations Organisation (UNO). This pattern has 50 movements to symbolize the 50 countries which founded the United Nations Organisation in San Francisco, USA in *1945*, after the 2nd World War. The diagram represents peace.

Sun-Duk is named after Queen Sun-Duk of the Silla dynasty Queen Sun Duk was known for bringing martial arts from China to Korea. Sun-Duk has 68 movements which refer to the year 668 AD *when the Silla Dynasty united Korea*[247] and the diagram represents 'Lady'.

---

[247] This is all my own addition, but explains the year (668 A.D.) and thus the number of movements within the pattern better, as without the explanation it doesn't really make sense in that regards.

Bibliography

— Ackermann, Marsha; Schroeder, Michael; Terry, Janice; Lo, Jiu-Hwa; Whitters, Mark. *Encyclopedia of World History*. Facts On File Inc., 2008

— Ahn, Moon-hye; Suh, Sang-mok. *Dosans Way To Leadership*. Bookorea Publishing, 2011

— An, Chunggŭn. *A Treatise on Peace in the East*. Thesis, 1910 translated by Professor Kim Chŏngmyŏng, 1979

— An, Chunggŭn.. *The Story of An Ŭngch'il*. 1910 (Biography)

— Anslow, Stuart. *Ch'ang Hon Taekwon-do Hae Sul: Real Applications To The ITF Patterns, Vol 1*. CheckPoint Press, 2006/2009

— Anslow, Stuart. *The Encyclopedia Of Taekwon-Do Patterns, Vols 1,2 & 3*. CheckPoint Press, 2010

— Anslow, Stuart. *Ch'ang Hon Taekwon-do Hae Sul: Real Applications To The ITF Patterns, Vol 2*..CheckPoint Press, 2012

— Armstrong, Charles. *The Koreas*. Routledge, 2006

— Armstrong, Charles. *The North Korean Revolution, 1945-1950*. Cornell University Press, 2004

— Ballard, Admiral George Alexander. *The Influence of the Sea on the Political History of Japan*. Greenwood Press (Reprint), 1972

— Best, Jonathan. *A History of the Early Korean Kingdom of Paekche*. Harvard East Asian Monographs, 2007

— Best, Jonathan. *An annotated translation of The Paekche Annals of the Samguk sagi*. Harvard East Asian Monographs, 2007

— Buswell, Robert E. *Encyclopedia of Buddhism*. Macmillan Reference USA, 2004

— CC Books. *7th-Century Heads of Government: Yeon Gaesomun, Eulji Mundeok, Yeon Namsaeng, Yeon Taejo, Yeon Namgeon*. LLC Books, 2010

— Cheoyong. *The Song of Cheoyong*. Poem, compiled by Iryeon, 13th Century

— Choi, Gi-eok. *Leadership of King Sejong, CEO of the Nation*. Easybook, Year Unknown

— Cho, Hee Il. *The Complete Tae Kwon-Do Hyung, Vol 1*. Master Hee Il Cho, 1984

— Cho, Hee Il. *The Complete Tae Kwon-Do Hyung, Vol 2*. Master Hee Il Cho, 1989

— Cho, Hee Il. *The Complete Tae Kwon-Do Hyung, Vol 3*. Master Hee Il Cho, 1984

— Choi, Hong Hi. *Encyclopaedia Of Taekwon-Do*. ITF, 1993

— Choi, Hong Hi. *Taekwon-do*. Deaha Publication Company, 1965

— Choi, Hong Hi. *Taekwon-do And I: Vol 1*. ITF

From Creation To Unification
The Complete Histories Behind The Ch'ang Hon (ITF) Patterns

— Choi, Hong Hi. *Tae Kwon Do: Art Of Self Defence.* ITF, 1972

— Chu, Yo-sŏp. *Kim Yusin; the Romances of a Korean Warrior of 7th Century.* Mutual Publishers, 1947

— Cumings, Bruce. *The Origins of the Korean War: Liberation and the Emergence of Separate Regimes, 1945-1947.* Princeton University Press, 1981

— Daehwan, Noh. *The Eclectic Development of Neo-Confucianism and Statecraft from the 18th to the 19th Century.* Korea Journal, Winter 2003

— Edens, Bert. *ITF Pattern History - With Korean.* 1st Degree report, 2006

— Gardiner, Kenneth. *Legends of Koguryŏ : Samguk Sagi, Annals of Koguryŏ.* Korea Journal, 1982

— Griffis, William Elliot. *Corea: The Hermit Nation.* 1882

— Ha, Tae-hung; Sohn, Pow-key. *Nan Jung Il Gi (War Diary of Admiral Yi Soon-Sin).* Yonsei University Press, 1977

— Hawley, Samuel. *The Imjin War: Japan's Sixteenth-Century Invasion of Korea and Attempt to Conquer China.* Royal Asiatic Society, 2005

— Heron, Maria. *Interview with General Choi Hong Hi, Founder of Taekwon-do.* The Times, 1999

— Il-yeon. *Samguk Yusa: Legends and History of the Three Kingdoms of Ancient Korea,* translated by Tae-Hung Ha and Grafton K. Mintz, 2006

— Jeong, Byeong-Jo. *Master Wonhyo – An Overview of His Life and Teachings.* Diamond Sutra Recitation Group, 2010

— Wanna, Joe; Choe, Hongkyu. *Traditional Korea, A Cultural History.* Hollyn, 1997

— Kang, Won-Sik; Lee, Kyong-Myong. *A Modern History of Taekwondo.* Bokyung Moonhwasa, 1999. *Translated by Glenn Uesugi*

— Kim, Djun Kil. *The History of Korea.* Greenwood Press, 2005

— Kimm, He-Young. *Hong Hi: A Tae Kwon-Do History Lesson.* Taekwondo Times Magazine, January 2000

— Lankov, Andrei. *From Stalin to Kim: The Formation of North Korea 1945-1960.* Hurst & Co, 2001

— Lee, Bae-yong. *Women in Korean History.* Ewha Womans University Press, 2008

— Lee, Hyun-hee; Park, Sung-soo; Yoon, Nae-hyun. *New History of Korea.* Jimoondang, 2005

— Lee, Joogsoo James. *The Partition of Korea after World War II: A Global History.* Palgrave Macmillan, 2006

— Lee, Kenneth. *Korea And East Asia: The Story Of A Phoenix.* Praeger, 1997

— Lee, Peter; De Bary, William. *Sources of Korean Tradition: From Early Times through the Sixteenth Century.* Columbia University Press, 2000

Bibliography

— Lewis, Sanko, *An Introduction To The Philosophy Of Chon-Ji*. Totally Tae Kwon Do Magazine, August 2010

— Lone, Stewart; McCormack, Gavan. *Korea Since 1850*. Diane Publishing Company, 1993

— McKenzie, F. A. *The Tragedy of Korea*. Yonsei University Press, 1969 (Reprint)/ originally printed, 1908

— Moses, Vincent (Dr.). *Oranges and Independence: Ahn Chang Ho and Cornelius Earle Rumsey, An Early East-West Alliance in Riverside, 1904-13*. Bright World Foundation

— Prinz von Hohenzollern, Carl, *Meine Erlebnisse Während Des Russisch-Japanischen Krieges, 1904-1905*. Ernst Siegfried Mittler und Sohn, 1912 (Translated Title: *My Experiences During The Russo-Japanese War*)

— Rutt, Richard. *The Bamboo Grove: Introduction To Sijo*. The University of Michigan Press, 1998

— Rutt, Richard. *The Flower Boys of Silla (Hwarang)*. Korea Branch of the Royal Asiatic Society, 1961

— Seth, Michael J. *A History of Korea: From Antiquity to the Present*. Rowman & Littlefield Publishers, 2010

— Shin, Chae-ho. *Joseon Sanggosa (Ancient history of Korea)*. 1948

— Shimpei, Ogura. *The Song of Cheoyong*. Poem (originally by Cheoyong), reconstructed into Hangul, 1929

— Shultz, Edward J; Kang, Hugh; Kane, Daniel. *The Silla Annals of the Samguk Sagi*. The Academy of Korean Studies, 2012

— Thiébaud, Jean-Marie. *La présence française en Corée de la fin du XVIIIème siècle à nos jours*. Harmattan, 2005 (Translated Title: *The French Presence in Korea in the Late Eighteenth Century to the Present Day*)

— Various. *Encyclopaedia Britannica (32 volume Set)*. Encyclopaedia Britannica (UK) Ltd, 2009

— Vitale, George. *Why Is Taekwon-Do's History So Hard To Find?* Totally Tae Kwon Do Magazine, January 2010

— Vos, Frits. *Kim Yusin, Kim Yusin, Persönlichkeit und Mythos: Ein Beitrag zur Kenntnis der Altkoreanischen Geschichte*. Publisher Unknown, 1954 (Translated Title: *Kim Yusin: Personality and Myth: A Contribution to the Knowledge of Old Korean History*)

— Wasserstrom, Jeffrey. *Student Protests in Twentieth Century China*. Stanford University Press, 2000

— Yoon, Byŏngryŏl. *The Collected Biographies of Patriot An Chunggŭn*. Ministry of Patriots and Veterans Affairs, 1999

— Yoshihisa, Tak Matsusaka. *The Making of Japanese Manchuria*. Harvard University Asia Center, 2001

From Creation To Unification
The Complete Histories Behind The Ch'ang Hon (ITF) Patterns

— *Web Sites:* www.ahnchangho.or.kr, www.dosan.org; www.kaedc.com, www.koreanhero.net, www.populargusts.blogspot.co.uk; www.raynerslanetkd.com; www.san-shin.org; ww.sooshimkwan.blogspot.com; www.wikipedia.org

Other Books By The Author

The Encyclopedia Of Taekwon-do Patterns
The Complete Patterns Resource For Ch'ang Hon, ITF & GTF Students Of Taekwon-Do, Vols 1,2 & 3

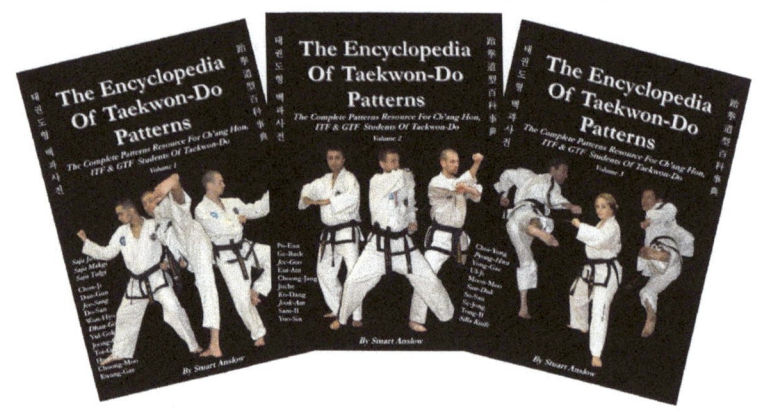

The Encyclopedia Of Taekwon-Do Patterns is a unique series of books that feature the complete works of General Choi, Hong Hi; Creator of the Ch'ang Hon system of Taekwon-Do and founder of the International Taekwon-Do Federation; as well as the patterns further devised by some of his most talented and legendary pioneers; Grandmaster Park, Jung Tae and Grandmaster Kim, Bok Man.

This 3 volume set is the only series of books in the world to feature all of the 25 patterns created by General Choi and his Taekwon-Do pioneers (including both Juche and Ko-Dang), as well as all 3 Saju exercises, the 6 Global Taekwon-Do Federation patterns developed by Grandmaster Park, Jung Tae and the Silla Knife Pattern instituted by Grandmaster Kim, Bok Man.

Bibliography

- Lewis, Sanko, *An Introduction To The Philosophy Of Chon-Ji*. Totally Tae Kwon Do Magazine, August 2010
- Lone, Stewart; McCormack, Gavan. *Korea Since 1850*. Diane Publishing Company, 1993
- McKenzie, F. A. *The Tragedy of Korea*. Yonsei University Press, 1969 (Reprint)/ originally printed, 1908
- Moses, Vincent (Dr.). *Oranges and Independence: Ahn Chang Ho and Cornelius Earle Rumsey, An Early East-West Alliance in Riverside, 1904-13*. Bright World Foundation
- Prinz von Hohenzollern, Carl, *Meine Erlebnisse Wahrend Des Russisch-Japanischen Krieges, 1904-1905*. Ernst Siegfried Mittler und Sohn, 1912 (Translated Title: *My Experiences During The Russo-Japanese War*)
- Rutt, Richard. *The Bamboo Grove: Introduction To Sijo*. The University of Michigan Press, 1998
- Rutt, Richard. *The Flower Boys of Silla (Hwarang)*. Korea Branch of the Royal Asiatic Society, 1961
- Seth, Michael J. *A History of Korea: From Antiquity to the Present*. Rowman & Littlefield Publishers, 2010
- Shin, Chae-ho. *Joseon Sanggosa (Ancient history of Korea)*. 1948
- Shimpei, Ogura. *The Song of Cheoyong*. Poem (originally by Cheoyong), reconstructed into Hangul, 1929
- Shultz, Edward J; Kang, Hugh; Kane, Daniel. *The Silla Annals of the Samguk Sagi*. The Academy of Korean Studies, 2012
- Thiébaud, Jean-Marie. *La présence française en Corée de la fin du XVIIIème siècle à nos jours*. Harmattan, 2005 (Translated Title: *The French Presence in Korea in the Late Eighteenth Century to the Present Day*)
- Various. *Encyclopaedia Britannica (32 volume Set)*. Encyclopaedia Britannica (UK) Ltd, 2009
- Vitale, George. *Why Is Taekwon-Do's History So Hard To Find?* Totally Tae Kwon Do Magazine, January 2010
- Vos, Frits. *Kim Yusin, Kim Yusin, Persönlichkeit und Mythos: Ein Beitrag zur Kenntnis der Altkoreanischen Geschichte*. Publisher Unknown, 1954 (Translated Title: *Kim Yusin: Personality and Myth: A Contribution to the Knowledge of Old Korean History*)
- Wasserstrom, Jeffrey. *Student Protests in Twentieth Century China*. Stanford University Press, 2000
- Yoon, Byŏngryŏl. *The Collected Biographies of Patriot An Chunggŭn*. Ministry of Patriots and Veterans Affairs, 1999
- Yoshihisa, Tak Matsusaka. *The Making of Japanese Manchuria*. Harvard University Asia Center, 2001

From Creation To Unification
The Complete Histories Behind The Ch'ang Hon (ITF) Patterns

— *Web Sites:* www.ahnchangho.or.kr, www.dosan.org; www.kaedc.com, www.koreanhero.net, www.populargusts.blogspot.co.uk; www.raynerslanetkd.com; www.san-shin.org; ww.sooshimkwan.blogspot.com; www. wikipedia.org

Other Books By The Author

The Encyclopedia Of Taekwon-do Patterns
The Complete Patterns Resource For Ch'ang Hon, ITF & GTF Students Of Taekwon-Do, Vols 1,2 & 3

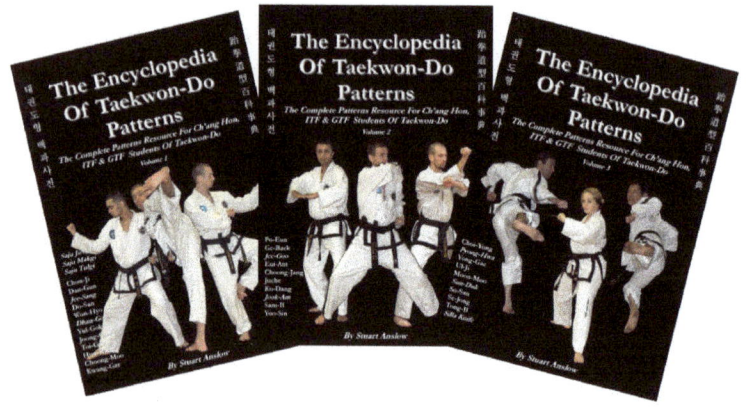

The Encyclopedia Of Taekwon-Do Patterns is a unique series of books that feature the complete works of General Choi, Hong Hi; Creator of the Ch'ang Hon system of Taekwon-Do and founder of the International Taekwon-Do Federation; as well as the patterns further devised by some of his most talented and legendary pioneers; Grandmaster Park, Jung Tae and Grandmaster Kim, Bok Man.

This 3 volume set is the only series of books in the world to feature all of the 25 patterns created by General Choi and his Taekwon-Do pioneers (including both Juche and Ko-Dang), as well as all 3 Saju exercises, the 6 Global Taekwon-Do Federation patterns developed by Grandmaster Park, Jung Tae and the Silla Knife Pattern instituted by Grandmaster Kim, Bok Man.

Other Books By The Author

Utilizing over 5,800 photographs the student is shown in precise detail, each and every pattern from beginning to end, including useful tips on their performance and things unique to particular organisations (such as Kihap points etc.). Displayed in full step by step photographic detail, which displays not just the final move but the 'in-between' motions as well making each book ideal to learn or revise your patterns, no matter which organisation you belong to.

Volume 1 takes the student of Taekwon-Do on his or her journey from 10th Kup White Belt through to 1st Degree Black Belt, including the first of the Black Belt patterns, as well as a *True and More Complete History of Taekwon-Do* chapter.

Volume 2 takes the student of Taekwon-Do from Po-Eun (1st Dan) to Yoo-Sin (3rd Dan) and includes both Ko-Dang and Juche as well as the Dan grade patterns required by the Global Taekwon-Do Federation (GTF).

Volume 3 takes the senior student of Taekwon-Do from Choi-Yong (3rd Dan) to Tong-Il (6th Dan) and includes both Pyong-Hwa and Sun-Duk (required by the GTF), as well as featuring the first weapon form of Taekwon-Do: The Silla Knife Pattern.

No matter which Taekwon-Do organisation you belong to, the Encyclopedia Of Taekwon-Do Patterns covers all you need to know to take you from White Belt to Taekwon-Do Master.

Ch'ang Hon Taekwon-do Hae Sul
Real Applications To The ITF Patterns, Vol 1

This ground breaking first book studies the history and development of the Ch'ang Hon (ITF) Taekwon-do patterns as devised, taught and developed by the founder of Taekwon-do General Choi, Hong Hi.

Ch'ang Hon Taekwon-do Hae Sul is an in-depth study of the Ch'ang Hon Taekwon-do patterns, their history, their roots, Taekwon-do's evolution, its genetic make up, its differences with other martial arts and the techniques and movements which define the system, detailing for the first time since its inception, realistic

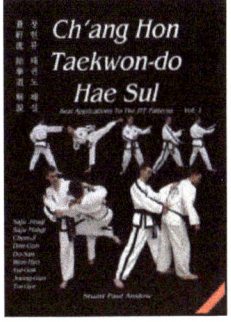

From Creation To Unification
The Complete Histories Behind The Ch'ang Hon (ITF) Patterns

interpretations for the patterns Chon-Ji, Dan-Gun, Do-San, Won-Hyo, Yul-Gok, Joong-Gun and Toi-Gye, as well as Saju Jirugi and Saju Makgi.

Over the 17 chapters, covering 350 pages, with 600 photographs, the patterns are examined, dissected and rebuilt to help both students and instructors understand the applications that are really contained within the Ch'ang Hon patterns, many of which were previously unknown and undocumented.

Learn what the techniques and combinations of each of the Ch'ang Hon patterns are actually for, in step by step photographic detail, and how turn your patterns into a realistic way of training actual self defence techniques that work and turn them into something much more than they are practiced today.

Along the way, the reader is treated to a fascinating insight into the history of the Ch'ang Hon patterns as well as Taekwon-do itself, with many of its previously unknown, undocumented or understudied principles revealed. Read what helped to shape the art which became so feared on the battlefield of Vietnam that enemy soldiers were told not to engage the Korean soldiers, whether armed or not, due to their knowledge of Taekwon-do.

A historical study of Taekwon-do and its patterns, a training manual and an encyclopedia of realistic applications make this book a must read for all those that study and practice Taekwon-do.

A milestone for the development of Taekwon-do.

"I know of neither a Western nor a Korean author who has gone this far to publish a book on Chang Hon Taekwon-do tul/ pattern analysis ... "
— Yi, Yun Wook, Taekwon-do Instructor

"Ch'ang Hon Taekwondo Hae Sul should be in the library of all practitioners of ITF Taekwondo. Read on, learn and enjoy!"
- Iain Abernethy

Other Books By The Author

Ch'ang Hon Taekwon-do Hae Sul
Real Applications To The ITF Patterns, Vol 2

Ch'ang Hon Taekwon-do Hae Sul: *Real Applications To The ITF Patterns*, Vol. 2 continues where the ground breaking Vol. 1 left off.

In Vol. 2 the senior patterns of the Ch'ang Hon System up to 2nd Dan, have gone through the same in-depth analysis as the lower grade patterns originally did, with each one having been examined, dissected and rebuilt to help the student of Taekwon-do to understand what is really contained within the patterns we practice in Taekwon-do.

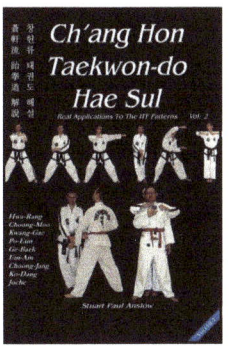

Patterns Hwa-Rang, Choong-Moo, Kwang-Gae, Po-Eun, Ge-Baek, Eui-Am, Choong-Jang, Ko-Dang and Juche have been examined in-depth to find more realistic applications for their movements - based upon what the author refers to as their 'DNA'. In this volume, even the ready postures and stances have been examined and the results are documented in step by step photographic detail, using over 2,200 photographs.

Comprising of over 350 pages, this book not only shows more realistic applications to the Red Belt, 1st Dan and 2nd Dan patterns, but also explains how it is possible to achieve these applications in the first place, why General Choi, Hong Hi, the founder of Ch'ang Hon Taekwon-do couldn't make the same conclusions, as well as expelling a falsehood that has been with Taekwon-Do since its inception!

After reading this book, the patterns of Taekwon-do no longer seem just a collection of movements, performed in a dance like fashion for competitions or gradings, but become realistic techniques that can actually be utilised as real world self defence applications - making this a must read companion to Vol. 1, for all students who study and practice Taekwon-do.

> *"... the art merely became like a domesticated wild cat, content to sleep whilst still retaining a savagery at its heart enabling it to bare its teeth when required."*
> *- John Dowding, 4th degree*